Culture,
Crisis,
and
Creativity

Culture, Crisis, and Creativity

Dane Rudhyar

A QUEST BOOK

*This publication made possible
with the assistance of the Kern Foundation*

THE THEOSOPHICAL PUBLISHING HOUSE
Wheaton, Ill., U.S.A.
Madras, India / London, England

First Quest Book edition, 1977,
published by the
Theosophical Publishing House, Wheaton, Illinois
a department of
The Theosophical Society of America

Library of Congress Cataloging in Publication Data

Rudhyar, Dane, 1895-
    Culture, crisis, and creativity

    (A Quest book)
    Includes bibliographical references and index.
    1. Theosophy — Addresses, essays, lectures.
    2. Culture — Addresses, essays, lectures.
                    I. Title.
BP570.R82   218   76-43008
ISBN 0-8356-0487-X pbk.

Printed in the United States of America

TABLE OF CONTENTS

For Leyla

that she may grow in creative strength and happiness in the fulfillment of the responsibility she has assumed.

DR

1.

WHERE DO WE STAND?

THE GREAT Hindu Holy man. Sri Ramana Maharshi, demanded of all those who came to him for spiritual guidance that they ask of themselves what he considered the most basic question: "Who am I?"

The German philosopher, Martin Heidegger, built his book *An Introduction to Metaphysics* around what he thought was the fundamental question in philosophy: "Why is there anything, instead of nothing?"

Today, I believe, another question has acquired an essential meaning and a character of urgency: "What is my stand toward the culture which has formed me, the questioner?"

Any question has to be formulated in words. Words belong to a language which is the most primordial expression of a culture. This culture forms the mind of the child and crystallizes a set of values, a type of thinking, a way of life, which is forced upon the child from birth by the example and the language of those who surround and direct the development of his consciousness; thus, in the broadest sense, psychic and mental as well as physical, his environment.

Sri Ramana Maharshi's question asked of Hindus, by a Hindu of Southern India and in an Indian environment, is loaded with millennia of Hindu concepts, devotional feelings, images and values. If this question is asked in English, it implies that "foreigners" from another culture have come to India seeking in the country they once conquered and pilfered, spiritual values which they feel are no longer present in the Anglo-Saxon culture. It is this historical background which gives to the question its true and vital character of urgency. It is not asked in the abstract—that is, in a historical vacuum. It is asked by a Hindu today, to individuals living today, whose coming to India in the first place implies an unvoiced question. In the spiritual fashion, the Hindu Sage answers by asking another question. The question means: "Why have you come to me in India? What it is essential for you to discover is who you think and feel you are as an I." Such a discovery can be pertinent if the would-be disciple of the Hindu yogi thoroughly understands that he was impelled to go to India by the present state of his culture and the manner in which, consciously or unconsciously, he is reacting to it. And if Sri Ramana's question is addressed to a modernized Hindu devotee it spurs him to return to the ancient Indian realization of *atman*, the transcendent Self.

The German philosopher, Heidegger, lecturing in a University between the two World Wars, sought to impress his students with an urgent need to study and reconsider with a free, unconditioned mind what he considered the primary source of our Western civilization, the Greek culture which preceeded Plato — especially the Greece of Heraclitus and Parmenides. He felt that European culture had lost the deeper meaning of what he called "being" (Sein) and had misinterpreted the essence of the Greek philosophical tradition. He saw European culture becoming increasingly materialized, superficialized, and vulgarized. He sought therefore to sound again the original keynotes of Western civilization as the great minds of ancient Greece had tried to formulate them in an especially expressive and, in his view, "spiritual" language. Therefore Heidegger's question should also be seen in its historical context. It asks German students to return to the root-concept of "being," the loss of which in Christian European culture — he felt — had drastic repercussions; these now should be thoroughly understood and evaluated in all their implications.

But India is not limited to one tradition. When Gautama, the Buddha, in the sixth century B.C. taught what is now known as the *anatma* doctrine, he challenged the old Hindu concept of *atman* and denied the reality of a permanent and transcendent entity somehow superior to man's existential being. His aim presumably was to break down the crystallized form which the concept of an individualized *atman* had taken in the collective consciousness of the India of his time. To this end he presented an existential approach to the meaning of selfhood in which the compound nature of the human and the absolute power of karma were emphasized. Also, if we consider the problem of "being" which preoccupied Heidegger, we should realize that, while this problem has haunted the mind of most European philosophers, it may have become relatively irrelevant to the American mind trying to emerge from intellectual bondage to the old Greco-European concepts and to develop a new, more inclusive philosophy of existence. In such a philosophy, being and nonbeing cannot be separated, any more than in Chinese philosophy *Yang* can be separated from *Yin*. *

The problem we are facing today, not only in the Western world but all over the globe, is how to constructively and significantly evaluate our present-day position as we deal with the ideas and the values we

---

*For a discussion of this concept, read my book *The Planetarization of Consciousness*, especially Part Two (ASI Publishers, paperback edition, 1977).

have inherited from the past, that is, from cultures which should no longer demand our total and unquestioning allegiance because either they have lost their existential base of operation — thus their roots and their actual livingness — or they have seen their relevance to the contemporary conditions of existence radically challenged by a tide of vulgarization and rebellion against all formal cultures. This is the reason for the question I have posed. This question confronts every thinking person with the imperative need to try to evaluate objectively and in terms of the world-situation the character of his or her relationship to the national culture in which he or she has been born and educated. This culture — as impressed upon our nascent consciousness by parents and teachers — not only surrounds and affects us now physically and socially; it has conditioned, if not totally determined, our mode of thinking and our feeling-responses. It has formulated for us our conscious or unconscious answer to the philosophical problem of the nature and purpose of existence. It has provided us with basic religious beliefs which we have used in building our "self-image."

Today we can no longer *blindly* accept any of the formulations of past traditions. We have to ask basic questions, for whatever a human mind considers obvious and unquestioningly takes for granted imprisons that mind, however beautiful the prison walls may be. At first human beings are bound by their culture, its language and its traditional way of life, almost as inescapably as they are bound by biological imperatives (hunger, self-aggrandizement, sex, etc.) But a time comes in the evolution of human societies when the development of kingdoms and cities, travel, commerce, and intermarriage bring tensions, internal conflicts, and a state of confusion. The "self-evident" truths and paradigms, the traditions, the once-revered institutions of the culture, become shells, mostly irrelevant, empty of meaning, and binding to ever more individualized and restless persons. As the culture reaches such a critical point in its evolution, the individual person is confronted with the need to make a choice. Different and often sharply divergent paths present themselves to minds open and sensitive enough to realize — however dimly — that immobility means death. They must move on.

They should realize, but most often do not, that the character and orientation of the paths from which they must choose are defined primarily by the manner in which they relate to the familiar culture. They can do this consciously, if they are able to think objectively and to feel deeply; or they choose unconsciously, if—being still unaware, confused, or afraid—they feel compelled to accept implicitly, or dare not question, the validity of the social, cultural, and religious attitudes of their parents or group of friends. In such a situation, the most decisive factor is the individual's ability or inability to conceive, vividly imagine, or intuitively envision *a frame of reference for human life and consciousness transcending the strictly cultural level.*

What is implied by a *transcultural* level of consciousness and activity will be discussed throughout this book. In the next chapter a contrast will be drawn between "culture" and "civilization," placing these much used and abused words in a relatively new historical or evolutionary context. Here I shall only state that in our moment of worldwide crisis a deeper and more inclusive—and even a more cosmic—use of the term *civilization* is imperative, if we are not to entirely lose our faith in the value of what we call "Western civilization."

Civilization, in the context of the "cosmic" philosophy of existence which I have presented in a number of books, is a process of planetary scope. It affects the whole Earth and mankind as a whole. Therefore I do not speak of this or that "Civilization" as the English historian, Toynbee, does, but of a global *process* of civilization which began in man's ancient past. However, it was not until a relatively recent date that this process could operate in a focalized and public manner. The turning point was the sixth century B.C.—the century in which Gautama the Buddha, the last Zoroaster (the esoteric Parsee tradition speaks of a series of 12 Zarathustras extending over many millennia) Pythagoras, probably Lao-tze, and other great spiritual leaders lived and sought to fecundate the minds of a few receptive men with a radically new approach to the meaning and possibilities of human existence.

Some six hundred years later Jesus, and in India the seer-philosophers of Mahayana Buddhism, added an essential touch to the process. But just as Greek philosophers and statesmen had betrayed the deeper spirit of the revolution of thought that had given to the mind of man a central and dominant importance, so Christ's vision of universal love and the compassionate ideal of the Boddhisattva became perverted. The institutionalized and dogmatic Catholic Church gave refuge to the negative aspect of Greek rationalism and could not stop European people from using religion to give an aura of sanctity to their crude and violent egocentric passions—the worst instances being the Inquisition and the wars of religion. The quest for God burning in the souls of a few mystics turned into the craving for gold which led the Spanish conquistadores to the brutal conquest of America and the genocidal torturing of thousands of human beings; the treatment of our Indians during and after the conquest of the land, as well as the gold rush, did not show much more of the Christ's spirit of universal love.

What we call "Western civilization" has been built on the basis of an intellectualistic and analytical mind—concerned since the Renaissance with the control of material forces for the improvement of man's physical everyday living—and a restless drive for change and ego-centric expansion. Our Euro-American society has produced technological wonders and enormous cities filled with violently competitive, atomistic, and proud egos whose greed for material power and conquest knows no limits. We call all this individualism, freedom, equality—and civilization. Yet it is only the shadow aspect of *the first phase* of the public and world-wide attempt at establishing the collective consciousness of mankind at a level transcending the compulsive realm of biological values and instinctual imperatives—the realm in which cultures are born, mature, crystallize, and die.

Civilization is not the opposite of culture. The process of civilization interacts with the genesis and development of local cultures all over our globe. We need to understand how this interaction operates, and how metabiological and spiritual modes of activity are able to transform and dephysicalize the products of land-based and always local cultures, and the purpose of such a transformation. This is today a matter of extreme importance, for only such an understanding can help us to attune the deepest area of our being and consciousness to planetary and cosmic rhythms revealing, behind the tragedies of our social, cultural, and personal crises, the vast and imperturbable Harmony, foundation of all existence.

In moments of ecstasy, and in some cases through what is loosely called "meditation," the consciousness of a particularly sensitive and open person may resonate to the normally inaudible "Sound" which can also break upon the mind as transcendent light, but when this seemingly timeless experience ends—as it always must—what of the aftermath? How will the ego-mind deal with it?

Whether the after-effect of the transcendent experience will prove truly constructive or confusing, not only for the experiencer but for those to whom it will be emotionally or verbally conveyed, always depends upon both the cultural level and the mental-emotional state of the experiencer, and the condition of the culture at the time. However universal and seemingly timeless Spirit is understood essentially to be, the *acts* of this Spirit—and as a result the "revelations" dispensed to human beings—deal always with particular persons and particular situations. The outcome of these acts and revelations depends upon the answers which a particular individual, implicitly if not explicitly, gives to the fundamental question: Where do you stand, here and now?

2.

CULTURE-WHOLES AND THE PROCESS OF CIVILIZATION

IF WE ARE to understand clearly and convincingly the significance of what we are facing as human beings seeking to orient ourselves in a confused and cathartic world-situation, it is most important for us to differentiate between what belongs to the realm of *culture* and what should be referred to the larger planetary rhythm of the process of *civilization*. These two italicized words have been variously defined and often interchangeably used—a practice which actually has confused basic issues. It is therefore imperative to state unequivocally and as precisely as possible the meaning I am giving them in this book. In so doing I may have to overemphasize some of their contrasting features, but where there is contrast there is also complementarity and interrelationship. The meaning of such a relationship *today* is what we have primarily to understand, so that we can consciously and deliberately take a meaningful stand.

The word *culture* can be used in both a subjective and an objective sense. It has a subjective meaning when we speak of "a man of culture"; that is, of a person displaying certain qualities of breeding, education, and refinement of manners. The meaning is subjective in the sense that it refers to the character and feelings of human beings. On the other hand, the meaning is objective when we speak of *a* culture and its development. In order to avoid any possible confusion I am using here the term "culture-whole" in order to emphasize the objective and organismic character of *a* culture.

A culture-whole can be defined as an organized field of collective human activity having specific characteristics and operating within more or less clearly marked—even if in most cases gradually expanding—boundaries. The definite characteristics of that field, the culture-whole, are derived from a set of philosophical-religious and psychological premises which in turn are conditioned by racial or genetic features, and by geomagnetic, climatic, and environmental factors. A culture-whole is, in the broadest sense of the term, an organism; it is born and grows amidst struggles; it matures and cystallizes during a classical age; it develops internal conflicts, and gradually disintegrates, even though its remains may endure until they are absorbed into a new culture-whole.

A culture-whole depends upon what the particular region of the biosphere in which it was born has to offer in terms of natural resources. These are provided by the soil, the water, the flora and fauna of the region; and they condition, if not entirely determine, the way of life of the people of the culture-whole. The region is the home of the people; its land is the foundation of all they consider precious and significant, once they have settled upon it and the character of the culture-whole begins to assert itself. They are rooted in it almost as profoundly as trees in the soil. The village the people build is for them the center of the world. All cultures are *locality-centered*.

The people living in the space in which the culture-whole gradually takes form have in many instances — perhaps always in relatively recent times—at least two or three different racial origins and original languages; but these languages combine in an often harsh and violent interplay to form the official language of the culture-whole, as the latter grows to maturity and seeks to formulate its basic character and to develop more effective forms of communication. Any fully developed culture has also a dominant "religion"—in the broadest sense of this term. It accepts as basic, and most of its members take for granted, a number of metaphysical ideas, psychological attitudes, and socio-ethical principles, and it features a number of "rituals," festivals, and collective modes of behavior—a way of life which at least in some respect is uniquely or characteristically its own. Such a way of life is an answer to basic needs collectively felt and physically experienced by the people held together by the psychomental magnetic field of the culture-whole. This answer manifests in a myriad of forms, which have almost a "living" quality as they express the particular character that the deeply generic urges of the human species as a whole have taken as they have faced the conditions and the challenges of a particular environment.

Everything that strictly belongs to the realm of culture has a fundamentally biological character. It is a product of a collective human response to the rhythms of the biosphere in the particular locality in which the culture-whole has taken form and developed. Man, however, has the capacity to express biological responses to nature in a symbolic form, which serves as means of communication making possible group cooperation and a collective way of fulfilling biological needs and meeting the everyday challenges of human existence. Most and perhaps all animal species have such a capacity in at least a rudimentary state, and it may exist even in the vegetable kingdom; but the rootedness of plants and trees in the soil obviously restricts the possibility of cooperative action to the barest minimum. In mankind this possibility acquires a new dimension. As Count Korzybski stated in his early book *The Discovery of Man*, man is endowed with a "time-binding" faculty which seems to be lacking in animal species.

Such an apparently innate faculty makes it possible for human beings not only to communicate with each other by means of symbolic gestures and vocal sounds, but also to transfer to their progeny the knowledge resulting from individual and group experiences. Some kind of transfer of knowledge is in some degree possible for animals; but it presumably is limited to what the young learns from its mother and the adults of the group during a very brief period of education through imitative behavior. The symbol-generating capacity of human beings, even at the primitive cultural level, goes much further. In man, biological urges not only have psychic overtones, but these overtones can in turn act as fundamental tones acquiring a degree of independence from biological drives and needs. A new, and let us say "higher" or biology-transcending type of *needs* results from such an independence. Gradually, as mankind evolves, this independence and the needs it engenders produce a new realm of human activity. To use a now familiar term, a *noosphere* develops with characteristics and potentialities of its own.

Some philosophers and scientists have seemed to picture this noosphere as above and surrounding the *biosphere*; and perhaps the concept is valid. It is valid if we think of vibratory frequencies—that is, of lower and higher vibrations (of fundamental tone and octaves of overtones of increasing frequencies). But we should realize also that what is "above" penetrates what is "below." It does so at least until the center of consciousness is irreversibly shifted from the realm of "below" to that of "above"—from the biosphere to the noosphere. Then the above completely *detaches itself* from the below. The process, which will lead eventually to the detachment of the noosphere from the biosphere, is what I call civilization. When we consider mankind as a whole, civilization is an extremely lengthy process; yet, some relatively rare individuals are able to go through it in a special manner and at a very accelerated pace.

Generally speaking, what we today call civilization refers only to the *first stage* of a planetary process which, probably after millions of years, should utterly transform not only mankind, but the entire Earth and the type of matter to which we are now accustomed. This first stage has been extremely disturbing to the condition of the biosphere, and today we are faced with a large-scale poisoning of this biosphere as the result of the vast complex of human activities which we consider to be "civilization." But is this really what should be called civilization? Is it not rather the result of the first wholesale impact of the process of civilization upon a type of culture which brought together special types of human beings in a particular land, Europe, and at a time in the evolution of mankind which called for such an impact?

What then do I exactly mean by the process of civilization?

In France and England during the Classical and post-Classical period of the Enlightenment—the eighteenth century— the word *civilization* was used in contrast to barbarism. Europe was bringing to barbarian or pagan people "the blessings of civilization," and these of course included Christianity. In America, the European colonists who were invading Indian lands were also bringing such "blessings" to the "uncivilized" pagan tribes. This traditional use of the word *civilization* was linked with the concept of linear progress, which dominated the mentality of nineteenth century historians and philosophers—and, after Darwin, of natural scientists. The great English historian, Arnold Toynbee, after World War I, made a slightly different use of the word, studying what he called (almost interchangeably) past and present Societies and Civilizations. In his view, mankind at a certain point of its evolution reached a phase of development permitting the growth of a type of social living and organization which he characterized by the word *civilization*. This occurred less than 10,000 years ago, and since then a number of Civilizations (or independent great Societies) have been formed, have matured and disintegrated. Toynbee gives to these Societies a quasi-organic character; and in his great work, *A Study of History* (London, 1934) he analyzes a process of growth and decay which he claims is to be found in each and all of these Societies or Civilizations, including our present Euro-American Society. The development of these Societies is "organic," because each of them ends in a situation with a twofold character.[1] While the Society disintegrates and its institutions break down, a "universal" type of religion is born and develops which, like the seed of a yearly plant (whose leaves fall and decay when autumn begins) becomes the spiritual foundation for a new Society. The new religious movement provides the future Society with great symbols and myths which constitute its soul—i.e. its principle of integration.

What Toynbee calls Civilizations is approximately what I mean by culture-wholes. The idea that these culture-wholes, as they follow one another, are linked serially by a spiritual seed-harvest was developed in my booklets "Seed Ideas" written in 1928-29 and published in book form as *Art as Release of Power* in 1931. It had occurred to me while a student in Paris in 1912 when I wrote a book, of which only the least important section was published, *Claude Debussy et le Cycle de la Civilization Musicale*. I used then the word *civilization* in the prevailing French sense. At the same time in Germany, the German historian, Oswald Spengler, was writing his once famous book published in English under the title *The Decline of the West*. In this book, whose two volumes appeared in Germany in 1918 and 1920, Spengler extolls the typically German concept of *Kultur*, and gives to the word *civilization* a totally negative and indeed destructive meaning. According to him, civilization is much like a disease which attacks cultures that are losing their vitality and strength because of inner conflicts and the declining power of an aristocracy whose task it is to uphold the "Prime Symbols" and great myths which ensoul the culture.

For Spengler a culture is an independent socio-spiritual organism which arises spontaneously in a particular land. It may be somewhat influenced in a superficial way by other cultures, but it is not directly *apparented* to any; nor will it have a socio-spiritual progeny in a future culture. The men of a culture can never be truly understood by those of another culture whenever basic issues and beliefs are discussed, for these deal with deep-rooted feeling-responses which are essentially uncommunicable.

Spengler's historical picture was pessimistic, and in it our civilization—and particularly our modern big cities—appeared in a purely negative role. Perhaps this was a partly prophetic reflection, of what was to happen to Germany, and as well to our Western world and humanity as a whole. Toynbee's picture, on the other hand, was essentially optimistic, inasmuch as it was based on a belief in a progressive evolution of the basic character of human society. According to him three basic phases in this evolution can be defined: the primitive stage at a more or less tribal level; the stage in which a number of civilizations develop and decay, transferring their spiritual harvest to a progeny; and a still future stage, which he does not clearly depict, in which the whole of mankind will somehow be integrated.

This sequence is not unlike the one which Karl Marx and Friedrich Engels envisioned. According to these men writing in the middle of the 19th century, the historical development of mankind has a "dialectic" character and passes through three stages: the stage of *tribal societies* in which a compulsive unanimity prevails, at first under matriarchal principles of organization; *a period of class-conflicts* during which each of what the Hindu would call the four castes of human beings in turn predominates (warriors, clergy, merchants, proletariat); and, after the revolutionary proletariat finally has seized power, *a classless society* in which peace, abundance, and the happiness of all people theoretically should flourish.

Each of these historical pictures came at a time when events were calling for them. They were visions of a future which then seemed to the prophets an ideal that could be striven for. This ideal had to be formulated in quasi-messianic and millennial terms because such a formulation might bring, and indeed was intended to bring, to a clearer focus the potentialities which then had begun to be perceptible.

The ideal of civilization vs. barbarism and of a straightforward historical progress developed when the humanistic and scientific spirit inspired the men of the 17th and 18th centuries and made the hearts of nineteenth century scientists, sociologists, and philosophers (except Nietzsche) beat with joyous expectation—an expectation whose validity the first World War brutally challenged. The millenial expectations of Marx and Engels, wherein the "virgin masses" of workers of the world would triumph, were an answer to the horrible conditions which the Industrial Revolution had brought to the working class, an answer whose validity the Russian Revolution was to disprove, at least considering the way it worked out in a world in conflict. And Spengler's pessimism was a reaction to the trend of events in Europe and America as World War I was being ushered in. The Nazi movement may have used Spengler's ideas as an inspiration; unfortunatly this led to drastic results produced by an unholy mixture of the neotribal and pagan spirit of German Kultur and the cold laboratory and industrial techniques of a dehumanized civilization-oriented mentality. Interestingly, Spengler refused to accept the rise of Hitler as that of the great Caesar-type of personage which he had announced. He thought of Hitler as a comic opera hero, and if he had not died of a heart attack in 1936, he certainly would have been sent to a concentration camp.

In contrast, Arnold Toynbee is a representative of the English character, whose indomitable spirit made his nation stand successfully against the German onslaught during World War II. But his expectations for the future are confused and biased by his Anglo-Christian tradition. Nevertheless these expectations reflect the seemingly inescapable trend toward the global organization of human society and, first of all, of big business and finance, a field in which England was the most successful pioneer.

The concept I am presenting in this book, and which I have discussed to some extent in previous writings,[2] is also an answer to our time and the deepening crisis in which all the culture-wholes of the world are now involved. This answer is founded upon principles that are implied and partially formulated in various Oriental and esoteric traditions, and more particularly in the encyclopedic, but often greatly confusing, work of H. P. Blavatsky, *The Secret Doctrine*. This answer differs from the ones given by Western historians, sociologists, biologists, and most present day philosophers and scientists trained in our Euro-American universities in that it refuses to limit man's field of activity and man's consciousness to the realm of events perceived by our senses, as these are normally constituted in this period of human evolution. For modern science this realm is the only valid foundation for knowledge, and such an exclusivism is to me unacceptable.

Western archaeologists and historians painstakingly try to unearth and discover records of events; but these, and above all their interconnections, can be interpreted in many ways. Witnessing what industrialization, the development of huge cities, the flight from the land of masses of people, and an increasing vulgarization of great ideas, symbols, religious myths, and behavior had been doing to the old European culture, Oswald Spengler interpreted these factual developments as a process of decay. If we adopt his strictly cultural and aristocratic point of view, the presence of decay is evident. Such an approach extols the trinity of "blood, land and folk"; and in their own primitive and pure ways, all typical tribal societies—including the American Indian tribal society—have been molded by it. The question is whether the total, and indeed the most characteristic potentialities inherent in Man's essential nature, can be actualized through such a cultural way of life.

The ideals such a way of life glorifies belong to the biosphere and are overtones of the deep fundamental urges and needs of the realm of "life." Can there not be another realm which does not relate to particular *local* conditions of race, soil, climate, natural resources—a realm which has been prefigured by the intuitions, the visions, the discoveries of great human minds reaching after *universal* principles, cosmic laws, and an understanding of rhythmic processes transcending the birth-growth-decay cycle of culture-wholes? Just as the vast period covered by the evolution of the entire human species on this Earth far transcends the birth-maturity-death cycles represented by the life-span of particular human organisms, can there not be a larger planetary pattern of all-human evolution within which the cyclic series of historical phenomena constituted by culture-wholes would fit, and thereby acquire a new meaning?

In fact, both the Marx-Engels' and the Toynbee concepts of human evolution introduce a broader frame of reference according to which the development of human societies takes on a quasi-dialectical character. The evolutionary picture I am presenting retains such a character if seen from a broad and holistic point of view; and it is by grasping what each of the three stages of thesis, antithesis, and synthesis represents that we can most easily understand the character of the relationship between culture-wholes and the process of civilizzation.

The Dialectics of Human Evolution

The stage of "thesis" is represented by human societies totally bound to the local biospheric environment where they are born and develop. At this tribal stage a society reveals an internal and psychic harmony, a unanimous consensus in all vital matters, and complete dependence upon nature. However, at this stage man endows nature with a double character, psychic and physical. In Medieval European times this dualism was expressed by the terms *natura naturans* and *natura naturata*: the realm of psychic energies representing the active-formative aspect of life, and that of material bodies controlled by these *biopsychic* forces personalized as gods, nature-spirits, *devas*, guardian angels, etc. At this biopsychic stage of sociocultural development there are of course fights between tribes for land, water, and means of survival; but these fights parallel, at the human level, the constant struggle for survival between animal (and also vegetable) species. They have exactly the same meaning and ultimate value.

The second stage of "antitheses" in which mankind is still living today is characterized by a process of *internal differentiation*. It is also a process of individualization—an essentially difficult and often tragic process. These two processes begin as the results of a variety of natural causes—tribal expansion, conquest of weaker cultures, slavery, inter-marriage, even climatic changes. These causes lead to important changes in the structure of tribal societies; cities and kingdoms are born. But are these changes the result of natural and social causes alone, or do they not reveal the very gradual workings of an impulse which operates as a type of purposeful activity whose character transcends that of the biosphere—a transforming, fiery activity which develops as it were, *in counterpoint to* the cultural process? This is the crucial question. Is there a mysterious *Yang* factor operating in polar opposition to the *Yin* factor in natural, biopsychic and harmonic development when evolving human societies reach the stage of "antithesis"? I believe there is; and this Yang factor is the process of civilization.

The next question is: what does this civilization factor seek to bring about? The basic answer is that *it seeks eventually to develop in human beings their inherent potentiality of operating at a level of existence transcending that of life*, as we know life in terms of biospheric conditions on this Earth.

Superphysical does not mean supermaterial or immaterial. We know today that matter is only a relatively steady form of energy, and it is rather senseless to take for granted that only one form of energy can exist, thus one type of "matter." In fact, until the Classical period of European society, every human society has firmly believed that matter does exist at a superphysical level, and that superphysical organizations of subtle types of matter can be perceived by at least some human beings who innately possess that ability or are willing to undergo specific training in order to develop it.

To repeat in a slightly different way what has already been stated: Civilization, as here defined, is a process whose purpose is to develop in human beings the capacity to operate at a life-transcending level of existence in an organized field of consciousness and activity depending for its support on a superphysical type of matter. Such an operation essentially implies the transfer of the center of consciousness and of the sense of individual identity from the biopsychic level of Earth's nature to a "higher"—because more inclusive—level which we may call, for lack of better terms, spiritual-mental.

The center of a person's consciousness and identity has to be raised to a new level; or, from another point of view, a new frame of reference for the sense of being I has to appear to the consciousness. This appearance often, but not necessarily, takes the form of an illumination which provides for the illumined mind a new perspective and therefore the capacity to interpret all the facts of human existence in a new light. In any case, if the process is to operate on a conscious, steady, and permanent basis, a strong and adequately formed mind should have been previously built. This is why civilization's first task is to build well-organized and integrated minds. Unfortunately this is a slow and difficult undertaking; and as it proceeds it tends at first to produce very disturbing, and often destructive results.

These results occur because the development of a well-organized and potentially independent mind begins in the context of a powerful system of biopsychic energies. Biological urges are intense, and as they dominate the field of the human organism in which this new mind at first weakly develops, the latter is seized upon by the biological drives—by the tremendous power of life, of which modern man today has but a most attenuated realization. The nascent new mind becomes the servant of the life-urges; it is a remarkably effective servant, but the new power it gives to these life-urges corrupts them and at the same time distorts the mind. The ownership of a slave perverts the master, who in the long run may be destroyed by his slave.

We are witnessing now, on a global scale, such a destruction of life by the products of a collective mentality, either at the service of biopsychic urges and passions, or at least unable to free itself from the conditioning they produce. The principal way in which this collective mind of Western mankind has been able to seemingly free itself has been by escaping into a realm of intellectual abstractions in which all that belongs to the life-field is denied importance and even reality. Another way has been religious asceticism.

Denial, however, is not a valid solution. Saying that a diseased life-condition does not exist at all is not a sound way of restoring health. It pushes back the biological reality into the unconscious depths where it may fester and poison the roots of consciousness. The development of a new level of mind-activity should enlarge the consciousness so that it becomes able to encompass both the anabolic and catabolic manifestations of life in physical nature, and those of the transcendent level. In other words, the basic problem is how to establish an adequate and valid *relationship* between what in us belongs to life and what is developing as a potentially independent factor in our total field of existence—a mind able to operate according to its own rhythm and purpose. There are, however, several levels, or realms, of mind activity; and the recently formulated concept of noosphere is much too simplistic and undifferentiated as understood by the majority of the people using it as a basis. We should rather say that, just as several kingdoms of life exist in the biosphere, several types of mental processes operate in the noosphere. A symbolic kind of correspondence between the biospheric and noospheric levels of activity may help us to better understand the character of the different kinds of mind-processes which man today can experience.

There are in the Earth's biosphere three basic modes of existence: mineral, vegetable, and animal. Organic life results from the harmonic and hierarchical interactions of the activities related to each of these levels. Plants are composed of chemical substances which they raise to the level of biological integration within specific and generic forms of life and consciousness. Animals feed on plants and breathe the atmosphere which the vegetable kindgom has generated; and animals help the fertilization of plants and the spread of seeds.

The mineral kingdom reaches a special state of existence in the crystal. In a somewhat analogical sense man, at the strictly biological-tribal level, occupies the place of the crystal, for at that level he brings the tremendous life-energy and the mobility of the animal kingdom to *a perfectly formed* state in which cosmic harmony is reflected in material art-forms and even in the building of villages. Some cultural objects have a "sacred" character because they are felt to act as means of communication between the psychic-cosmic realm of life-gods and the human-tribal sphere of existence.

Human beings can also become sacralized and mediums for the transmission of vital messages. They can be consecrated or offered in sacrifice to tribal gods who symbolize and personify various aspects of the great power of life. Every event can be given a symbolic and revelatory character by the mind which, crystal-like, reflects the light of divine intent and purpose. As higher overtones of cultural activity and consciousness are sounded, this capacity for reflecting the light of divine Beings takes the form of what we now call devotion or *bhakti*. But when that devotion not only reflects, but uses for collective purpose the supreme power of the highest psychic realm—light—the devotee has reached a state corresponding to the vegetable state; because as we know, plants capture sunlight and transform it into potential food for the animal kingdom, while also releasing oxygen for animal breathing.

In the animal kindgom, life becomes free motion, and emotion. The rudiments of intelligence and of the abilities to produce tools and to construct useful structures develop, and definitely social patterns of behavior prefigure the rise of the primitive types of human culture. What the animal kingdom brought to the biosphere parallels and symbolizes what occurred when a type of mind appeared which gave rise in man to the individualized experience of "I am" and to the urge to reach beyond the essentially passive reflectivity of the strictly biopsychic cultural mentality.

This emergence of the I-am consciousness has been considered by most ancient traditions to be a supreme, even if potentially tragic gift to mankind, a gift involving a great sacrifice performed by a divine or semidivine being. In Greek mythology this is the Promethean gift for which the giver had to suffer ever-renewed tortures. When Prometheus, out of compassion for animal-like and earthbound human beings, gave them the fire of the gods which he had stolen from heaven, he incurred the wrath of Zeus, the Sky god, who chained him to a peak of the Caucasus mountain range and had a vulture repeatedly tear open his breast and devour his liver. As soon as this was done, the liver grew again, and once more, cycle after cycle, the vulture fed on it.

The symbolism of the myth should be clear: in ancient Mediterranean cultures the liver was considered the location of the life-force and the vulture is the symbol of the death process. Thus Prometheus, who gave to mankind the possibility of transcending the animal compulsions of the realm of life and, as we shall presently see, of achieving a superphysical kind of at least relative immortality, has to expiate for his compassionate deed by having his own life-center endlessly torn, rebuilt, and torn again by the bird of death. He who wishes to transcend life must accept the possibility of tragedy in some form; and whoever incites and teaches men how to proceed to the path of life-transcending metamorphosis makes an enemy of the god of life. In Greek mythology, Jupiter symbolizes an already culturalized and socialized aspect of life, but in Hebrew Genesis, the god who gives to man the "breath of life," (after which Adam "became a living soul" [2:7]) is most definitely the ruler of the biosphere. This is the realm in which all living organisms, and (in their original character) all culture-wholes, are born, unfold their biopsychic powers, and die. This Hebrew god is the Tetragrammaton, the sacred four-letter word, Jod-He-Vau-He, once translated as Jehovah and now as Yahweh.

This god of life and of all tribal cultures, worshipped under the many names which each culture has given him, appears in Genesis *only at the second chapter*. He is "Yahweh Elohim"—only one of the Elohim, as Elohim is a plural noun. On the other hand, the creative process depicted in the *first chapter* of Genesis should be understood as referring to creation at the level of archetypes. The second chapter deals with the creative process *only* as it operates at the physical level of the biosphere, and particularly with reference to mankind.[3] Archetypally man is essentially different from animals, because, as male-female, he is "created" *within the divine Mind* in the image and likeness of the entire Elohim Host — the spiritual-cosmic Seed of a previous cosmic cycle (or in Sanskrit a *manvantara*). The archetypal potentiality of being Godlike is inherent in archetypal Man; but the Yahweh aspect of the creative God that dominates the cultural evolution of mankind, until another aspect reveals itself to Moses in the Burning Bush, is only able to give to natural man the power of life. It is not concerned with the power of free and responsible individual selfhood.

This is not a new concept, as it can be found in all Gnostic and Alchemical traditions. These also point out that the "first Adam" was neither male nor female. "Its" consciousness but passively *reflected* the harmony of Edenic life; even if it was intuitively able to "name" (i.e. to sense the innermost character of) animal species. The formation of Eve was necessary in order to actualize the archetypal potentiality of Man mentioned in the first chapter of Genesis (1:26-27)—the potentiality of developing a consciousness which, through the experience of duality (which includes sexual polarization), could learn to transcend dualism and the conflicts it generates, and to *consciously and deliberately* enter the realm of divine unity.

Life is rooted in unity, however differentiated its multiple aspects; but the only kind of consciousness which life *of itself* is able to produce can only passively reflect that unity. What most people, clergymen included, seem to have forgotten is that at the center of the Garden of Eden *two* trees stood: the Tree of Life and the Tree of the Knowledge of Good and Evil. The god of the biosphere, Yahweh, tried to frighten Adam from the latter by telling him that by eating of its fruit he "would surely die." What this means is obvious: the dualism of Good and Evil is reflected in the dualism of living and dying—of anabolic and catabolic activity. Nevertheless a positive, individualized, and responsible type of knowledge can develop only when both the constructive and destructive consequences of any activity are lucidly and fearlessly considered. The essential character of living can be known only through the conscious experience of death.[4]

The living-dying process is cyclic, and thus is symbolized by a serpentine and sinusoidal motion. The knowledge of cycles is a knowledge of the constant interaction of two opposite and complementary principles, which Chinese philosophy named Yang and Yin. The Tao consciousness is nondual; yet it can be attained only *through* the full experience of duality. This means the experience of relationship and mutuality. Where there is self, there must also be a not-self—the outside world, and in a concentrated form, the Beloved or the Adversary. The fruit of the Tree of the Knowledge of Good and Evil is the consciousness of relationship; and this means *all* relationships and not merely sex-relationship, though sexualization provides a most characteristic field for what relationship at its deepest level implies.

The two trees at the center of the Garden of Eden symbolize the two levels at which man can operate: the level of life and culture, and the level of civilization based on knowledge acquired by a mind able to deal with the constructive and destructive aspects of existence. The crucial question is *how* that mind deals with relationship. Any relationship—thus any interaction between self and not-self, and between "I" and "the Other"—can either be given a positive, integrating character or approached with the fear and insecurity which are the twin roots of war, hatred, and indeed of all evils. *Civilization is a process based on relationship.* How individuals and collectivities approach, face, interpret, and resolve the problems engendered by relationship determines the character which this process will have.

The animal lives in a biosphere where "eat or be eaten" is the basic, impersonal, accepted law. Man, as he comes to a point in his collective evolution at which he is impelled, by inner growth as well as by outer sociocultural developments, to *individualize his consciousness*, is faced by the alternatives "love or hate." He can choose. As man collectively and individually chooses, so civilization develops as a blessing or a curse. It can be a little of both at the same time, yet one polarity must prevail.

During the yearly cycle either the day or the night must be longer, except at the "magical" moments of supreme choice, the two equinoxes, when day and night are equal; but even then, at the spring equinox the basic momentum is toward more daylight, while at the fall equinox the trend toward an increase of darkness is inescapable. The two equinoxes are *polarized* in opposite ways. Autumn must bring the decay of vegetation. It brings also the fall of the seed into the humus pungent with the scent of disintegration. Cycle after cycle a time comes in the development of culture-wholes when the increasing inner emptiness and outer rigidity of its "Prime Symbols," having become institutionalized, are revealed. Then the process of civilization overcomes the organic biopsychic character of the culture. At such times, whether or not they are aware of this compulsive fact, the people of the culture-whole are forced to face a crucial symbolic choice: to disintegrate with the leaves, or to participate in the formation of seeds, foundations of a future cycle of vegetation—a cycle that will begin with their ritual death, germination.

What is always at stake is the quality of all human relationships and the character of man's allegiance. It is what mankind—and every individual able to envision the possibilities open to him or her by the Promethean gift of the fire of selfhood and responsibility—will do with that ambivalent gift and its inherent potentialities. Today, more than ever, the state of conscious individualized existence may mean alienation from the universe, the inability to enter into and maintain meaningful relationships, tragic isolation, and a frightened regression to the law of the biosphere, "eat or be eaten," which at the level of the mind and of civilization becomes not only internalized, but far more cruel and implacable. It may also mean the attainment of supreme and all-encompassing consciousness through a mind that, because it fully accepts relationship, is illumined by a love relating all opposites and contradictions to a universal and all-inclusive principle of Harmony—a love within which all colors experience their multifarious essence in white light.

Civilization may lead to the megalopolis (the Biblical Babylon) where cultural values are vulgarized, poisoned by greed, fear and loneliness, and where the jungle-existence of tenements borders the pompous yet vacuous displays of "the beautiful people" with empty souls. But the process of civilization could also lead to the Holy City, the New Jerusalem "descended from heaven"—the world of divine Archetypes and universal Principles of Order and all-encompassing Harmony: two alternatives and one essential human choice, ever repeated through the myriad of opportunities for relationship that living in the biosphere presents to us all, human beings touched by the fire of individualized consciousness.

The old myth states that Prometheus, chained on the Caucasus mountain, can and will be released from his torture. He can be released only by Christ-like men and Boddhisattvas whose universal, impersonal, nonpossessive and redeeming love offers the one and only way to overcome the catabolic and tragic aspects of civilization.

This love does not *deny* life. It transmutes its energies and transubstantiates its physical basis. By so doing, it establishes a harmonic relationship between "life" and "mind"—between culture and civilization—by accepting both, yet not being attached to and compelled by the rhythms of either one. This universal love allows the power of a divine Will and of universalistic forms of existence (Archetypes) to manifest *through* the mind and to fecundate a matter which then begins to assume a superphysical character.

Such a form of matter has been called "astral"; but today this word has been misused and its meaning debased, and there may be value in using the Sanskrit term, *akasha*, though it too is being materialized by pseudo-occultists and self-styled clairvoyants claiming to be able to read "akashic records." Astral means "of the nature of the stars," and the realm of stars symbolizes for man the possibility of existence of radiant forms of consciousness and organized fields of energy in which the principle of universal Harmony is manifested in its many aspects. When at long last this principle operates in man, what was a tyrannical ego-master swayed by biologic, emotional, and sociocultural impulses, becomes a gradually more perfectly formed and translucent lens of pure crystal *through which* divine Light radiates upon an Earth whose materiality has become transfigured, as Jesus's body is said to have become transfigured when the Christ-spirit pervaded his total being on the Mount of Transfiguration.

This is the stage of "synthesis" in the dialectical process, not only of human but of planetary evolution. It is that stage which Teilhard de Chardin envisioned and formulated in terms of his Catholic background as the Omega state. At critical times in the history of a culture-whole, men dream of it as an approaching millennium. They do not seem to understand that it can occur only when they themselves have transcended the bondage of biological drives and intellectual ideologies—of emotional passions, dogmas of both science and religion, and of the craving of their egos for the joys and sorrows of separate individual existences.

Civilization is a means for man's liberation from biopsychic bondage to the narrow boundaries of a land-based, traditional culture, which determines his basic emotional responses and his collective moves; but liberation and freedom have only the meaning which the kind of use man makes of them determines. In themselves they have no meaning. Civilization is a means to an end. It is a process; not a fixed state or a consummation. The end is beyond *both* culture and civilization.

At the close of his great work, *The Life Divine*, Sri Aurobindo attempted to make us participate in his epic millennial vision of what he called the Gnostic Society. Over forty years ago, in a large unpublished book, I sought to base on a total picture of human and cosmic evolution the expectations for a future "Age of Plenitude" that would succeed our present "Age of Conflicts". More recently, in my book *The Sun is also a Star* (Dutton, N.Y. 1975), I have spoken of "the Galactic Community" prefigured in the theosophical concept of the White Lodge, the spiritual seed harvest of humanity. These may be dreams, yet in some sense and at some level, they must be realities—existential realities. The future *does* polarize the past. It draws to itself whatever, in the ever-altered present moment, strives however uncertainly to discover a guiding star by which to orient and consciously direct its efforts. It is the direction that is important, not the star itself.

Once on the path cut through the jungles of the biosphere, mankind may well rest, sing and dance on the fertile banks of great rivers, but the Promethean imperative will ineluctably seize new generations; and if the cities which men have built on the river banks have become monstrous cancerous growths, many will die—so that a few may live and continue the cyclic journey toward whatever culmination of human achievement is possible upon, or even beyond, our Earth.

What is most important for us, today, is to know, clearly and unequivocally, where we stand, individually and collectively. It is consciously to assess the value of what we so long have taken for granted in passive, uninspired worship. It is to realize what point in the cyclic relationship of culture and civilization we have reached, so that we may be able to understand how to use the mind which civilization has built for us in a manner that may open a way toward the formation of a new and more inclusive culture, even while the end-products of the cultures of the past slowly disintegrate under "autumnal" skies.

3.

THE CYCLE OF MAN ACCORDING TO THE SYMBOLISM OF NUMBER

ACCORDING TO the prevailing beliefs concerning the evolution of mankind, in its first stage man lived in small groups as "food gatherers," existing on what they could find to eat in their immediate environment. Whether in the beginning this food was strictly vegetarian or included the flesh of captured animals, sooner or later men began to hunt with clubs, spears, bows and arrows, nets and traps.

The use of tools and the eating of flesh most likely increased in importance when human beings, instead of being frightened by fire, as all animals are, began to use and produce it artificially. At this point the process of civilization began. It is probable that men started to plant seeds and to plough land before the wide use of fire in melting metal began. But in any case, two basic lines of development are essential in the formation and growth of culture-wholes: agriculture and industry. *Agriculture*—and with it cattle-raising and the domestication of animals—deals with the power of seed-multiplication inherent in vegetable and animal life. *Industry* is based on the transformation of matter through the use of fire.

In previous books I have discussed the meanings and the eventual results of these two primordial modes of human productivity. Man, as food producer uses both; but the relative importance of agriculture and industry in the formation, development, and transformation of cultures can greatly vary. Industry, which at first had but a secondary importance, and whose products were mainly concerned with agricultural activities and warfare, has come in recent centuries to occupy a primary role as determinant of the character of the culture. In the Bible, the two lines of human development are sharply differentiated as the descendants of Seth and those of Cain, and the god of life, Yahweh, always favors the former and the pastoral life. The men who use fire and forge weapons somehow end by building cities, which in turn become "dens of iniquity."

According to the Biblical narrative, which simply condenses in a strictly symbolical form long ages of human development, the process of civilization takes a special and far more dangerous form when the

Ben Elohim appear among human beings, "marry the daughters of men," and giants are born displaying great powers, sooner or later being used for selfish and perverted purposes. The term *Ben Elohim* (apperaring in Genesis 6) has been translated "Sons of God"; but according to esoteric tradition, these beings "emanated" from the Elohim who, in Genesis 1, are shown to create the *Archetypes* of male-female human beings. They were "sons" not of Yahweh, the *fashioner* of physical and biological man, but instead of Elohim, the *creator* of the universe at the level of the divine Mind. They had within them the "fire"—the power of creation and radical transformation—which characterizes this divine Mind. In that sense, they correspond to the Greek Prometheus, but they are far more precisely related to the *Kumaras* who, according to the ancient Hindu traditions, brought to animal mankind the "fire" of individual selfhood, at least in a *latent* state.[1]

With the coming of these *Kumaras* the process of civilization began to operate at the mental-spiritual level where it essentially belongs. The potentiality of conscious, responsible, and free individual selfhood was "grafted" upon the human species. One might also say that the Tree of the Knowledge of Good and Evil was *fertilized* by the coming among men of these "divine" beings. Today, when the coming of "space people" from other planets or solar systems is widely believed in, many people reading these words will probably think that these beings were cosmic visitors. In fact, some esoteric doctrines assert that they came from Venus; but it is not at all clear whether the name Venus refers to what we see in the sky as a material celestial body, or to a transcendent realm of consciousness having a special relationship to the type of human existence having emerged from the Earth's biosphere.

Such a concept obviously can only be accepted with great difficulty by college-trained minds or religious traditionalists; but it would not startle people whose mentality had been formed by any older culture. I shall add that in relation to this present discussion, it does not matter a great deal whether the idea of a spiritual fecundation and potential transformation of the human race by superior extraterrestrial or metabiospheric entities is to be considered a myth or a factual reality which can be related to a definite period of human pre-history. All great myths are based on a few facts. These facts often have left no physical records available to historians, nevertheless they have brought to a focus basic changes in human consciousness and collective activity, and it is such changes that concern us here. The original events in time became interpreted and expanded into symbols of deep and everlasting significance. These symbols always acquire a tremendous psychic power; they move multitudes, and though seemingly forgotten for centuries in a particular culture-whole, they may be resuscitated in a modified form, and new meaning and power may be poured into them. This happens whenever the new collective needs of a people, and now perhaps of humanity as a whole, can be adequately and significantly met by these symbols in their new avataric embodiment.

Today the need that underlies all more superficial problems is to reassess the fundamental assumptions and the religious-ethical dogmas on which Western society, and all the older societies which it has conquered and traumatized, are basing their ways of life, their deep emotional responses and their mental assumptions. This means first of all, a reassessment of the relative value of the way of culture and the way of civilization.

Extremists deny to one of these ways a basic significance. Some, following Spengler and numerous other modern thinkers, believe that civilization is essentially evil and that human salvation can come only through an uncompromising return to the land, to "natural" values and behavior, and to more or less local or at least regional cultures depending for their power upon "the Earth-mother"; and this, not merely as a temporary regathering of vital power, but as a permanent way of life for all human beings. Other extremists are looking eagerly to a future in which industrial technology and an ever-greater dependence on the type of thinking on which modern scientific procedures and conceptualizations are based will almost totally absorb and overcome man's subservience to natural conditions and deeply vitalistic and emotional responses.

In the first instance, if extremists had their way, Western technology and industry, and their far-reaching psychosocial results, would be given a secondary importance if not almost totally tabooed; in the second case, agriculture would become almost entirely industrialized and chemicalized, and the whole globe would be made into a vast agglomeration of huge cities, with the natural spaces between them considered mere playgrounds tor sophisticated recreation and fun —zones for the release of tension. Should the Earth prove too polluted for man's well-being, then the human elite would be shipped away to conquer new planets and bring to whatever life-forms may grow on them the doubtful blessings of our present-day or day-after-tomorrow human civilization.

Between these two extreme positions, a variety of solutions are possible. Whatever they are in practical detail, they should be based on the intuitive realization that a harmonious interrelationship and interaction between culture and civilization will be possible only when man is

able to see that both have a definite part to play in the gradual achievement of a state of being which transcends them both. I have already
presented such a "vision" of a perhaps distant human and planetary
future in my book *We Can Begin Again – Together* (Part Two). What
should be clarified is the way in which the process of civilization
interacts with the development of culture-wholes.

Culture forms; civilization transforms. Cycle after cycle, the transforming process of civilization broadens and raises the level of the
formative power of culture. Yet, as it performs such a task, it also saps
the foundations of the institutionalized patterns of culture-wholes
which have become rigid and devitalized. Wherever life operates in
organized systems of rigidly structured activity, these systems automatically induce the power of transformation which, at the level of the
biosphere, operate as death. But—as already stated—in man death can
be experienced in life. Man's *mind*, when organized by a life-transcending *will*, can experience death without breaking its basic relationship to the biological organism.

Because it is the product of human activity, a culture-whole can also
consciously and deliberately *accept* the transformation activity of
civilization, and retain its basic identity even though it has experienced
a collective cultural death. This occurred in China, in "greater India"
(*Aryavarta*), and in Egypt. The Greco-Roman Mediterranean culture-
whole was not able to experience death-rebirth, because the shock of
Christianity was too radical. It is possible that our Euro-American
culture-whole will have the same fate, because the shock produced by
modern science and its technology since theReformation may be too
devastating not only to our own and all ancient cultures but to the
biosphere itself.

This is possible, but neither necessary nor fated. However, I firmly
believe that the possibility of experiencing a death-rebirth process
entirely depends on man's ability to clearly envision a metabiological
state of existence transcending what until now mankind has assumed to
be—and desired to be—the only possible foundation for all cultural
activities. That life-transcending state is *not* civilization as we know it
today or have ever thought of it. Civilization is only the necessary
means to so radically transform culture-wholes that, after many historical cycles, they may become what seers and prophets have symbolized
as the New Jerusalem, the Holy City, or the Gnostic Society of the Age of
Plenitude.

Civilization is a means to an end. It kills any living organism which,
because it neither can envision that end nor understand its eventual
inevitability, is unable to work toward its existential realization. What

we need today is neither more civilization nor a permanent and idealized return to nature. What we need is to allow the process of transformation to act so deeply in us, as individuals and as collectivities, that we can lose enough of our sense of bondage to the biosphere and its compulsive drives to gain the vision of the transcendent state, not as a mere ideal but as a planetary reality on an equally transformed or transfigured Earth.

Alas, what today we call civilization, while it inspires us to look beyond our past subservience to biospheric imperatives, also makes it impossible for our civilized minds to picture such a "beyond" except in materialistic and self-defeating terms of physical comfort and technological prowess and power. This is the great tragedy of modern man. His much acclaimed scientific spirit frees him of the compulsions of subrational and subconscious states of mind, only to bind him to an empty rationalism and a quantitative analytical intellect, both of which actually entomb him in a sarcophagus filled with only the mimicry of life. This sarcophagus is the "megalopolis" — the monstrous city.[2]

Numbers as Cyclocosmic Archetypes

I shall develop further what is implied in the preceding statements, but it seems necessary at first to try to clarify in broad lines the relationship between culture, civilization, and a state of human existence transcending both. To that end the use of a traditional type of numerical symbolism should prove very revealing, provided one realizes that when using numbers in such a manner, one thinks of archetypes and levels of being at which fundamental *qualities* operate, but not of quantitative measurements and merely intellectual classification. Pythagorean, Kabalistic, and alchemical systems dealt with numbers in such a way, and recent Theosophical or, broadly speaking, occult descriptions of cosmic and biopsychological processes have stressed the importance of this kind of analysis.

Here three numbers are of special importance: 4, 5, and 6. They acquire their most basic existential meaning in terms of a sevenfold frame of reference widely used in the study of cyclic processes, as it is a most valuable foundation for the study of the structure of physical systems of organization and of the sequential phases of their development.

In order to understand the essential meaning of number 7 we have to start from the premise that all forms of existence imply the operation of two basic principles. As these are constantly interacting, a third principle — the principle of relatedness — must also be considered. If now we try to understand how these three principles operate we see that they can be combined in *four* ways. If A, B, and C represent the three principles, we may have the following combinations: AB, AC, BC and ABC.

Let us say that A stands for *the principle of individualization*, according to which whatever exists operates as a whole (a unit); and B for the principle of *collectivation*, according to which units tend to gather into more inclusive combinations. C would then stand for the power that keeps the two principles in a state of dynamic, ever-altered, but fundamentally harmonic relationship. If now we consider this power of harmonization as it acts within the individual, such an action is represented by AC; when operating within a "collectivity" it is symbolized by BC. If we dealt with the *physical manifestation* of the process, we would have the combination ABC.

There are therefore three basic principles and four combinations. Number 4 refers to the concrete actualization of all cosmic possibilities. This is the square; and, in three dimensions, the cube with its six faces — the perfect Stone whose symbolism is developed in all religious and metaphysical or occult systems. At one level, number 4 therefore stands for the physical world, the Earth, Nature; at another it symbolizes the human person considered as an individualized whole, a microcosm.

A circle can be entirely surrounded by and tangent to six circles of the same size. This is a well-known geometrical design (which any one can test by using seven dimes touching one another) and a profound symbol. If, however, we pass from the static archetypal level of geometrical figures to the dynamic realm of existence in which motion and change are unceasing, we have to think of *cyclic processes* instead of circles. These processes have three essential phases: beginning, middle, and end.[3] A seven-beat rhythm operates within these processes and the mid-point of the cycle comes during phase 4. During that phase, physical matter is the foundation of existence, and physical bodies develop to the fullest extent possible on solid planets, at least some of which have a biosphere.

Number 4 thus symbolizes our Earth and the fundamental vibration characterizing all life-processes with the biosphere. However, if we can think of the Earth as a cosmic whole encompassing far more than the present physical mass which our senses perceive and our instruments survey and measure, and if we try to imagine *the entire cycle* of its development, we should realize that in this development, there were three phases which, in terms of time, preceded the present stage 4 — or, as American Indians say, "the Fourth World" which human beings are now inhabiting. During these first three phases of the entire planetary cycle *an original Creative Impulse* gradually becomes more concretely manifested in solid physical matter. The subjective vision and purpose of a creative center of metacosmic consciousness — a Creator, Logos, or *Ishvara*—infused with an immense, yet finite amount of energy, gradually becomes more explicit, more objective. This vision and purpose "formulate" themselves in cosmic, planetary and eventually biological forms of increasingly denser and more solid matter — mineral, vegetable, animal, protohuman.

We may speak of phase 1 of the cyclic process as purely spiritual or dreamlike. The one original vision retains its homogeneity, though already differentiation occurs at a level we can hardly imagine. Phase 2 begins when the colors that have differentiated from the original one light *reflect* themselves in the materials that were left from a previous universe and are being "churned" or wheeled around in response to the original Creative Impulse and the energies it released. The dualism of spirit and matter dominates this phase; but as phase 3 begins a power of relatedness begins fully to operate. It is the power of the integrative and formative Mind, organizing matter in direct and immediate response to what now have become definitely differentiated and multifarious expressions of the original creative Impulse. If that Impulse is seen as a creative "Word" (*logos*), the multitude of "Letters" that were *implied* in the meaning of the Word are now clearly *explicated* as definite *qualities of being*.

It was at the end of that phase 3 of our planetary process that, according to Hindu traditions, the *Kumaras* entered the planetary field of our Earth and brought to humanity-as-a-whole the *potentiality* of attaining an individualized type of consciousness and mind—thus, the possibility of relating all experiences to a center of consciousness and, as a result, of developing a sense of independent identity, of "being I." Such a possibility, once actualized, can operate in two directions. Indeed, every new release of power can always be used either constructively or destructively. The use is constructive when it is in tune with the original creative Impulse — or in religious terms, God's Will. It is destructive when, ignorantly or more or less deliberately, it works against the divine Purpose. It does so when it operates for the mere satisfaction and/or aggrandizement of an individualized center of consciousness in which separative tendencies have overcome any deep feeling of belongingness to a whole — a whole in which the individualized self occupies an archetypal function, somewhat as a cell performs an organic role within a living body.

Phase 3 of a cosmic or planetary process refers therefore to a period during which the principle of relatedness and the direction in which it operates are all-important. The end-purpose of relationship, and in general of existence itself, is taking form in the consciousness. What the gradually more structured field of consciousness envisions as life's purpose becomes a determining factor. Thus, the inability to picture a divine purpose for the universe, and for man an equally divine condition as the *ultimate* result of his individualization can have a tragic outcome as phase 4 begins and everything that the mind has pictured tends to become a concrete physical fact. A failure of vision — which at the level of the personal life is often called a "failure of nerves" — almost inevitably leads to destructive results. Phase 4 actualizes in physical, biopsychic terms what was potential during the preceding phases. It concretizes all relationships and brings them to a point at which decisions and choice have to be made, individually and collectively.

In the mythology of occultism (which does not mean that the myths are not based on actual events!) this phase 4 refers to the Atlantean period and the struggle between white and black Adepts able to wield the enormous power of a humanity of giants living close to an immensely prolific soil. What made these Adepts of the white and black Paths, was the *quality of their vision*, which in turn concretized itself either into total faith in the divine Will and Purpose, or into tragic insecurity and the fear of losing control of the tremendous energies inherent in life, sex and imagination — energies which in that period were operating at a level of intensity we can hardly conceive today.

During phase 4 the original creative Impulse given by the Demiurge or Logos can *reflect* itself in its totality within a human organism, which, as this occurs becomes a "whole Person", an Avatar. The keynote of that evolutionary period is *personification*. Because men realize that within them a capacity of total response to the creative Word inheres, they unconsciously project this sense of totality upon whatever seems to act independently and purposefully.

The whole Earth, and especially its biosphere, is attuned to this cosmic vibration 4; and so are all culture-wholes rooted in the soil and controlled by the compulsive urges and needs characterizing a biospheric or biopsychic state of existence. Each culture-whole *personifies its innermost potential of being as God*. But at the tribal level of social organization this God is only the god of a particular tribe; and the center of the tribal village is not, as tribesmen believe, the center of the whole world. In time, however, the tribal vision tends to become a global, planetary realization of the oneness of mankind, and "universal religions" (as Toynbee calls them) arise. They arise only after new levels of consciousness are reached by a mental-spiritual vanguard of mankind, and geniuses, seers, prophets and God-revealing personages fecundate the collective consciousness of their own or the following generations with flaming ideals and seed-ideas.

This creative-transforming vanguard, though living in bodies resonating to the vibration 4 of the Earth's biosphere, somehow becomes attuned in consciousness, imaginative power, and will to the vibration 5. They herald the eventual appearance of new faculties and a new mind. Through them the process of civilization operates. It operates in culture-wholes that have attained a critical state in their evolution; and we have already seen what this operation leads to.

The important point for us to realize now is that phase 5 in any cyclic process, be it microcosmic or macrocosmic, constitutes a dynamic transition between phase 4 and phase 6. The creative Impulse which, after passing through the above-described phases 1, 2, and 3, reached the stage of concretization in physical organisms and personification in human consciousness, has to *dephysicalize itself* through the operation of mind — that is, of *metabiological fields of conscious activity.* If we consider the first three phases of the cycle as a "descent" of spirit into matter (a confusing, yet widely used image), the last three phases of the cycle—5, 6, and 7—represent the "ascent" of individualized fields of conscious activity to a planetary or cosmic level of operation. We may speak also of a "universalization" of consciousness implying a conscious and active participation in the planetary or cosmic "greater Whole" to which these individualized fields belong.

The first half of the cycle is involutionary; the second half evolutionary. Spirit *involves* itself in organic forms which are concrete manifestations of its many and varied aspects — each aspect operating as an archetypal quality of individualized being and relatedness. Then consciousness *evolves* and expresses itself in always purer, more definite, yet more universally applicable forms of mind and of what Sri Aurobindo called overmind and Supermind, which refer respectively to vibrations 5 and 6.

In the second and ascending half of the cycle, phase 5 corresponds to phase 3 in the first and descending half. Phase 4 is the "bottom" of the cycle. The main task of vibration 5 is to *mobilize* what had become earth-bound, institutionalized, and static in its inertial worship of the *reflected* power of the creative origin of the cycle. It is to set in motion what had become self-complacent and set along rigid traditional lines. Mobilization in wartime is a highly disturbing and crucial process for the soldiers-to-be; and wherever vibration 5 acts in a focalized manner — that is, through an individual person radiating a Promethean spirit — the status quo is challenged and a more or less cathartic type of crisis takes place. It may occur in the life of single persons or small groups;

but it affects the entire society and culture-whole when their institutions and their paradigms have become rigid and no longer susceptible to gradual, *natural* modifications or mutations. Then Promethean spirits, whose symbol is the five-pointed star, appear in increasing number, and civilization *at the same time* opens the gates of the collective consciousness to a new vision and destroys whatever resists radical transformation.

I should stress at this point that while the several phases of a cyclic process are sequential, they also interact and interpenetrate to some extent. The future phase draws to itself the present state of consciousness, while the unfinished business and the failure of vision of the concluded phases permeate the present in the form of memories that tend to revitalize the past — or, we might say, as *karma*. During the large planetary cycle of the Earth's evolution which began millions of years ago, the vibration 4 gives to the biosphere and to mankind as a life-species its fundamental character. Yet after a certain point in that evolution the vibration 5 also begins to operate. It operates as the process of civilization. This process is to some extent conditioned by what occurred when vibration 3 was the fundamental tone of the Earth and of humanity. If there was a failure of vision during phase 3, as vibration 5 begins to operate as an overtone of the Root-fundamental of our planet, it will tend to be deviated (made "out of tune") by the karma or unconscious memory of that failure.

According to the "holarchic"—i.e. holistic and hierarchical—picture of the universe and its workings, every existential whole at the same time contains lesser wholes and participates in the organic activity of a larger field of existence. This picture is valid in the dimension of time as well as in space. That is to say, every cycle—a unit in the time-process of universal existence—contains sub-cycles. Thus while the large planetary cycle (let us call it the eon) is in its fourth basic phase, that phase has also seven subphases, and each of these has sub-subphases. As a result, a situation may arise in which the eonic process as a whole operates under vibration 4, the subphase operates under vibration 5, and the sub-subphase under vibration 6. Indeed, we live today at a time when this situation is beginning to be experienced by mankind, or at least by a sizeable section of mankind.

It is when vibration 5 starts to operate *at any level* (eon, subphase of sub-subphase) that the process of civilization begins to affect the consciousness, and eventually the activities and ways of life of human beings. This process operates through "civilizers," men whose constitution and character can *resonate* to the vibration 5. A time came during *the fifth* subphase of the planetary eon when the vibration 5 could begin to operate. This allowed for the appearance within the planetary field of the Kumaras-Prometheus who brought to man the fire of individual selfhood and therefore the possibility of developing a new type of mind freed from the compulsions of the biosphere. These beings, whatever names we may give them, were the first Civilizers. But because mankind as a whole and the Earth were fundamentally operating under the eonic vibration 4, and the coming of these Civilizers occurred in the third subphase of the large planetary cycle, the incoming vibration 5 could operate only at the level of Archetypes (number 3), thus as only a potentiality that could be concretely actualized only at a much later time.

When, during the fourth subphase, the fifth sub-subphase began to operate at a crucial moment in the development of the mythical Atlantis, the process of civilization was given a new and far more concrete impetus. Both its positive and negative (anabolic and catabolic) possibilities were developed by groups of Civilizers—the Biblical "giants"—some of whom used their "vibration 5 minds" to direct the intense powers of a tropical biosphere into destructive channels of self-gratification and tyrannical power-seeking. This led to the war between the "white" and the "black" Adepts which destroyed Atlantis, but also to the first stage in the development of a new humanity in which vibration 5 eventually became a strongly emphasized first overtone of the fundamental vibration of the eonic process still being ruled by vibration 4.

I stressed the word eventually because it was only when the fifth sub-subphase of the fifth subphase began that a large proportion of mankind actually became emotionally and intellectually dynamized at a personal and social level by the power of the Civilizer's mind, vibration 5. This process began around 600 B.C. and it can be related to the impulse given by such great men as Gautama the Buddha, Pythagoras, the last of the Zoroasters, and to the Greek culture as a whole. During the preceding sub-subphases the involutionary first half of this process had taken place. Strictly speaking, the Greco-Latin and Mediterranean period of human history can be considered in some of its outer aspects as operating under a strong vibration 4; yet the power that was released in the sixth century B.C. began to work within the consciousness of a relatively small elite, and basic concepts were provided for a later, more widespread and more concretized development of the Civilizer's mind during the 16th and 17th centuries in Europe. Generally speaking, whenever vibration n operates fully, vibration n +1 begins to act within the vanguard of mankind.

It is difficult to formulate clearly in existential terms how the whole process operates and the interplay of culture and civilization takes historical-social forms. Yet the archetypal principle implied in the process is extremely simple. It may also be illustrated by a musical analogy.

The sociocultural forms defining the collective way of life, feeling-responses, and intellectual assumptions of human beings within a culture-whole can be analyzed in a manner not unlike the way in which an acoustical specialist analyzes the timbre (or quality) of a musical instrument. He isolates the fundamental tone and the various overtones which, in their combination, determine the specific character of the sounds produced by the instrument; and he particularly studies the relative strengths of these constituting elements within the complex instrumental tones. A family of instruments tends to emphasize a certain set of overtones, sometimes even at the expense of the fundamental or "root-tone"; another family, another set. Every instrumental family can thus be characterized by a particular formula of relationship between fundamental and overtones. Likewise any culture-whole stresses a certain set of assumptions, values, concepts, and feeling-responses which determines its collective way of life—and, musically speaking, its "timbre." Nevertheless individuals may operate in a way which appears to be, and at the higher level of their total being actually is, much in advance of the stage of development reached by their society or even by the human race as a whole. At the biological level of man's common humanity, their bodies—and in most cases, their "personalities," in the usual sense of the word—still experience the normal pressures and impulses of human nature, but the consciousness of these individuals no longer gives to these pressures and impulses the importance and/or the meaning which they have for the average human being. In some relatively rare cases, these men or women have actually transferred the center of their consciousness and therefore their sense of identity from the biopsychic level to a spiritual-mental level.

It is at that level that the great Civilizers have their consciousness focused; nevertheless, if they are to act as a civilizing, mobilizing, and transforming power, they have to use what the culture-whole in which they are born can provide. They have to give a cultural form to their culture-transcending visions or inspirations. Whether in concepts and words, in artistic creations, or in deeds which, as symbols and myths, become the foundations of sociocultural or religious institutions, these men must formulate what often is in fact unformulatable at the mass level of their culture. Because they radiate a mental or supermental light upon the opaque and rigid mentality of their contemporaries, one of the almost inevitable results is the appearance of a shadow as deep as the light emanated from their minds or souls is strong. They fascinate a few people, perhaps a large section of their community, who follow them, even at the cost of at least a relative type of martyrdom; but they also usually arouse equally strong opposing forces which focus the inertia inherent in the phase 4 of any cycle.

I repeat that number 4 symbolizes a concrete and solid state of existence. It must be solid in order to generate a sense of security, not for any particular living organism—because the biosphere has no concern for individual organisms which are always expendable—but for the species as a whole. The phase 4 of the human cycle brings the energies and functional activities of life to a point of dynamic equilibrium at which an individual person can reflect the cosmic harmony of the universal Whole. But the kind of material substance which can serve as a mirror is so coarse and so muddied by a constant unresolved (because unconscious) state of conflict that, save in the rare and exceptional cases of "avataric" beings, the reflection is very poor and usually distorted.

As vibration 5 begins to operate at the level of mental activity and creativity, the reflected forms become more definite and their meaning clearer, but this vibration 5 almost inevitably induces conflicts and provokes the inertial resistance of the biopsychic level of existence operating under vibration 4, and another kind of problem arises. I am referring here to what often manifests as the Civilizer's "double personality." This occurs because, even if his consciousness has become recentered at the 5 level, it is still operating in a natural body, from whose energies and need the "vibration 5 mind" cannot totally separate itself, except in very rare cases.

That mind finds itself in a state of transition, and therefore of conflict. It is pulled by the memories of past moments of beauty, happiness and fulfillment, yet irrevocably drawn toward a future state which it usually cannot clearly or convincingly envision. Number 5 is a symbol of transition. It can be represented by an up-pointing or a down-pointing five-pointed star—the former, a symbol of "white magic"; the latter, of "black magic."

Civilization is a process of transition. As already stated, it is a means to an end; and that end becomes realized only as vibration 6 begins to operate within the mentalized consciousness of man. Civilization fails when this vibration 6 does not operate at least as an ideal and some sort of utopian vision. But today mankind is still (and has been for a very long time) operating at the fourth stage of the vast planetary cycle. Thus the 6-inspired *vision* in most instances remains vague and elusive because unformulatable in biopsychological terms, except through often more confusing than revealing attempts at symbolization; and the *ideal* inspired by vibration 6, and those extremely rare beings who can transmute or radiate some of its power—Gautama the Buddha, Sankaracharya, the Christ, and a few others, known and mostly unknown— become personalized and institutionalized. Their message is diffused and emotionalized by the glamor of religious worship.

The very few beings, far ahead of human evolution, who brought to our planet at least the "prologomena"—the prophetic vistas—of its sixth phase, appeared in places where vibration 5 was particularly strong. This was true, for instance, in the India of the Age of Philosophy, and in the midst of the Jewish society that, though worshipping the typically vibration 5 experience of Moses in his encounter with the "I am that I am," nevertheless was still dominated by the rigid legal formulas of the tribal state. The Buddha attempted to desystematize and "metabiologize" Hindu life, still oppressed by a caste system which once, in its ideal form, was meant to reflect the fourfold order of the cosmos as seen from the perspective of a life-centered consciousness. Christ sought to spiritualize, deintellectualize and deformalize the consciousness of the people to whom he had come, and to extoll above every other law the principle of universal love. But how little is left of Christ's vision and ideal! And probably how inaccurately understood has been the meaning of nirvana (the state of liberation) which the Buddha sought to convey to his followers, even though, later on, Mahayana Buddhism stressed the ideal of total compassion in terms of an existential reality, which nevertheless had a somewhat remote and rarefied field of application!

On the one hand, whatever the vibration 6 of consciousness brings to the human mind always tends to be physicalized and dogmatized so that it may give a sense of security, transcendent though it be, to the man of our "fourth World." On the other hand, when, through the development of intellectual analysis and objectivity, the vibration 5 succeeds in bringing to a culture-whole a workable sociocultural system making possible the development of individuals in at least relative freedom and equality before the law, it also fosters technological advance, a passion for physical comfort and ego-satisfaction, a craving for social, cultural, and political fame and power, and the uncontrolled growth of monstrous cities in which existence becomes thoroughly artificialized and in the end bitterly disruptive of health, harmony, and security. Then a reaction sets in, and the only form of salvation which a new generation of city-dwellers and suburban commuters can envision is a chaotic return to the "natural" life and a glorified sexual freedom which is essentially not free, because it is an escape from emotional conflicts and from an intellectualized sense of futility or despair.

In saying this I am of course dealing with generalities always susceptible of being modified by conditioning particularities of personal or group living. But at this point in history, not only in the Western world but everywhere on the globe, the need for a vision, in which vast and inclusive currents of human consciousness and activity are seen moving to almost inevitable ends against a cosmic background, seems imperative. These currents actually operate within each and all individuals, whether consciously or not; and it is essential that we should be clearly conscious of what these currents mean and to what they are leading. Understanding is essential, and our physical sciences and our various and conflicting psychological schools do not give us the kind of understanding we need. They are obsessed with particularities, personal case histories and existential data. These, if well treated, may help individual persons to feel better and calm their emotional crises. But today this is nonessential. A greater vision of what existence is and what it means to us all, now, in our global state of crisis, is necessary for human survival. We have to go ahead, not backward. Yet we have to include the tragic past of mankind in our departicularized consciousness, and through an understanding of where this past fits when seen as a phase of the total process of planetary development, to accept it, even with all its tragedies—including our own as individuals.

To do this without being affected by it and emotionally drawn into it is difficult. But, as I see it, this is the only way—not "out," but forward; the conscious way of total acceptance. There is no way out, no possible escape. Even the ideal of living totally, exclusively, spontaneously in the present—the now—can be an escape from the conscious acceptance of responsibility. This is not the way of creativity. A truly creative activity has meaning essentially because it brings forth a new and transforming solution to the problems which the past has tried to evade or failed to meet squarely and fearlessly. The popular Hindu imagery which depicts the universe as the play (lila) of Brahma in which He takes all the parts under a myriad of masks has a beautiful child-like naivete. It glorifies life in its innocence—the fourth stage reflecting, but only reflecting, the original Edenic unity of all beginnings. It has not yet discovered the Tree of the Knowledge of Good and Evil.

Man must leave the original Eden in order to become Man. He eventually will make of the whole Earth a garden, not a reconstructed wilderness. Within that garden the many castles his many culture-wholes have built, and for a brief time inhabited, will again stand, illumined by the myriad of lights of multifarious human understanding. But Man will no longer need any castle, for he himself will be the one archetypal Castle, the great dream actualized, potentiality totally fulfilled on a transfigured Earth in all-encompassing plenitude of existence.[4]

4.

TOWARD A COMPANIONATE
ORDER OF RELATIONSHIP

THE PROCESS of civilization brings to the field of human activity in which culture-wholes operate a radically new approach to interpersonal and group relationships. This approach is responsible for the most basic features of the transformation which humanity as a whole, and particularly our Western society, is partially experiencing; but most people fail to understand at its deepest level the difference between the ways in which interpersonal relationships operate, on the one hand in tribal groups of cultural societies living close to nature, and on the other hand in the lives of human beings who, having achieved a relatively individualized state of consciousness, come together for the purpose of gradually realizing a deliberately chosen ideal of life.

In order to elucidate the character of this difference, let us mentally picture two gatherings of human beings. In the first case, a close family group in a conservative European or American town is found at Christmas time around a tree laden with presents. These people are related by kinship; they speak the same language; the same religious, cultural, and geomagnetic influences have molded their personal development. They are now exchanging gifts in a loving traditional spirit, rejoicing in a quasi-instinctual communion of feelings arising from a *common rootedness in a collective past.* Whether or not they are aware of such a grounding in a past, it is that sameness of origin that psychically unites them. It acts as a more or less compulsive force which operates underneath and through the more conscious feelings of personal likes or dislikes.

In the second case, we have a meeting of delegates at the United Nations headquarters discussing an international problem. Here we see educated individuals coming from different continents, races, creeds, and cultures, yet intent on working for the realization of a common purpose through days and nights of deliberation and compromises. In the end, a formula may emerge which will solve a crucial international problem and establish a more lasting peace.

The family gathering at Christmas is marked by the *basic similarity* of all the participants. The United Nations meeting reveals at first *seemingly unresolvable individual differences;* yet these differences may become harmonized and, ideally, an integrating solution acceptable to all should be reached. In the first instance unity is a primary fact which precedes the meeting and underlies the collective mood it produces. It is "root unity." The functional activities operating within living organisms are rooted in that kind of unity; all such organisms originate in one common ancestral cell, a seed or fecundated ovum. In the second instance, we start with basic differences; unity is at first only an ideal and an often distant goal which may or may not be realized. When realized we should speak of "multiunity"—or, in the recently popularized phrase, "unity in diversity"—rather than of simple and singular unity. This potential state of multiunity requires constant effort and vigilance for its implementation and maintenance. It can never be taken for granted.

Unity achieved at the group level as the outcome of a difficult process of harmonization of individual differences has assuredly not the same character as unity resulting from an initial sameness or basic biological similarity. While in the latter case the relatedness of a multiplicity of persons is the result of a *process of differentiation* which began in unity, in the United Nations group we see at work a *process of integration* which, it is hoped may end in the establishment of a single world-community. Such a process can be seen operating also, but in a somewhat different manner, in the type of communities formed by people of perhaps different races, cultures, and religious backgrounds, who have come together in order to work for the establishment of a type of society that would operate at a higher level of inclusiveness and consciousness. In such a community the actual patterns of organization and the implications of a new society may not be clearly envisioned by many of the participating individuals, yet the basic feeling that a new type and quality of interpersonal relationship can be worked out serves as an integrative force producing a union.

The envisioning of an ideal democracy by free thinkers of the eighteenth century and some of the founders of our nation when speaking of liberty, equality, freedom of opinion and association, and justice for all, was an attempt to demonstrate the possibility for human beings of various races, cultures, and religions to come together for the avowed purposes stipulated in the Preamble to the Constitution.[1] When a truly democratic society is consistent in its everyday application of what it officially professes, a *common purpose* should orient the consciousness and the actions of all its citizens and draw them toward the future. This future is not "given"; it has to be created. The vision of the ideal goal must be constantly upheld by the members of the community—at the local as well as the national level—as something *that is yet to be fully realized*, for quite obviously its realization is, at best and for a long time, partial and subject to reverses and crises of readjustment. Such a community should have an essentially dynamic character, because it should never take perfection for granted. Because it did not begin in actual physical unity, but in diversity of backgrounds, the only essential unifying principle must be the common goal; and this fact should *polarize* all the interpersonal relationships operating in that community and define their character. They should be deliberate and purposeful, because the joining of individual lives and efforts should be dedicated to the task of actualizing and substantiating what is as yet only a future possibility.

Such a type of interrelating is fundamentally different from that operating in tribal societies. These societies may be dynamic, at least during the first periods of their life-span, but what is at work is a dynamism of growth. The germinal impulse *unfolds* its inherent genetic potentialities. Everything is *given* in principle. A unity of origin differentiates into a multiplicity of cells according to a prearranged structural plan. The only basic uncertainty is whether or not the gradual development of the tribe and its culture proceeds *correctly* (right—*rita* in Sanskrit) according to the original seed-potential and the characteristic nature of the root-energy.

All tribal cultures speak of their Golden Age which they glorify in myths and rituals. It is the age of creative beginnings when gods or demigods walk with men. It is "sacred" time in contrast with "profane" time.[2] The latter refers to the type of growth-processes which are under man's uncertain and often perverting control. Thus, a typical culture displays an inherent spiritual inertia, and so do all living organisms. The physical seed in the beginning will have to be reproduced in the equally physical seed in the end. The unfoldment of the plant may be a success or a failure, depending on environmental conditions and according to the manner in which the different human cells within the plantlike community or culture-whole fulfill their functions; but nothing can be expected to take place that was not potential in the divine act of creation in the beginning of time.

The type of order prevailing in tribal communities is what I shall call *organic order*. It is the order of life: biospheric order, biopsychic and cultural order. It is order rooted in the past, manifesting in organic growth, maturity, and decay: a cyclic type of order. In contrast to such a type of order, we can speak of a *companionate order* whose manifestations should be associated with the process of civilization[3]; but, as already said, this process can be destructive as well as constructive, and its destructive aspect is particularly evident in the present-day *megalopolis*—the "tentacular," ever-spreading, and devouring city. Its constructive and transcendental aspect has been symbolized by the New Jerusalem and, in Asia, Shambhala.

The most characteristic manifestation of the companionate order has been exemplified in what has been called occult or universal Brotherhoods, a not too adequate designation as it uses a biological characterization "brother" to characterize a meta-biological and transcendental type of relationship. One of these occult Brotherhoods was the Druze Order founded in the 13th century by El Hamza. This Brotherhood united men and women of various races and religions who sought to build a spiritual community free from the religious conflicts of the period. The Druze Order operated in the Lebanon mountains of Syria, and Druze communities still exist today; but apparently much of the spiritual foundation of the Order has vanished under the pressures caused by the need for survival in a land constantly disturbed by religious conflicts and wars of conquest.

Last century an Oriental sage defined a universal Brotherhood as "an association of 'affinities' of strong magnetic yet dissimilar forces and polarities centered around a dominant idea." Around the same time, the English art critic and philosopher, John Ruskin, stated the same concept in different words: "It is the great principle of brotherhood not by equality, not by likeness, but by giving and receiving; the souls that are unlike and the nations that are unlike being bound into one noble whole by each receiving something from and of the other's gift and the other's glory." And after World War I, a remarkably perceptive and idealistic American woman, M. P. Follet wrote in her book *The New State*: Group-organization, the solution of popular government: "Each must discover and contribute (to the group) that which distinguishes him from the other, his difference. The only use for my difference is to join it with other differences. The unification of the opposites is the eternal process."[4]

At about the same time the then highly controversial idea of "companionate marriage" was upheld by Judge Kinsey in a book which at the time became quite famous. It stressed the idea that marriage could validly be based on a revocable contract between a man and woman who deliberately agreed to unite their lives for a consciously held common purpose. This purpose could include the procreation of children as well as any other common goal, but the basic factor in this new type of marriage was that it was considered an association of two *individuals* who of their own accord and for purposes strictly of their own as individuals—and not as members of a biological family and a social or religious community, financial class, race, or nation—*freely chose to work together.*

We usually forget that until about one hundred years ago (and much more recently in many places) the choice of a marriage partner was almost never decided by a boy and a girl acting as individuals free from external parental and social or religious pressures. Marriage was a taken for granted event in the natural lives of normal men and women, and the two partners did not deliberatelyly come together as individuals and for the purpose of achieving an individualized goal to which they were eager to consciously devote their joined lives. The one purpose of any marriage (except in rare instances) was to perpetuate the human race and a particular sociocultural and religious tradition endowed with a divine origin. To this "culture-marriage" we may therefore oppose a "civilization-companionship." The opposition is not to be thought of as absolute in terms of the physical, biological, and social consequences of the two types of man-woman union; these consequences may be outwardly the same in both cases, yet the intent and the essential character of the two participants radically differ in the two types of marriage. Not to realize what the difference is and how basic it is implies a failure to understand the difference between culture and civilization. And one can never sufficiently emphasize that without such a realization, the present all-human crisis cannot be given its true meaning.

Having said this, I must add at once that in our historical period most human beings respond in some degree to both types of order, organic and companionate. Human consciousness has for a long time resembled the mythical Roman Janus, one of whose two faces looked toward the past, the other toward the future. In Greek mythology we have also the twin brothers, Epimetheus and Prometheus, who can respectively symbolize the traditionalist oriented toward the past and the prophet whose vision seeks to pierce the as-yet-unknown future.

The pull of the biopsychic roots must be felt even by the "seed man" who is still attached to the plant of his culture. He can be free of that pull only when he has developed a mind and an experience of individual center allowing his transformed consciousness to leave the plant and, like a seed, to fall into the soil. Even then, as long as this culture-liberated individual operates in and through a physical body, he is still subject to the pressures and desires that characterize physical organisms within our biosphere. The two pulls coexist, and as a result conflict is unavoidable. Thus, a potential state of war exists within every individualized person; the biospheric self makes demands which the mental-spiritual self tries not to accept. Compromises are required if the unity of the personality is not to break down. Crisis follows crisis when new levels of adjustment between the conflicting forces become possible.

This sacred place is Man's consciousness; but in order to act as an alchemical vessel wherein the process of transformation can effectively operate, consciousness has to be *individualized and formed*. A place set apart and isolated from the mass-vibration of the culture-whole is required for the process to operate. The alchemical vessel—mind—has to be structured according to archetypal principles inherent in Man and in the universe to which we can relate. The consciousness of a particular human being has to be "formed" into a mind *open to the above as well as to the below*. Because, within this mind, the above and the below cannot only enter into contact, but can interpenetrate; it becomes a sacred place, an altar, an alchemical vessel. Only within such a formed consciousness can the symbolic union of Heaven (archetypal reality) and Earth (biopsychic human nature) occur.

It is in the minds of only a few individuals that the process of civilization acts upon the evolving culture-whole. Through these minds, and to the extent that the global state of the biosphere makes it possible at that particular time, civilization universalizes the culture of a particular group of human beings. What the creative minds are able to *formulate* in terms intelligible to the participants in that culture becomes then a mutating ideologic seed that, sooner or later, will germinate and affect other minds. By a process of mimesis, and more significantly of resonance, the latter in turn reproduce and multiply the new images and the new quality of relationship embodied in, or at least symbolized by these images and concepts.

We are dealing therefore with the interaction of two processes. The *evolutionary* biopsychic growth and eventual decay of a culture-whole is a continuous process; but at various times during its unfoldment, and especially as it reaches a stage of incipient degeneration, it is affected, and we might say fecundated, by a creative impulse emanating from centers of consciousness belonging to a far vaster planetary process. This process which I identify with civilization discontinuously releases into a few ready and open minds of culture-born persons new seed-ideas, symbols charged with an immense potentiality for transformation. New forms are visualized by the minds within which this metamorphic process of civilization has become, for a time, gradually focused—a time which operates in a different dimension from the time of our biosphere.

Form is the expression or concretization of relationship. Thus a new quality of relationship must inevitably produce new forms. Any basic change in the consciousness of human beings calls for a process of "trans-formation"—a process of metamorphosis. Because the life within the form develops a great deal of inertia, such a metamorphic process requires a concentration of energy, thus of energy-directing will. The release of energy produces motion and internal heat. The tremendous amount of energy released and heat produced in a hydrogen-bomb explosion is a fitting symbol of the crisis of transformation in which all human beings are now involved, whether or not they accept this fact and act intelligently and creatively in order to keep pace with the vast release of possibilities now open to mankind.

But how to keep pace, and where are we to go? The direction should be clear. It can be only toward the companionate order of relationship. First, the quality of interpersonal and intergroup relationships has to be changed so as to allow for a resonance of human consciousness to the consciousness of what is more-than-man—a metabiologizing of consciousness which transfigures the relationships of the life-sphere without, as in asceticism, violently belittling or repudiating them. Then, one must be open to the appearance of new forms concretizing the new character of relationships. But to be open to the advent of new forms, we should understand what is implied in the concept of form. We should grasp the meaning of the dualism of internal and external forms, of forms based on exclusion and forms demonstrating, at least in a relative sense, the character of all-inclusiveness. We should consider forms operating in terms of space and forms referring to the sequence of phases in processes inevitably implying time. We should understand the difference between "proportional form" and "expressive form"—a basic difference not only in the arts but in the art of living—forms derived from the differentiation or parceling of space, considered as fullness of being, and forms projected upon theoretically empty space by the emotions or the creative will of the artist. We could also discuss the meaning of form in the language of the modern physicist, and that of *gestalt* (or configuration) in twentieth century holism and psychology.

The subject is almost endless, for existence is relatedness, and the modes of existence are infinitely varied, each calling for a different approach to form. We shall therefore have to limit and restrict ourselves to those aspects of form which can reveal the operations of culture and civilization, particularly in the domain of the arts considered as a revelatory symbol of the organized activity of human communities.

At first the demands of the organic order cannot be dismissed. "Natural man" triumphs over "civilization man," and the ideal of metabiological and "noetic" existence according to the principles of the companionate order can but weakly challenge the power of the tribal roots. What is even more serious and eventually tragic is that the biopsychic drives of "natural man" succeed in using the mind that had envisioned a companionate ideal to satisfy their aim more excitingly. The deviated future-oriented drive becomes perverted and in turn it exacerbates and poisons the natural biopsychic energies. As this happens, the civilization process turns negative. It prostitutes itself. A totalitarian law-and-order worship—a brutal and obscene caricature of the companionate order— is gradually forced upon individuals rendered helpless by the products of a technology which have become the uncontrollable progeny of a civilization obsessed by materialism. Sadism and torture are accepted by a vast number of people as matters of no real consequence, even as matters of policy. Brutalizing civil wars rage, and when human beings refuse to unite in world-wide companionate love, their bloods have to unite on global battlefields. The symbolic (and probably also actual) battle of Kurukshetra described in the great Hindu epic, the Mahabharata, is to be fought again on a panhuman scale. The Biblical Armageddon may yet occur.

The blend of civilization and culture has innumerable destructive results, as long as the compulsive drives operating in a natural and balanced manner in the biosphere are able to intrude in the realm of the companionate order in a forceful and dominant manner. And they will intrude in a variety of unsuspected, confusing or lightly dismissed ways until the two principles of order and their corresponding levels of consciousness are not clearly distinguished and evaluated for what they are and are meant to be. But while coexistence must be a fact as long as human consciousness operates in a biological body, it is possible for any human being to alter, transform, and refine the quality of the results of such a coexistence. This quality basically depends on the manner in which the coexistence is interpreted, thus *on the origin, meaning, and purpose which are attributed to it.*

To say that a human being is both angel and beast is an emotional interpretation. To state, with Oswald Spengler, that all that is good is related to culture and everything destructive of value comes under the label, civilization, is an equally emotional and biased judgment based on a tragically incomplete grasp of human evolution. The two orders of relationship (organic and companionate) have their place in present-day mankind. They can be harmonized, but only if human beings are able to stop "thinking-feeling" in terms of either an absolute kind of presumable spiritual transcendence, or a glorification of a compulsive and essentially cruel state of nature, in which physical strength or intellectual cunning is the guarantee of survival.

Man is not a combination of angel and beast, of spiritual soul and coarse, unredeemable body. Man is fundamentally Mind, but not what our materialistic scientist and philosophers think of mind. Archetypally, man is that through which material bodies can be transmuted into structured fields of energy, and physical nature can be alchemicalized into soul. Man is an alchemical retort. In and through man a process is going on; but the character and the purpose of this process are not yet readily understood, because we witness everywhere the whole human material fermenting; and the fermentation throws off an ugly scum which hides the end purpose of the transformation. This alchemical process is civilization. Civilization begins with individualization and the stressing of differences, mind providing the heat required for the individualizing operation. But these differences *can* be harmonized once human beings accept the fact that Man is not merely an evolutionary product of the biosphere ineradicably and unconsciously determined by life's compulsions, but a vessel (a sacred place," *maqom* in Hebrew) within which these biopsychic imperatives can be consciously and objectively understood and evaluated, then repolarized and transmuted by their contact with metabiological spiritual forces.

This sacred place is Man's consciousness; but in order to act as an alchemical vessel wherein the process of transformation can effectively operate, consciousness has to be *individualized* and *formed*. A place set apart and isolated from the mass-vibration of the culture-whole is required for the process to operate. The alchemical vessel—mind—has to be structured according to archetypal principles inherent in Man and in the universe to which we can relate. The consciousness of a particular human being has to be "formed" into a mind *open to the above as well as to the below*. Because, within this mind, the above and the below cannot only enter into contact, but can interpenetrate, it becomes a sacred place, an altar, an alchemical vessel. Only within such a formed consciousness can the symbolic union of Heaven (archetypal reality) and Earth (biopsychic human nature) occur.

It is in the minds of only a few individuals that the process of civilization acts upon the evolving culture-whole. Through these minds, and to the extent that the global state of the biosphere makes it possible at that particular time, civilization universalizes the culture of a particular group of human beings. What the creative minds are able to *formulate* in terms intelligible to the participants in that culture becomes then a mutating ideologic seed that, sooner or later, will germinate and affect other minds. By a process of mimesis, and more significantly of resonance, the latter in turn reproduce and multiply the new images and the new quality of relationship embodied in, or at least symbolized by these images and concepts.

Repeat of p. 44 —

We are dealing therefore with the interaction of two processes. The *evolutionary* biopsychic growth and eventual decay of a culture-whole is a continuous process; but at various times during its unfoldment, and especially as it reaches a stage of incipient degeneration, it is affected, and we might say fecundated, by a creative impulse emanating from centers of consciousness belonging to a far vaster planetary process. This process which I identify with civilization discontinuously releases into a few ready and open minds of culture-born persons new seed-ideas, symbols charged with an immense potentiality for transformation. New forms are visualized by the minds within which this metamorphic process of civilization has become for a time gradually focused—a time which operates in a different dimension from the time of our biosphere.

Form is the expression or concretization of relationship. Thus a new quality of relationship must inevitably produce new forms. Any basic change in the consciousness of human beings calls for a process of "trans-formation"—a process of metamorphosis. Because the life within the form develops a great deal of inertia, such a metamorphic process requires a concentration of energy, thus of energy-directing will. Energy being released produces motion and internal heat. The tremendous amount of energy released and of heat produced in a hydrogen-bomb explosion is a fitting symbol of the crisis of transformation in which all human beings are now involved, whether or not they accept this fact and act intelligently and creatively in order to keep pace with the vast release of possibilities now open to mankind.

But how to keep pace, and where are we to go? The direction should be clear. It can be only toward the companionate order of relationship. First, the quality of interpersonal and intergroup relationships has to be changed so as to allow for a resonance of human consciousness to the consciousness of what is more-than-man—a metabiologizing of consciousness which transfigures the relationships of the life-sphere without, as in asceticism, violently belittling or repudiating them. Then, one must be open to the appearance of new forms concretizing the new character of relationships. But to be open to the advent of new forms, we should understand what is implied in the concept of form. We should grasp the meaning of the dualism of internal and external forms, of forms based on exclusion and forms demonstrating, at least in a relative sense, the character of all-inclusiveness. We should consider forms operating in terms of space and forms referring to the sequence of phases in processes inevitably implying time. We should understand the difference between "proportional form" and "expressive form," a basic difference not only in the arts but in the art of living—forms derived from the differentiation or parceling of space, considered as fullness of being, and forms projected upon theoretically empty space by the emotions or the creative will of the artist. We could also discuss the meaning of form in the language of the modern physicist, and that of *gestalt* (or configuration) in twentieth century holism and psychology.

The subject is almost endless, for existence is relatedness, and the modes of existence are infinitely varied, each calling for a different approach to form. We shall therefore have to limit and restrict ourselves to those aspects of form which can reveal the operations of culture and civilization, particularly in the domain of the arts considered as a revelatory symbol of the organized activity of human communities.

5.

FORM AND CREATIVITY

THERE ARE essentially two ways of defining what is implied in the concept of "form." Form, we may say, results from the manner in which a number of elements are interrelated. These elements may be dots, lines, surfaces, masses, entities of whatever type and size. The particular way in which a number of such elements are arranged produces a form. Such a group can be called a whole within which many interdependent parts are linked. This whole may exist geometrically in space; it has an organic character if a living entity is considered. One can also refer to a group existing in time, as a definite sequence of interrelated elements or units constituting a whole unfolding its potentialities; for instance, a melody in music, or a seed developing into a plant according to a definite schedule of transformations. One can also speak of the form of a theory or system of concepts within which a number of ideas are interrelated.

While the form of a whole is the result of the particular organization of its parts, this whole is not alone in space. It exists in the midst of a multitude of other wholes which, by exerting upon it various kinds of pressure, contribute most basically to the determination of its externally perceptible form.

Thus the form of any compound entity—any whole having component parts—should be considered the result of two kinds of arrangements: an internal scheme of interconnections between the components of the whole, and the sum total of the interactions between this whole and other surrounding wholes or various forces operating in the environment. We have therefore to distinguish between *internal* and *external* factors when we consider any form, or the process of formation giving rise to forms; this at any level whatsoever, whether it be atomic, organic, psychological, conceptual, or cosmic.

If we take the simple case of a unicellular organism living in the sea, we see that it consists essentially of a small amount of sea-water separated from the ocean by a flimsy membrane, usually with two openings: one through which some kind of foodstuff is ingested, and one through which waste products are excreted. Any biological or biosocial organism (for instance, well-defined cities) can likewise be said to depend upon the existence of three factors: some sort of membrane, physical or conceptual, separating the organism from its environment; some kind of opening (precisely located, or extending over a relatively porous membrane) through which what is needed by the organism for survival and expansion is absorbed; and another type of opening through which what the organism cannot assimilate, or must reject as toxic waste-product of its activity, is excreted.

Within the boundaries of the organism, organs and cells are constantly active. This is an internal activity and it follows a definite plan and schedule. The organism is also active within its environment; it must get food—whether biological nutriments or emotional-mental "food" for its psychic well-being and development—and in order to do so it must enter into relationship with other entities and adjust to or control forces operative within that environment. And there is a social-cultural, psychomental environment as well as a biological one.

These relationships with external entities can be peaceful and constructive, or they can demand strenuous effort, aggressiveness, and violent fights for survival or for the achievement of what the organism wants in terms of a relatively individualized consciousness and ego-satisfaction. Such external relationships condition, and in many ways even determine, the form of the organism and its psychomental character just as much as the internal relationships linking all its internal parts define its generic functional rhythms and shape, and—especially in a human being or a society of human beings—its psyche and its particular psychomental responses to life.

Boundaries: Closed or Open

Boundaries, separating the inner from the outer field of activity, can be of many kinds. They may be very concrete and solid, porous, or transparent. They may be those of conceptually or legally defined systems, or they can be defined by differences in electromagnetic polarization or even in emotional group-responses and behavior. What is most important, they can be seen to serve two theoretically opposite functions. Boundaries *isolate* the inner from the outer; but they also *relate* the inner and the outer. At the circumference of a circle, the space within the circle is in contact with the surrounding space. Through the skin of an organism, exchanges between the interior of this organism and the universe at large—and perhaps most specifically some other organism—take place. At the skin, and through certain differentiated areas of response, a man feels cold or heat, loves a woman, shakes hands with friends or is wounded by enemies.

A more or less well-defined zone in which contact and communication can be established surrounds any organism; it exists also at one level or another wherever socially, politically, or conceptually organized systems of activity operate. When the boundaries of the form consist, for instance, of a fortified wall, there may be a moat extending for some distance outside of the wall, and a drawbridge for incoming and outgoing traffic. We are now aware of the existence of an aura around living organisms; but, at the conceptual level, a well organized theory sharply and logically defining a particular interpretation of data of human experience is always surrounded by the possibility of the intrusion of conflicting and inadmissible facts which, if presented to the builder of the theory, are often given a rather doubtful and tendentious interpretation, or rejected *a priori* because they are inimical to his conceptual approach.

The potentially dual character of the boundaries of a form is a most important factor in the development of consciousness. Any system of life-activity or thought-feeling can be characterized by the nature of its boundaries and by what takes place at these boundaries. We often refer to an "open" or a "closed" society; but the ego of an individual can also be surrounded by fortified walls which close upon and rigidly isolate its psychic contents and make difficult, if not impossible, communication with other persons and the flow of love—a spiritual "commerce," an interchange of feelings, sensations and values. Yet a man's ego need not act as a medieval fortification; it can have open boundaries through which all kinds of interchange take place.

Closed ego-boundaries produce deep-seated, even if masked, loneliness, and a sense of separativeness and alienation from the environment. On the other hand, too open and inadequately defined boundaries may lead to an invasion to the field of consciousness by unassimilable influences, and in some cases to psychic possession. This often happens when the organism, the individual consciousness or the conceptual system, does not have a well established center, or lacks cohesion and consistency; thus, when the interior field has not stabilized its own functional rhythm and defined any central purpose. If this is the case, insecurity is felt and the organic response may be the erection of fortified walls which seem necessary to insure independence and acceptance on one's own terms—unclear or irrational as these may be—by the environment.

A strong individual has either a powerful center (will) directing and radiating the energy building up within the inner field of his personality (in which case fortified boundaries are not necessary) or he has built impressive and menacing ego-walls and an aggressive ego-will able to launch violent predatory attacks of limited scope upon his environment. Real security, however, does not depend mainly on strong and rigidly defined boundaries. It depends on the character and quality of the consciousness which pervades the form; and as consciousness develops in terms of relatedness, what is at stake is the character and quality of the relationships operating within the field of activity limited by the boundaries of the organic, psychological, social, or even conceptual form. Problems nevertheless may arise when relationships of this kind and the form they spontaneously take are at variance with the character of the relationships normally acceptable to the environment.

In a strictly biological environment such as our planet's biosphere, teeming with lives and filled with dangers, *the organic order of relationship* described in the preceding chapter is normally the more sound and effective, in terms of adaptation to outer circumstances and of biological survival. This is why the *family* pattern of organization has so far proven indispensable, at least as a foundation for interpersonal relationship, sociocultural interactions, the development of group-consciousness and the transmission of knowledge from generation to generation. But man is not only a biological system, a body. He is also and, at least ultimately, even more a mind. He is an organized form of consciousness, rooted in biology, yet able metabiologically to develop "mind seed" and even the seed of his own archetypal immortality, relative as immortality may be. Such a development implies a shifting from organic order to *companionate* order; thus, from the exclusiveness characterizing all family and tribal patterns of relationship to the inclusiveness of an open society of open minds — minds that are centered in self, yet interpenetrate and unite in love.

This graudal, yet discontinuous and periodic shifting of the gears of human consciousness, which control the reactions and operations of the engine of personality, is what is described in this book as the process of civilization. Radically altered relationships demand and sooner or later produce new forms of organization, whether it be in the lives of individuals, in the social, political, and cultural fields, or in modes of thinking and conceptual systems such as logic and mathematics. The process of change often is extremely painful at the personal level, revolutionary and cruel in politics, and confusing in the fields of religion and philosophy. We are now in a period of accelerated, indeed critical, change of gears. The road is rough, filled with obstacles and ups and downs, and mankind, the driver, is inexperienced, confused, and hesitant; the grinding noise is often appalling. We call it a "world war."

The League of Nations, the United Nations, UNESCO, and also the big international corporations are new forms of sociopolitical relationships. The concepts of "companionate marriage," unlegalized child-bearing associations and group-marriage — revealing a basic change in the collective consciousness of woman — and those at the root of non-Euclidian geometry and Einstein's Theory of Relativity are parallel developments. Probably none of these have reached an even relatively final stage. They are compromises between the compulsions of the biosphere and the rhythms operating at the cosmic or archetypal level of the mind.

Carl Jung — and before him philosophers and religious leaders — has validly stressed the need for "integration." Nevertheless the ultimate problem confronting us is not merely that of integration vs. loose aggregation; it presents itself to man as he realizes that for him several levels of integration are possible. Today we should be clearly aware of what two of these levels imply in terms of personal, interpersonal, and intergroup organization; but others are conceivable and, what is more, we have also to deal with sublevels existing between the two fundamental ones, "life" and "mind." Each of these sublevels constitutes important and presumably necessary intermediary stages. The worm does not at once become a butterfly; and the driver changing gears has first to go into neutral.

In actual living the process of transition is far more complex than these symbolic illustrations suggest, because for man the transition from the biological to the mind realm does not mean a total relinquishment of the values directly or indirectly referring to life and its urges, as long as the human being operates as a physical organism. What is involved is a shift in weight and polarization. Psychologically speaking, the Yang of consciousness never totally overwhelms Yin. What changes is the *relative strength* of the two pulls within the total person: on one hand, the individual's attachment to life experienced in a body as a separate field of organized activities and drives; and on the other hand, the individual's eagerness or determination to operate as a "free" center of consciousness in a mind-form detached from all that living as a biological organism psychically as well as physically implies.

The Metaphysics of Form

What has just been stated should be expanded, I believe, to cover every conceivable mode and form of existence, cosmic as well as human. Existence implies a dualism of forces or pulls, opposite yet complementary. To say it does not is the greatest illusion, the supreme *Maya*; yet human beings at times, in periods of crisis, may need such an illusion — the belief that absolute Unity can be reached in some sublime form of *individualized consciousness and being*. Hindu philosophers have spoken of *manvantaras and pralayas* — long cosmic periods of Manifestation, and equally long (but can "length" mean anything in a timeless state!) periods of Non-Manifestation. Yet this cosmic or divine in-and-out-breathing is inconceivable, unless in the assumed periods of total Non-Manifestation the principle or the "seed" of Manifestation exists within the Absolute. Thus it is said that "before" the beginning of a universe God "desired" to create, to reveal Himself to Himself. Yet such a desire could not occur if the idea of duality had not remained within the One; thus it could not be an absolute One. The desire for the Many may "sleep" within the One; yet this simply means that the One and the Many — Non-Manifestation and Manifestation — represent essentially inseparable polarities. The human consciousness separates them in its attempts to overcome the pull of the Many (i.e. the pull of material biological existence) and to center itself resolutely, yet most often blindly, around *a* One — the "I" or Self. Every system of Manifestation begins in a One; but there can be no *absolute* One.

With reference to space, we can say that *ideally* Space can be conceived as *infinite multidimensional extension* or as the *mathematical point* without dimension and extension. But both concepts are futile abstractions as soon as we think of actual existence. Space can never reach *either one* of these two extremes, for this would deny the possibility of existence and of a mind thinking the concepts. Existence presupposes duality and relatedness between existents; and these existents — whether they be atoms, galaxies, or human beings — *have form*, because *any* field of relationship has form. To speak of "formless" existence is as absurd as to speak of "timeless" processes.

Yet Hindu philosophers and modern "esotericists" speak of *rupa* and *arupa* realms, words translated as form and no-form. Such terms refer only to what a person, whose consciousness is totally controlled by biophysical experiences and operates within a mind subservient to the life-and-death patterns of existence in the biosphere, aspires to become. For primitive men, wind was formless. *Pneuma* (breath) implied "spirit," and the world around them was filled with unseen presences they spoke of as spirits or angels. Anything that was felt, yet unperceived by the senses, could only be considered formless. Yet the clairvoyant's inner eye seems to perceive entities with eerie and evanescent forms, forms of light or darkness, forms that may instantaneously change their apparent shapes, disappear and reappear. When a clairvoyant sees such forms, the clairaudient hears unspoken words, or a "clairthinker" receives new ideas formed and ready for expression, what is seen, heard, intuited is the manifestation of a *relationship* between the human person and a realm of existence transcending concrete biophysical living. To call that realm *arupa* or formless is needlessly confusing. Since the advent of the Theosophical Movement a century ago, many people speak of "thought forms." Clairvoyants claim to see such thought forms; but what they describe is *an interpretation* — in terms referring directly or indirectly to the realm of their physical experience — of *formative processes* operating in the field of mind-activity.

When the Sufi mystic describes his experience of an exalted state of consciousness in terms of intoxication, wine, and the thralldom of total love, he is using symbols or metaphors to interpret what to him is ineffable. Likewise, the wings of angels in Christian paintings, or of devas in Persian-Hindu miniatures, are interpretative symbols making use of man's experiences of birds, whose field of existence is this mysterious, seemingly formless air, *pneuma*. They are forms that express the fundamental relationship between the normal level of human consciousness and a transcendent field of existence. If the clairvoyant's relationship to such a field is less dependent upon human experiences at the biological level, he or she may perceive the angels as elongated forms of light, or nature-spirits as pulsating currents of energy. Yet because the seer is somehow aware that consciousness inheres within these indescribable forms, he or she can hardly avoid sensing soul-revealing "eyes" and perhaps facial features, simply because this is the way a human being perceives consciousness in an exteriorized state. Some feature in the transcendental form must *express* consciousness; and because transcendent consciousness is not an *individualized* kind of consciousness but (we are told by the most believable Occultists) is the consciousness of a large group (or spiritual Hierarchy), we find that the "eyes" of representations of spiritual beings, or even of the great "Masters" of whom Theosophy speaks, all have a similar super-individual quality. They are like deep pools of light and love — gates *through which* our consciousness is called upon to enter a superhuman realm of activity as well as of being.[1]

The function of these forms is to convey to still biologically compelled human beings the possibility of becoming more-than-human. They are *transhuman* forms; and by this term I do not refer to something "beyond" the human as much as to what, operating "through" a human form, draws sensitive individuals toward a higher state of consciousness and a supersensual type of relationships in which the exclusiveness of the tribal and strictly personal level is replaced by the inclusiveness of pure and unwavering compassion.

Personal Expression and Space-Differentiation

At this point in our discussion of the various meanings and implications of form it is essential for us to distinguish between *expressive
forms* and what we might call geometric, or (more significantly) cos-
mometric or *cosmogenetic* forms.

Expressive forms imply the existence of a "formative agent" existing
prior to the process of formation. By means of such a process this agent
seeks either to "express" himself or to achieve a self-conditioned or
precisely self-determined purpose. On the other hand, cosmogenetic
forms can be considered inherent as potentialities not only in Space
itself — they occur spontaneously (and in a sense automatically) as the
result of an impersonal process of differentiation — that is, of the
parceling of Space according to the structuring power of cyclic Time.
These two approaches to creativity are opposite, yet also complementary. It is essential that they should be clearly understood.

When a painter, facing what to him is the blank space of a canvas,
projects upon a space he considers empty forms which he either sees in
his imagination, or feels to be characteristic means to convey to other
people a strong emotion or belief, the forms he paints are "expressive."
He, their creator, fills them with whatever space is conveniently available or fits his creative purpose. He creates art-forms which, in their
concrete physicality, are exterior to him.

This concept of *exteriority* is capital in the arts of our Western culture. It reflects the metaphysical belief in a God exterior to the universe
He has created. This God creates the universe and Man with only a
portion of His infinite being, and after the creation He remains "separate." This concept of God and His creation may have found its first
formulation in India's *Bhagavad Gita*, whose original unwritten form
is undoubtedly far more ancient than obvious biased Western archaeologists with their Christian and European background would want to
acknowledge. It characterizes what is called "theism," the conceptual
and emotional foundation of the recent great religions born in the
Near-East.[2]

It is also the foundation of the individualistic and the Romantic-Ex-
pressionistic approach to artistic creation — whether in literature,
music or the plastic arts. As the artist creates he (or she) projects some of
his personal being and psychic energy into the art-form; yet he remains
separate. The potentiality of many more creative acts remains within
him. Likewise man's Soul is believed to be exterior to the physical
organism — or even, for Spiritualists and students of Oriental philosophies, exterior to the total "personality" conceived merely as a
temporary vesture of this Soul seeking experiences or ·"working out

past karma" in the more or less dreary field of existence we call the Earth.

Such an interpretation of the nature of the creative process obviously is based on the experience of the procreative act at the biological-sexual level. The male projects his semen and some of his psychic energy into the receptive female womb which, in every menstrual cycle, is re-virginized; a child is born, and the father remains separate and capable of many more fecundative acts. In the theistic concept God is the Father of the cosmos; and at a superphysical level, He is also the Father of male-female Man made in His image and likeness (Genesis I). The creative artist likewise is thought of essentially as a male power fecundating, at one level, his material for creation — a material extended through empty space — and at another level, the virgin field of his culture, his public. He is, according to the Romantic interpretation, a microcosmic God, who creates in order to "release the torment of his plenitude" (cf. Nietzsche in *The Origin of the Tragedy*). He not only desires to create; he is inwardly *compelled* to project some aspect of his being into artistic forms. These, therefore, for onlookers or hearers vividly experiencing them, are potentially revelatory manifestations of the artist's inner being. If this artist is truly a Representative Man, the revelation should also throw much light upon the inner being of a spectator, hearer, or reader who is thus able to experience by proxy a release of psychic contents which, though within him, he had perhaps not as yet the courage to face and deal with in his personal life.

The other basic approach to creativity is founded upon the realization (or intellectual belief) that Space is *fullness of potential being*. It can be thought of as an "Ocean of infinite potentiality." Ancient philosophers have spoken of it as "the One Life"; but the word Life, even if capitalized, seems confusing, for while it is a cosmic extension and metaphysical generalization of what we experience within the Earth's biosphere as living processes, it should not be thought to have the same characteristics as what we know as life at our physical-material level. Other more recent philosophies, such as American New Thought, speak of the Divine (or Cosmic) Mind; but there also the term *Mind* is confusing, for it tends to give modern human beings an unrealistic feeling of the value and power of the human mind at its present stage of development.

A concrete illustration should clarify the abstract concepts. Consider a fecundated ovum in a female womb. It constitutes one cell. It occupies space. This cellular space represents Space in a bounded and finite condition. A dynamic fullness of potential life is within that limited space, and at once a process of cellular differentiation takes place. The one original cell divides itself (*mitosis*), multiplying itself through generation after generation of cells, thus by geometric progression. After a relatively few generations, billions of cells will have been formed, each potentially fulfilling a special function in the fast developing organism.

How did the fecundated ovum — the finite space filled with life-potential — originate? Was it "created" by some entity external to that space?

It should be quite evident, though the idea undoubtedly would upset many people, that the man and woman whom we call father and mother had very little to do, as individual persons, in producing the fecundated ovum. Human beings have no control over their sperm and ova. They copulate under somewhat personalized circumstances and may either allow biological processes in them to operate naturally or deviate and altogether block these processes; but this has little to do with the particular contents of sperm and ovum. These contents are determined by the totally impersonal processes of life as these operate unconsciously and to a large extent compulsively in human organisms. What "creates" is life in its generically human mode. Thus one normally speaks of the procreation of babies, not of their creation.

Religious believers will say that God created the Soul of this particular baby out of nothing and for, to us, incredible reasons. Students of Hindu philosophies or Theosophy claim that it is a reincarnating individual Soul that determines the character and destiny of the body within which it is born in order to further its long term development and/or achieve some particular aim.

This is the individualistic and "Romantic" theory, produced by a metaphysical philosophy and psychology personalizing most processes of existence. It presumably was in order to counteract, or at least complement and polarize, such a personalistic approach to existence that Gautama, the Buddha, presented his nonpersonalistic *anatma* doctrine. He denied the reality of a permanent Soul-individuality and spoke instead of the cyclic reappearance of karmic residua (*skandhas*), thus substituting for a creative God the cyclic emergence of finite compound wholes, out of the infinite Ocean of potentiality, space. He stated that these emergences occur according to a metacosmic and absolutely impersonal principle of Harmony; and that once emerged, the existential wholes unfold their innate potential according to universally valid laws of cosmic differentiation and functional specialization.

These laws operate according to Number and Proportional Form. They are not conceived or imagined by a personal or individualized

Creator-God. They operate spontaneously because they are inherent in Space; and their operation follows a rhythmic sequence, a cosmic schedule, also inherent in Time whose nature is cyclic. Such a philosophy is associated in the West with the name of Pythagoras and was basic in at least one aspect of Greek culture.

This metaphysical approach does not imply that there is no God. God is Number One; the fecundated ovum of the cosmos is symbolically referred to in some systems as the Cosmic Egg, *Hiranyagarbha*. The Divine Presence inheres in every microcosm, just as the genetic code formed in the fecundated ovum — cell number 1 — inheres in every one of the trillions of cells of a human body; but each cell can only realize — or "reify" and concretize — one of the myriad of aspects of this immensely vast, *yet finite*, genetic code or Word (*Logos*) . However, neither the cosmic-divine Number One (*Ishvara*, or the *Logos* of the Greek-Christian Gnostics) nor the human microcosm, the individual person, is *exterior to the form defining his existence*; and this is an essential point, though it does not constitute the entire picture.

The Cosmic Egg differentiates into a multitude of forms through a long process operating at level after level of complexity. The original cosmic Space vibrates into an immense number of large or small eddies (or whirlpools of energy) each having its own keynote, each an overtone (or one should rather say an "undertone") of the one cosmic Fundamental. At one level, such eddies are galaxies; at another, planets and their life-kingdoms (each an "organ" in the entire planetary organism); on still another, human persons. Every microcosmic egg or seed unfolds its inborn potentialities in a specific generic form; and as mankind reaches the evolutionary stage at which psychomental *individualization* is possible, 3each fully individualized person *becomes as it were an entire species*, thus truly a microcosm. But this can happen only when the individual is able to metabiologize his or her consciousness and free himself of biological compulsions, though he remains *conditioned by* genetic patterns and needs as long as this "liberated" consciousness operates in a body.

If this cosmic picture is well understood it should be clear that every entity in the universe essentially is the space it occupies. It is a particular space, a specialized and functional differentiation of the original cosmic Space — that is, of the Number One state of the universe being considered. However, in individualized human beings a new possibility emerges: the possibility to be *consciously and actively related* to a greater Whole of which this individual is a functional part — the possibility to be attuned to the rhythms and the consciousness of that greater Whole, and thus to become consciously and responsibly a participant in the greater space and the greater life of that Whole.

The Two Approaches in the Arts

How this cosmic picture affects the creative process in the arts may not be apparent at first. Nevertheless if this world-view were a potent factor at the deepest level of the artist's consciousness, it would profoundly alter his approach to the work he performs and to all creative processes. Even when the metaphysical foundation of the picture is not clearly perceived, something of its impersonality may be a most significant feature in the creative attitude. During certain periods of the culture's development, when it has stabilized its specific character and revealed it as a particular style, the artist (whether in the plastic arts, in music, or in literature) operates simply as the agent of the collective whole which the culture constitutes at the psychomental level. The style comes first; then the artist. The style is the substratum and the basically conditioning element in the creative act. A work of art is a particular personalized eddy in the vast impersonal current of the collective life, having taken form as a cultural style — whether or not the creative artist is conscious of and accepts this fact.

At another level we find the artist — particularly in the case of the sculptor confronting a block of marble or a trunk of wood — asking the material he is ready to use for an inspiration. The sculptor tries to "feel" the potentiality of forms hidden within the stone or the wood; and in an analogical manner the composer of music may seek in the character of the instrument he is using an inspiration for his melodies or chords. In a sense therefore the material, which is a particular form of space, comes first, revealing its inmost potential of form-production through the agency of the composer.

The two approaches to creativity which I have just outlined undoubtedly can, and often do coexist within the creative process. Yet each approach represents a very basic attitude toward life which has endless repercussions, personal and social.

On the one hand, an artist acting as a strict individualist considers space and the material he deals with as a "blank sheet" upon which he forcefully projects his vision or his emotional tensions or aspirations; and even if he accepts the fact that in order to find a response from a public he has to conform to certain collectively defined conditions and traditions, he does so reluctantly and as uncompromisingly as possible, for to him, only one thing really matters: that he express his own personal vision, character, and purpose by any means available, and with an absolute minimum of subjection to the nature of these means.

On the other hand, when, instinctively or deliberately, he adopts the cosmogenetic or collectivistic attitude toward creativity, the artist (or any producer of forms) sees himself and acts as a guide to a creative process occurring at a certain place and at a particular time, because Space itself (the whole cosmos) there and then is pregnant of as yet unrevealed *but needed* forms. In a sense he pictures himself as a mid-wife rather than an impregnator. Yet he also is both. He is the husband who not only has cared for the pregnant woman he fecundated as an agent of life and of the need for survival of the human species, but also who assists in the child's delivery. He is also the mother as she co-operates consciously and willingly with the birth process operating in her.

At the personal level, the love-making that created the child has characteristics caused by the man's and woman's individual tempera-ments and bodily natures; yet, if the two partners and cocreators live in a society whose culture has a fundamentally impersonal and biological character, they would be deeply aware that the procreative process has operated through them, rather than from them. The basic form of the creation was determined by the vast impersonal life-force operating through them in a human mode. The child is not "theirs"; it is life's child — and at a socio-cultural level, it is the child of the community and the family considered as long-lasting evolving social organisms. The child succeeds those who came before him and gave him a.bio-logical human form and cultural determinants, which in turn he has to pass on to a new generation of children of whom he will be the prede-cessor.

If we now consider the cyclic development of culture, we should readily see that there are periods of history during which the artist is like a peasant tilling his ancestral land in order to produce a crop needed for the sustenance of his people. The peasant selects the seeds he sows — the creative artist selects some particular sacred motive — after which they merely guide, yet also participate in the growth of the biological or cultural forms. The peasant lives in nature, attuning his acts to the rhythms of the seasons and of the internal processes of vegetable unfoldment from seed to seed. He lets natural forces operate, rather than controlling them. He lets life be the prime mover, though he evokes life's magical power of growth and self-multiplication, focusing this power upon a "sacred place" where the release is needed for the fulfillment of human needs; and he intuitively, subconsciously knows that the life-process follows cosmic principles and harmonic-organic proportions. He knows because he is a totally involved participant in these rites of life and vegetation, existing from time immemorial.[3]

Likewise the artist who sees himself as a servant of a religious, spiritual, or social-political purpose, consecrates himself or herself to the magical operation of giving a concrete form to forces with which he has become identified.

Life-processes were operating long before man cultivated the soil and boys and girls united in passionate loving. Likewise two-dimensional space existed long before painters drew forms on the walls of caves and temples. Three-dimensional space existed before architects envisioned the emergence, out of the plains or hills on which they and their people lived, of buildings needed for the life of their community; and time existed, scanned by the motions of planets and stars, before musicians gave a particular sense of direction, substance and meaning to its rhythmic flow by the melodies and thematic developments they created. Interpersonal and socio-cultural relationships are likewise *manifestations* of a four-dimensional reality whose essential characteristic is interpenetration. All human societies and all cultures are eddies in the moving tide of this four-dimensional space as it comes in contact with this rigid, yet expectant, form of three-dimensional space we call the Earth.

However, the forms which human beings call into being by the power of their imagination and will in answer to collective socio-cultural needs (even if they glory in the illusion of their being the sole self-determined authors) have only a limited span of existence. Human needs change, cultures that were intensely vital and aggressively expanding tend to become static and their long-unquestioned paradigms obsolete. A new creative impulse may be imminent; yet because socio-cultural institutions, organized religions and nations stubbornly resist change, a new type of creative person has to be called upon to act. The forms they produce and which concretize their special relationship to their collectivity — and, in a deeper sense, to Space and Time — have the characteristic features required if life is to be liberated from the meaningless and growth-frustrating perpetuation of what no longer fills its need.

Most human beings call such a liberation death or destruction, and dread all manifestations of its coming, because their consciousness is still hypnotized by a powerful internal feeling of the irreplaceable value of the condition of life-in-form. But this condition refers only to physical forms and the related patterns of ego-consciousness or to the limiting and normally exclusivistic forms of a particular style of art, of life and the related patterns of ego-consciousness. What human beings need is not a stoic and philosophical acceptance of body-disintegration and death, and (at another but related level) of cultural institutions, religious dogmas, and inherited class privileges. What is needed is the rapid yet wholesome development and expansion of a consciousness enabling them to envision, feel, and become committed in advance to an as-yet-unknown future, simply because they realize that this future is needed and (however delayed it may be) inevitable. It is needed because the once revered and indeed valid forms have proved empty and stifling. This future has to be understood as a *new gesture of life*, a new pulsation of the cosmos, a yearning of the eternal Virgin for new forms of existence — or as "God's will." The only factors that could be called evil are inertia, delays produced by fear and hesitation, and the inability of human beings to accept the unfamiliar while clinging individually and collectively to ghostly memories.[4]

Civilization, the Death-Rebirth Process

As already stated, shifting gears from one level of consciousness and activity to the next and more inclusive one, constitutes the process of civilization; and this process almost inevitably has two aspects. We call them destructive and constructive; they should rather be called, in order to avoid emotional connotations, *autumnal* and *adventive*. Under clear and lucent autumnal skies (at least in relatively high Northern latitudes) the soil is covered by both decaying leaves and seeds. Leaves and seed are products of a gradually ebbing tide of vegetation; but leaves are oriented toward inevitable decay (the humus that will be indispensable for future growth), while seeds are oriented toward the sacrificial rite of germination, which implies the rebirth of life-forms. Civilization is, at first, both leaf-decay and seed-rebirth. It is for human beings to choose the current to which they are inwardly, yet most often unconsciously, drawn.

As the symbolical fall ends, civilization operates in its "adventive" mode. It turns over and redirects the expectant nuclei of the seeds. It becomes the magical instrumentality for the new creative Word to sound *through*. In the cycle of vegetation the winter solstice is the Advent, for it is then that the cyclically renewed Sun begins to reassess its life-producing potency as it starts on its northward journey (in declination)[5]. In the cycle of a culture-whole the Advent refers to the coming of some powerful personage (or personages) who usually, some centuries later, becomes quasi-deified as the Father (or Fathers) of the by-then relatively stabilized political and religious-cultural organism of society. For instance, in our European Western Society, we might mention Pope Gregory the Great and St. Benedict around 600 A.D. and after them Charlemagne whose death marked the establishment of basic fields of racial-cultural tensions, later to become modern nations in ceaseless conflicts. At the higher spiritual-planetary level, the great adventive men are called Avatars. What these beings envision may take decades and centuries to be understood and rightly evaluated; but, while they live, they are focal points for the release of cosmic-spiritual forces into the biosphere and the noosphere of thisEarth. Today we may call these forces, symbolically at least, "galactic," for they refer to the greater cosmic Whole within which not only the Earth but the whole solar system lives, moves and has its being.

In the arts, we find men whose work of destiny is to help the disintegration of their culture by criticizing, ridiculing, or violently attacking the validity of the fundamental concepts and images of that culture. We call them iconoclasts and muckrakers. They destroy the glamor surrounding big names or great works haloed with cultural reverence and often idolatry. The forms they produce — be they books of criticism, musical works stressing all that "the School" forbade, paintings introducing combinations of colors and exotic shapes of primitive cultures to shock the viewers' sense of reality (Picasso), or the even more incongruous forms of Dadaism and Surrealism.

At a higher level, the challenge to the past comes also from geniuses who, intuitively sensing the need for a new type of culture, introduce a new approach to the old forms, extending their boundaries until these explode and release what they contained for a vaster, more significant type of integration. These men are the great mutants, whose entire being is polarized by the drive toward rebirth.

All adventive men are *transpersonal* beings. Space, Life, God, *act through them*, even if they are not aware of this fact. They often display what, to the superficial observer, may appear to be an extreme of individualism and even at times a boisterous, proud egocentricity. Yet one should realize that these men of genius in most instances have to be unconscious of the true source of their action if they are to perform disintegrative deeds. This is especially true of those iconoclasts whose function is to initiate or sustain cathartic processes, whether in politics, education or the arts. A clear consciousness of what impels them to act would confuse them. They have to be tough and perhaps violent in their catabolic passion for transformation in order to stand against the collective pressure, often the hatred and persecution, of "the Establishment" whose values (or lack of values) they challenge. The forms they produce — and also the form of their individual ego having developed through a deep feeling of compelling opposition to the status quo, often caused by personal tragedy — have to be strong, sharp, impervious to the many allurements with which society may try to seduce them; and these often appear in the classic and personalized shape of a "tempter" or temptress.

For similar reasons, the vital core of vegetable seeds must be enclosed within a tough envelope, without which they would at once be disintegrated by the strong chemicals within the autumnal soil. "Seed men" also must either be enveloped in what appears to be an intense and exclusive concentration upon their destiny — a psychic skin of imperturbability which may appear to be insensitive to those attempting to penetrate it — or else they must be so strongly integrated around a powerfully radiant center that the outgoing flow of energy and the power of the vision it manifests render the seedman impenetrable.

"Seed forms" appearing toward the fall period of the life-span of a culture-whole are intrinsically different from the artistic and institutional forms in which that culture comes to fulfillment; just as different as a seed is from a plant in full bloom. The characteristics of these two types of forms answer opposite, yet in a sense complementary needs, and these characteristics refer respectively to the inherent meaning and purpose of civilization and culture. A plant in full bloom has actualized its birth-potential. It reveals fully what it is and in many cases it is prolific and exuberant in the development of its fundamental nature. A seed, on the other hand, exists to carry a message from the species; a message from a particular type of life in the biosphere to the materials available on the Earth's surface — a message of integration, in which nevertheless the potentiality of mutation is latent if not explicit. This message is not superficially visible; it is hidden within the hard envelope of the seed — thus "occult." Within the seed is to be found only what is necessary to convey the message or to sustain those parts which will constitute the actual carrier. Bareness, condensation, internal necessity, and total consecration to the task to be performed characterize the seed-form and its contents. In it everything is as compact as in a modern man-made satellite loaded with instruments.

Here, however, we must not be confused by analogies. I am referring to the life-cycle of a culture-whole and to the fundamental character of the cultural forms created by men who, because they act as "civilizers" rather than "culture-men," make of their creations agencies for sociocultural transformation rather than fulfillment. Yet it is within flower-fulfillment that the seed is born. As the seed begins to grow, the yearly plant begins to die. The process at the level of vegetation may appear to be a Nietzschean kind of "eternal return"; but there are seeds in which mutations occur. In the human kingdom mutability is the fundamental law. In man the cyclic inertia of nature is challenged; the circle is meant to be a spiral, and this implies that civilization is active within the fateful biological circularity of living processes producing a culture-whole. It is active as a centrifugal power.

When this power is particularly active within a cuture-whole the latter assumes an intensely dynamic, but restless character. Our Euro-American culture-whole, especially in the West, has been characterized by what Spengler called the Faustian temperament. Human beings are periodically seized by a "divine discontent" and rebel against circular concepts and practice. This Faustian character, ceaselessly aspiring toward "more" and/or "beyond," has produced specific forms that reach toward an increase of complexity in relationship, because it is in and through relationship that changes occur. *Selfhood* — or at the cultural level, the Tradition — possesses inertia; it is and insists on remaining what it is; it resists change. On the other hand, *relatedness* produces change; yet the change may operate in opposite directions. In and through relationship the self can either lose its identity, or expand its field of activity and consciousness.

Selfhood may develop in depth without the challenge of relationships — which is why in the self-oriented culture of India the seeker after God insists on total solitude and concentration on the self. But the small field of human selfhood can concretely expand into that of the greater Whole only through a multiplicity of relationships, provided — and this is a crucial point! — the person is able constantly to refer his experiences of relationship to his own individual center. It is because this "reference to center" is often very difficult — which is why the process of multiple relationships is dangerous — that religious and cultural institutions have developed systems of morality compelling individuals to accept limitations to the centrifugal drive inherent in relationships; in other words, taboos and the concept of sin.

Within these "safe and secure" ethical boundaries the flow of cultural relationships can extend with relative freedom, and at any length. Thus cultural forms can develop and unfold their inherent potential of meaningful relationship for long periods of time, as in the case of India and other places where musical performances, involving a great deal of improvisation on ragas or similar bioenergetic tone-patterns, last for many hours. The musician is relatively free as an individual just because he feels secure in his rootedness in a tradition, and because in many cases, he is innately certain that by accepting its dictates he is following "laws of cyclocosmic activity," revealed to some illumined Ancestor or spiritual Teacher. Today, instead of divine revelation the musician or painter might speak of acoustical and (in general) natural laws, for instance, laws of symmetry and harmonic resonance. But the psychological result is the same in either instance.

Natural laws are *only* laws of the world we know and experience through our physical senses. Human cultures are local manifestations of the laws of a nature *we* can perceive, directly or indirectly, through our instruments; and each culture emphasizes some aspect of this nature and plays down other aspects. The result is a characteristic kind of form in which a particular type of relationship is concretized, other types being eliminated as irrelevant, alien, unwholesome, and therefore dangerous. Culture-forms, by stressing the type of relationships which the culture proclaims in no uncertain terms to be "good," are seen also to be "beautiful." They are based on the true knowledge derived from what to culture-men seems evident. The approach to culture-forms is therefore *esthetic*; just as the approach to culturally and religiously acceptable relationships is *ethical*, and propositions derived from the particular kind of experience and knowledge satisfying the collective cultural mentality are deemed to be *true*.

This is the basis of the well-known trinity of the Good, the True, and the Beautiful. All cultures define the characteristics belonging to each of the members of the trinity, and each does it in its own particular way. Nevertheless it is possible to discover many features common to most of these cultural formulations because each of the presently known local and psychically as well as geographically defined cultures is a specialized manifestation of the planetary nature of mankind *as it has been developing during the last millennia*, or as the Hindu would say, during our planetary Kali Yuga, a period of many thousands of years. Traditionally men whoe vision is focused backward to the One Root of our human cycle think of Kali Yuga as a dark period; but it is dark only in a certain sense. It is also the period of gestation of a new humanity through which the vibration 6 — of which I have previously spoken in the third Chapter — will more specifically and totally assume concrete form. Today, however, we can only dimly envision how the new cosmic-planetary vibration will manifest.

In the meantime the process of civilization is releasing into operation during this Kali Yuga, and more specifically and actively at the close of all cultural cycles, an array of forms needed to break down man's collective attachment to cultural images and values which have only a local character. These civilization-forms have a catabolic character; yet it is only *through* the crises they initiate that the seed-forms of a new culture, normally at a higher level of the evolutionary spiral, can reveal themselves to disenthralled or at least open minds. These civilization-forms are not to be approached from an esthetic, ethical, or truth-haunted point of view. They are there to perform a liberating and transformative function. In at least one sense of the term, they are magical forms.

In the following chapter, I shall attempt to clarify the contrast between magical and esthetic, between spiritual and religious, and be
tween evident truth and validity. But here this much can still be said
the concept of creativity applies as well to civilization-forms as to
culture-forms. Creativity releases and liberates as well as builds, and
having built, produces esthetic pleasure, the perfume of sanctity, and
the intellectual satisfaction that comes from "elegant" solutions to
scientific problems. There are times when men and women of courage
and open consciousness are faced by the grave and disturbing question:
What do you seek, liberation or happiness, transmutation or stability —
the forms that free or those that satisfy?

6.

THE MAGIC OF WILL AND
THE ESTHETIC EXPERIENCE

THE RECENT increase in the popularity of magical ceremonies and witchcraft has raised many questions and produced a variety of answers concerning the nature of magic. These usually fail to present magic in its most fundamental aspect, because they tend mainly to deal with a modern concept of magic based on a psychological—and especially Jungian—approach attempting to "dis-occultize" and psychologize what in the beginning of human societies had a vitalistic, naturalistic, and pantheistic character. The English writer on magic and occult philosophy, Dion Fortune, has been quoted as defining magic as the art of causing changes in consciousness in conformity with will. But primitive magic had essentially nothing to do with consciousness. It dealt with the focalized release of power in answer to vitalistic human needs.

In its most basic sense—a sense which can be expanded to cover cosmic processes and also all early manifestations of culture and art—I shall therefore define magic as *a purposeful release of focalized power through an effective form in answer to a need.*

This definition embraces a number of factors, each of which has to be defined with reference to several levels of activity, from the most cosmic (or cosmogenic) to the cultural and the personal or egocentric. We have to define the nature of the power being used and of the need being met, then the character of the forms used to bring the power to a focus.

Magic is not merely a *human* activity. Wherever and whenever power is being focused and released through a specifically conceived form in order to achieve a mentally defined purpose one can speak of magical activity. God's creation of a universe is the supreme magical activity. Through a "form," the creative Word, a cosmogenic power ("Light") is released. It is released in order to fill a metacosmic need. What this need is can be interpreted in two already mentioned basic ways: God may desire (or need) to create a universe in order to reveal the infinite complexity of His nature to Himself; or if one replaces the concept of a metacosmic God by that of an infinite Ocean of Potentiality in a transcendental state of perfect Harmony (Space in the most all-embracing and timeless sense) out of which universes periodically emerge and return, the need for the emergence of a new universe (and therefore of a new beginning of activity and time) results from the apparently inevitable fact that a preceding universe ended in a dualistic condition. We may speak of a dualism of "success" and "failure," or symbolically of "seed" and "decaying" leaves. However we may picture it in our minds, this condition is essentially disharmonic, and therefore a new attempt must be made to give to the waste products or the unfinished business of the past cycle a new chance to experience organic living and, in the end, a supreme Omega state of consciousness resulting from total and perfect integration at all possible levels.

We have already met these two basic interpretations in the source of existence when speaking of "expressive" and "cosmogenetic" (Space-differentiating) forms. In the first interpretation a cosmos-transcending God *expresses* His being in a universe or a multiplicity of universes; in the other, God is the first manifestation of the emergence of power and at least potential consciousness out of the infinite Ocean of Space. God is then pictured as the Unity aspect of the universe. In Greek and Theosophical mysticism, He is the Logos — the One Existent out of whose unitarian Being everything in the universe evolved.

Whatever interpretation one chooses to accept, at the beginning of any cycle of existence there is activity. This activity is not explosive and formless. Energy is released in a "package," the quantum of modern science. This energy inherently has form or structure. Out of an infinite, *and therefore essentially diffuse*, kind of metacosmic Ocean of potential energy, a limited amount of energy is focused and released according to some kind of internal structure controlling its differentiation; and it is released within a defined space of manifestation which its differentiated products will occupy for a definite period (a cycle) of time.

When we reach the biological level of activity we find that the one cosmic energy—which during the Vitalistic Age of mankind's evolution was referred to as the "One Life"—has taken the aspect of the life-force animating all biological organisms. Hindu philosophy speaks of it as *prana*. At this level we are confronted with a multitude of life's species and genera. In each of these the life-force operates according to a definite rhythm and within specific vegetable, animal, or human forms of varied types and sizes. The germination of a vegetable seed and the birth of an animal body are magical activities which begin with the fertilization of the flower and the formation of the fecundated ovum. These activities, like all magical activities, occur within a definite space. It is a "sacred" place, not unlike the small circle of light projected on a material surface when sunlight is concentrated by a powerful lens; and at this place heat is produced (i.e. intense molecular activity).

At this biological level, the power being released in a particular modality of the life-force operating in our biosphere; the effective form is the body as a whole; and the purpose of the new organism is to perpetuate the character of the species. Each species of life (mankind included) performs a definite function in terms of the harmonic workings of the total organism of the planet, Earth. We can speak of a *life-will* at work; it manifests within each organism as what we call instinct and as a few basic organic drives. These are mainly the drive for survival, the drive for expansion, the drive for self-reproduction, the drive for adaptation to environmental changes. The capacity for adaptation manifests as a biopsychic type of mind and intelligence or cunning. It may also produce mutations.

When we reach the level of primitive man there may at first seem to be no fundamental difference in the magical operations of the life-will. Hunting, eating, copulating are various types of magic, and are so regarded in early tribal societies; but with the special development of human language a new kind of mind gives a truly human form to consciousness—a consciousness that is potential in all life-forms. It also humanizes the fundamental biological drives for survival, expansion, and reproduction.

Vegetable organisms have devised a myriad of methods to insure the spread of their seed and, first of all, the production of an immense number of these seeds allowing for the inevitable destruction of the vast majority of them. Many species of animals also produce a prodigious number of eggs, of which only a relatively few develop as fully mature organisms; but mammifers, and particularly human beings, produce only a small progeny. Animals protect their young by various physical means—muscular strength, agility, venom, camouflage, and group-living to magnify the defensive and aggressive abilities of individual specimens.

Human beings not only live in family groups expanding into tribes, but the complex languages they have developed permit the cumulative transfer of a special type of knowledge. This knowledge is not only acquired from experience; it has a biopsychic dimension which seems to transcend the possibility of knowledge inherent in animal species, a holistic dimension. Man is able not only to perceive, remember, and convey to others what other living organisms *do*, but also to feel, realize, or intuit what they *are*, He is able not only to know, record, and transmit in detail to other men all the actions another living organism *performs*, but also to gain a direct understanding of what the *form* of the organism-as-a-whole reveals as to its intrinsic nature and character. This direct understanding is then expressed in a *symbol*; the organism is given a *name*. Often at first this name imitates the cry of an animal or the sound of a natural phenomenon; but, if so, these sounds are not considered merely as sense-data being reproduced by vocal imitation, but rather as revelation of the essential nature of the life-power animating the organism producing them.

What this means is that *the life* within man is able to resonate to, and at least relatively to identify itself with the life in the animal, or even in nature as a whole. The human senses, and the primitive biological mind that registers sense-data, provide information as to *activities* in the outer world; but this information can also become a pathway leading to a holistic intuition of *the life within the form*. It is to this life that, in magic, the name of an entity refers. Knowing that name gives power over the entity whose biopsychic nature it reveals.

The knowledge of a name—or of a mantram—is not merely a sense-based and phenomenological type of knowing. It is the life-consciousness within man that knows. In the same sense, in the Bible, a man is said to "know" his wife when he performs sexual intercourse with her. An "intercourse" ideally is a coursing (or flowing) of life-energy between (*inter*) two polarized human organisms. If unhindered by biopsychic-structural tensions and undisturbed by ego-generated factors, this interaction can evoke in each partner a realization in depth of the "tone" (or essential dynamic character) of the other partner.[2]

At the level of primitive magic, when a shaman (or medicine man) ceremonially utters the name of an animal he thereby attunes his life-consciousness to the characteristic rhythm of the animal's life-energy, and a response must come from that life-energy. That response gives the shaman power over the animal; for the utterance by the shaman of the animal's name deprives that animal of his protective covering—his existential mask or camouflage. In some manner, the animal finds itself exposed to the will of the magician, who can then kill or tame it according to his need.

The need to which the primitive shaman's activity refers to is biological, whether survival, or comfort and the utilization of what the animal has to offer to man, is concerned. Above all, the power he releases in the magical operation is not the personal will of an ego but the *life-will*. Primitive tribal man has no ego, no individuality. At this stage of human evolution it is the tribe as a whole, rather than the particular person belonging to it, which constitutes the psychic unit and sets the magical will into operation. This will has its origin in the root-unity of the tribe; it basically acts for communal purposes, even if this means the healing of a particular tribesman, for every tribesman is but a cell of the tribal organism whose total multipersonal life has to be cared for.

However, a process of differentiation is at work as soon as the primitive tribe develops a particular culture in and through which the essential characteristics and particular way of life of its people take exterior forms objectivizing and defining them. *Nature becomes overlaid and pervaded with culture.* "Man's common humanity" differentiates into more or less antagonistic and always (to a greater or lesser degree) exclusivistic culture-wholes; and in these a hierarchical order of natural functions sooner or later turns into a caste or class structure. The original life-will becomes a *collective will*: the will of a particular group or community. It becomes associated with an organized form of religion.

At least in its outer forms and rituals, religion is "culture-magic." It uses the collective will of the people to enhance, restore and glorify the deep-rooted sense of community, a sense having proven essential for collective survival and even well-being. Etymologically, the word *re-ligio* seems to imply a "binding back," thus an antidote against any centrifugal attempt of separate human beings which might disturb the tribal and cultural unity, for, as the often repeated phrase states, "in unity there is strength." In terms of such an integrative and holistic purpose, religion acts in a healing way; it keeps the collective body of the people whole and well, maintaining the communal health by the use of religious rituals, celebrations of the "sacred" origin of the group personified in a common Great Ancestor or tribal god, sports in which the group participates, and also war games or collective hunts and expeditions.

The collective will to culture-wholeness operates not only through religion and its magical ceremonies or festivals, but also in what at first is simply the special crafts of the community. The characteristics of the culture and of the organized religion (which actually is the internal superbiological and sanctifying aspect of the culture) take form in the special manner in which objects of utility such as pots, jars, tools, weapons, houses, etc. are made.

It has been said that the essential (or one of the most basic) characteristics of man is to be a maker of tools; but we now realize that some animals also use tools. Yet, they apparently do not sculpture or paint these objects of utility *for magical purposes*. That is to say, they do not incorporate in these tools and other deliberately shaped objects needed for biological purpose or group-convenience a *concretized realization of the meaning of their functions.* Somehow a consciousness emerges in the most sensitive tribesmen that life-functions can be objectivized and given concrete forms as "symbolic forms," just as the characteristic life-rhythm and power of an animal can be objectified in a name. These symbolic forms have magical power. They have power in the sense in which the image of the Cross, the figure of the meditating Buddha, the Tibetan mandalas, and in fact all the early manifestations of sacred Art—including mantrams, ritual gestures, epic narratives—are charged with the power to move and to change the destiny of nations.

The Sacred and the Profane

It is essential, however, to make a basic distinction between sacred art and the many differentiated forms gradually taken by the arts in which a developing culture exteriorizes and represents the various stages of its development. Sacred art is *magical and revelatory*; it arises from a single root. The cultural arts are produced according to changing styles for *esthetic* purposes. To ignore the difference between magic and esthetics is to be blind to an essential difference between two types of creative activity. The distinction is fundamental though often ignored. It is ignored first of all because culture-men tend to misinterpret and to shy from realizing the sacred character of the consciousness and mentality operating at the origin of and during the earliest stages of the evolution of the culture-whole to which they belong; and secondly, because the magical often shades into and blends with the esthetic elements. This occurs in all the arts; and as we shall see later on, it also happens in the art of living. It may be unwise to overstress differences where the characteristics of two levels of activity and consciousness interblend, yet this differentiation is particularly important at a time such as ours when the very purpose of art, and indeed of the individual existence of human beings, has become a crucial issue so often misinterpreted.

When a tribesman carves the menacing features of a god into the handle of a sword, his intention is not to make the sword more beautiful, it is to make it magically more effective, thus able better to kill the prey or the enemy. When he paints frescoes on the walls of a cave or a temple, or sculptures there, to us, strange but fascinating figures of gods or demons, he is not thinking of esthetic values, or of planes, angles, volumes according to some abstract concept; he is "feeling" the internal rhythm of the power *which it is the function of the object or the painting to release*. His mind and hands flow with that rhythm, embodying it in a concrete form. What operates within the creative act is not his personal will but the life-will within the human species; and when the culture-whole has reached a more social character, it is the collective will of the people. The creativity of the fashioner of art-forms is deeply and ineradicably rooted in the psyche of his culture-whole.[3]

In his outer personality the craftsman may display psychological traits which to some extent single him and his kind within the tribal community; but what really differentiates him is his openness and his yielding to the life-flow with which he is deeply identified, while many of the people around him tend to live and feel more rigidly in terms of social and family patterns. In and through the producer of magical forms, the creative process operates as a prolongation of the lines of force structuring the existence of entities living in the world perceptible to our senses, or in a more purely dynamic and preconcrete realm which we may call "psychic" or "astral" according to our basic philosophy and cosmology.

The essential point is that these men, and like them the truly so-called primitive religious artists, create according to *principles of formation* which are in no way basically different from those ruling the geometrical formation of crystals or the growth of plants. They do not "know" intellectually cosmic or biogenetic principles; they are unconsciously attuned to these principles. We should not consider them as individualized persons. *Life lives them.* Their creative acts are cosmobiological gesture of power. The works of sacred art are anonymous; but they are transpersonal, not impersonal. For this reason, the magical acts have a powerful effectiveness and inevitability which belongs to the realm of instincts and life-processes. To try to interpret or evaluate magical and primitive religious art in terms of esthetic values and concepts is as absurd as to attempt to psychoanalyze Buddha and Christ according to Freudian techniques.

In a more mundane and restricted sense it is like judging the activities of young children in terms of the values and motives ruling the lives of fifty-year-old men and women. Because a culture-whole develops essentially as an organic whole, the men and women of different periods in this development have a different cultural age. However, the organism of a culture-whole exists primarily at a psychosocial level and only secondarily in terms of the physical growth and multiplication of the people whose collective mentality, basic feeling-responses, and overt ways of life it controls. It is a noospheric rather than biospheric organism. As already stated, a culture overlays, pervades and gives form to a particular aspect of human nature. Culture is rooted in nature, but the particular character of the root is derived from a seed which, by germinating, impressed its life-potency upon a root that was born from it and immersed itself in the raw material of a new soil. This seed of a culture-whole is represented by the creative activity of a personage, or of several persons, *through whom*, before the beginning of the cultural cycle, the process of civilization operated, releasing a new transformative vision and power.

The vision and spiritual power of these civilizers or Avatars, and the Prime Symbols or Archetypes latent in them, are occult factors during what may be called the prenatal period and the infancy of the culture-whole. During such periods, the culture is still struggling to find and define its field of organic activity in the midst of slowly disintegrating older culture-wholes to which it is at least partly apparented, yet which it destroys, as the seed destroys the plant that bore it. The old cultural forms and institutions represent the "mother" side, while the activities of the Civilizers or seed-men constitute the "father" side of the new culture-whole.

In the mythology of most cultures, these Civilizers are given a divine character. They are true "Creators," for they stand at the *spiritual* beginning of the cultural cycle. They sound the creative Word, the mantram, of the culture-whole; and their lives become the source of symbols and scenes which, later on, the earlier religious artists will use as sacred themes for their magical productions. These in turn eventually lose their magical character as the artist's spiritual and transpersonal consecration becomes increasingly imbued with and deviated by sociocultural and egocentric considerations. Spiritual identification turns into religious devotion; the sacred, into the profane. The sacred time of the creative beginning—the time in which gods eternally create—changes into the profane time of constantly altered artistic and social fashions revealing the changes in the interests, the problems, and the collective moods of successive generations. The magical will is superseded by the esthetic mind moved by collective feelings.

The first indication of the basic change in art-motivation appears when magically inspired forms begin to be used in terms of *decoration and embellishment*. This change most likely occurs as the result of interactions between two or more cultures. Culture stresses the factor of *selfhood*; civilization that of *relatedness*. Selfhood is centripetal in the sense that it is dominated by the realization of centrality. The urge for relationship is centrifugal, dominated by the desire to commune with other selves. In selfhood there is power, magic, irreducible strength—and inertia. In relationship consciousness expands, activity differentiates; and the desire and stimulation for repeated transformation is a fire that can either destroy the self or transmute it and, through participation, absorb it into a vaster field of selfhood, a sacred Community at a more inclusive level of being. Selfhood remains what it is unless the particular self totally loses itself in the absolute SELF, the nirvana in which the flames of relationship are totally extinguished, though the extinguishment may not be permanent in a metaphysical or cosmic sense. On the other hand, relationship is perpetual, cyclic change, from level to level of participation; it implies involvement in the dualistic and cyclic aspect of being, which we call becoming or existence.

When intercultural relationships repeatedly take place, a new element develops in the communal psyche of the tribes: the factor of *competition*. It announces the more or less rapid disintegration or the sacred. It also becomes a wedge through which the process of civilization enters into the magical circle of the culture-whole. In such a magical circle the self of the culture-whole resides. It exists there, secure and illumined by an inner light that crystallizes into translucent magical forms. The transpersonal creative imagination of men haunted by the divine Presence in their midst plays, in childlike devotion, at exteriorizing that Presence in forms evoking the deeds and words of by then long disappeared seed-men and revealers of archetypal mysteries.

The negative—yet stimulating and transformative—aspect of civilization begins to operate when a culture-whole establishes more or less steady lines of commerce and places for interchange (markets and fairs) with other culture-wholes. This negative aspect acts through the competitive motive as a differentiating, separative, and individualizing factor. The men and women in each culture-whole who can best represent its particular character, its way of life and style of form-production, are impelled by their own people to develop their skills for the purpose of winning contests with the corresponding men and women of the other cultures. This gives birth to the urge for decoration, including the self-decoration of women.

Soon showmanship is born, and the will to be better than someone else. The competitive spirit triumphs. The profane overcomes the sacred, though the sense of the latter still remains alive at the core of the activities and in the creations of the greatest artists. But these by now have developed egos born of the competitive spirit and the psychology of "one-up-manship." The process of individualization—the first inevitable, withal essentially negative, stage of civilization—transforms both the society as a whole and its members now involved in attempts at displaying their superiority, or at compensating in devious ways for their inferiority. Superiority and inferiority at any level, including what passes for "spirituality," are quantitative evaluations. When quantity dominates a culture, or any form of activity *and of knowledge* (including what passes as scientific knowledge) quality is bound to take a secondary role, until we come to the absurdity of producing goods (*and indeed artistic products!*) in terms of "planned obsolescence." This is the most characteristic expression of a rapidly disintegrating culture-whole.

A classical period is ushered in when esthetic considerations begin to dominate the field of culture. Magic withdraws into the field of occultism. Sensate values in the arts and empiricism in science take control of the culture. Perspective and the pleasure of the eyes in the plastic arts, formalism in music, rationalism in the field of knowledge, are respectively developed by the great masters of the Renaissance, by the builders of musical counterpoint, fugues, and a rigid tonality system, and in science by Francis Bacon, Newton, and Descartes. In the world of dramatic performance a Shakespeare displays extraordinary gifts in depicting tragic problems of interpersonal relationship. Personality triumphs; whether it be the personality of the artist and of the characters he imagines out of his own experience, or the collective personality of a culture-whole now concretized and rigidly defined by an official language, a code of laws and national boundaries.

In every instance, the ego-will, or its collectivized projection, the national will (usually symbolized and made articulate by an autocratic king) supplants the life-will. What remains of magic gravitates unavoidably toward the satisfaction of the ego, which often takes grandiose poses to present itself as the "true I am"; the individual proclaims his will in magical ceremonies whose main purpose in most instances is the control of psychic or elemental forces for personal or at least personalized ends. The magical ceremony may not belong to the category of "black art" filled with the release of aggressive, acquisitive, ego-inflating or destructive energies; yet it seems rarely to be a transpersonally "theurgic" activity, except in cases where healing is the purpose. The men and women who participate in the ceremonies as a rule are mentally conditioned egos assuming the role of creative "godlets"—or else they are deeply confused mediumistic split-personalities open to whatever forces their particular type of confusion and emotional intoxication attracts. This is why most publicly known groups and organizations dealing with ceremonial magic in Europe and America have often led to tragic human failures.

This does not mean that in theory during the last millennia magic (whether of Asiatic, African, or Near-Eastern and European origin) has not answered to a basic human need; but what begins as a truly sacred type of performance in most cases tends to become a profane display of self-will, or else an attempt to balance, neutralize, or compensate for the utter artificiality of modern living in monstrous cities and assembly-line factories. In the latter case, ceremonial magic as practiced today is a part of the return to nature and to the uninhibited satisfaction of biological, emotional, and sensual urges. It is part of a conterculture which, in its polarized reaction against our culture, most often refocuses, in a nonrationalistic and nonformalistic manner, what in fact are still the hedonistic characteristics of the cultural attitude since the Classical period; thus, the basic desire for the "profane" and temporary enjoyment of forms. It is this wish that characterizes the esthetic approach to art.

Estheticism is based upon the concept of personal or collective *pleasure*, whereas the magical approach is founded upon the ideal of supreme and transformative *effectiveness* in the processes of transformation and transubstantiation. Let us consider what this dichotomy implies and reveals.

The Apollonian and Dionysian Attitudes

The characteristic feature of an esthetic approach to art is the expectation that the art-forms (whether in painting or in music and dancing) will elicit pleasing or pleasurable sensations; and emotional excitement or often relaxation from the routine of daily work, can be substituted or added to the more superficial sense-enjoyment. The types of art-forms which will satisfy the esthetic sense are those in which the characteristic type of mentality and/or personal or collective emotional feelings are objectified and glorified. At a more abstract level, and especially for esthetically trained individuals, the art-forms meet the desire to enjoy in a perceptual and contemplative manner the inner security and peacefulness produced by what appears to the mind to be a manifestation of cosmic harmony and the conceptual order of archetypes. Such an art may present "elegant" solutions either to baffling life-problems or to technical difficulties; and such elegant solutions may pertain as well to the field of pure mathematics as to that of complex polyphonic and counterpoint structures. They may involve the harmonization of inherently clashing colors or, as in the theater, interpersonal conflicts.

On the other hand, magical art is an act of will determined by a transformative purpose, which in most cases sooner or later leads to a crisis or catharsis. Magical art releases power; it is not concerned with personal enjoyment of forms in themselves; esthetic art seeks to produce sensual, emotional, or mental pleasure. It presents itself as an alternative to, and at times an escape from, the pressures of everyday life. Religion, in its organized cultural manifestations has often the same purpose, though it refrains from overtly mentioning it. Thus organized religion is the cradle out of which art emerges into the hedonistic formalism of the Classical period of all cultures.

We could use here the well-known opposition, emphasized over a century ago by Neitzsche in his *Origin of the Tragedy*, between the Apollonian and the Dionysian approaches to art and in general to meeting life-issues. Apollonian man seeks release from the state of tension inherent in earthly existence. He tries to obtain a feeling of inner security which he often derives from a contemplation of the sky where celestial bodies move peacefully according to a cosmic order making their position predictable—the impersonal order of unvarying laws and structural relationships. Dionysian man seeks depth-stirring stimulation and dynamic intensity. He welcomes change and insecurity, realizing that these are necessary implements to self-transformation, inner growth, and the transmutation of life into spirit. Such a transmutation can be structured by the aware and open mind, provided that the desire for it is intense enough to release into that mind the transphysical "hormones" of an unwavering faith in the individual's capacity to become more than he knows himself to be in a cultural and normative sense. Dionysian man enjoys the dynamic flow of power that thunders through human tragedies and all death-rebirth processes. He welcomes whatever is able to mobilize the energies which he intuitively feels to be as yet latent within him, even if he realizes that the cost will be suffering and possibly dying to this world, so certain is he that the "other world" can be reached only through conquest and total surrender of what men call normality and happiness.

Many human beings find in themselves elements belonging to both types; yet one of them usually dominates and if both are equally strong within the psyche, a stalemate can be produced with almost catatonic results. One should realize, however, that the Apollonian character can operate at a lower or a higher level of inclusiveness. Security obtained through predominantly static kinds of forms inevitably stresses exclusivism. What is important is *how much* it excludes as alien and unassimilable, and how artificial—that is, scornful of the natural energies of biospheric living—the security is. The typical "law and order" complex most often can be enforced only by police action. A Fascistic type of art can exist synchronously with a Fascistic political system. The rule of the C-major scale in classical music and equal temperament have a Fascistic character; the same can be said of Schoenberg's "tone rows" and formalistic polyphonic structures which for him, consciously or not, constituted a compensatory response to the cultural and political chaos of the dying Austrian Empire in which the composer reached maturity. We shall see in the following chapter that a musical approach to "tone" can develop on the basis of total inclusiveness. It was prefigured by the concept of *pan-tonality* which Franz Liszt tentatively conceived and Bela Bartok felt to be a necessity.

Apollonian man can also be the highest type of contemplative person who has reached a level of consciousness beyond duality, conflict, and tragedy. His mind may vibrate in perfect peace and serenity in attunement with the vast rhythms of the cosmos, once his emotional tensions have been calmed and his ego assuaged and made translucent to the promptings of the Divine at the core of his being. He rejects nothing because he experiences the place and function of everything in the supreme harmony of the universe and, beyond the out-and-in-breathing of universes, of That which is the forever inconceivable and unformulatable Ocean of infinite potentiality out of which the creativity of Gods and Logoi cyclically emerges and to which it returns as atabolic energy when the cosmic Form has ceased to reveal some particular aspect of the forever Unrevealable.

The Apollonian realization of, and response to, cosmic Form, especially when not securely purified from egocentric concerns, may co-exist with the Dionysian urge for cultural transmutation and personal metamorphosis. The clarity, objectivity, and serenity of the contemplative or illumined mind and the emotional stress and strain characteristic of ego consciousness not infrequently have their relatively separate areas of existence in the personality of the creative artist. The one polarizes the other and this polarization is seemingly necessary to establish a link (or line of communication) between the vibration of the higher mind (vibration 5) and that which animates the human masses and in general the Earth's biosphere (vibration 4). The archetypal form must "incarnate"; it has to send roots into the humus of man's common humanity. An alchemy of mind and life has to operate within the retort of the creative artist's personality, if the art-form is to draw a fairly large public able to assimilate at least some of the vital elements contained in the seed-form.

In this sense, an element of the magical will to transformation is inherent in all great art-forms. This element can use the personal desire for esthetic enjoyment and relaxation as a means to induce a lifting up of consciousness to a realm transcending the cultural and the personal. It is unfortunately an element which usually escapes the professional attention of either the art-critic in the esthetic field, or the moralist in the realm of religion and even more, secular ethics. The critic and the moralist have, as their official and culturally sanctified business, the task of analyzing the forms of art and of a person's feelings and behavior, then of passing judgment on their cultural or ethical value. Thus we hear critical pronouncements on whether a painting is or is not great art, or a performance is good or bad.

The art-critic *dissects forms* with the scalpel of an esthetically sharp mentality trained in the officialdom of universities, art-schools, or music conservatories. He or she *vivisects performances*, being always eager to catch or to miss the pulsation of a throbbing heart under the superficialities of finger dexterity. The moralist does the same with the life-performance and implied motives of human beings. He turns biographer and judges when dealing with famous personages. And all this is for the sake and the greater glory of the culture, of whose values and paradigms these critics and moralists assume themselves to be the custodians, or else, in periods of cultural disintegration, the scavengers.

Yet the deeper issue is never whether a form or a performance is good or bad, great or indifferent, but *whether it does what it is meant to do at a particular stage of a culture's development and of mankind's evolution.*

Magical forms have value if they can be used effectively to release the power necessary for the achievement of a valid creative or transforming biopsychic or spiritual purpose. Classical forms have value if they impress and inform the people who will perceive and experience them with the character of the culture which it is their task to make fully objective and to glorify. In Romantic periods, a work of art is significant and valuable if, by pouring his inner vitality and soul-passion into its form and its performance, the creative person becomes an exemplar or hero stimulating lesser human beings to catch fire and live more intensely as individualized and vibrant personalities always ready for self-transformation. And there are autumnal moments in a culture when a cathartic type of art is meant either to force upon the people who can stand its tragic implications the realization that the culture-whole is nearing its crisis of death and potential rebirth, or to open the consciousness of a relatively few men and women to the presence and the subtle impact of transcendent forces that summon to radical self-transformation and spiritual transmutation those who are ready, and assist those who are willing and able.

Everything in its proper place and at its appointed time is valuable if it brings to the concrete focus of an adequate form the essential meaning of that place and that time. Form exists to make the creative will objectively manifest and to reveal meaning; thus it has a creative and an informative function. Any significant and truly valid form is functional. But the function of art changes, as do the needs of a culture and the human beings this culture has "in-formed" and made into its image and likeness. Magical art in its sacred aspect creates, transforms, heals, or destroys according to the need of the place and the time, or the individual will of the magician. Esthetic art informs, reveals, satisfies through the forms it procreates, as the artist unites his power with the essential need or the fashionable expectations of his potential public.

Yet the magical and the esthetic, the sacred and the profane, the divine ("eonic") consciousness embracing a whole cycle of existence in the immediacy of an illumined moment and the fleeting experience intensely lived within an everchanging social and biopsychic context—these and all similar dualities can be harmonized in the counterpoint of an all-inclusive mental activity in which significant forms are spontaneously created, maintained, illumined, and destroyed. This is the "dance of Shiva," the in-and-out breathing of Brahma. This is existence in its prodigality of modes of manifestation and it always implied yearning for nonmanifestation. The great artist at any particular time catches a brief moment of this cosmic play or drama; and, if he has the power to impart to power-releasing or revelatory forms what his mind has experienced and his feelings have resonated to, his work—anonymous or personalized—endures as a living symbol of the ever-present possibility of man's becoming a transcendent seed sown in the womb of the Earth to carry and transmit the messages of God.

7.

MUSICAL FORM AND THE INNER SPACE OF TONES

IN OUR Euro-American culture, the concept of musical form occupies a central position. The new approach which, science has taken in this century, and particularly stressed in atomic physics clearly reveals the mental attitude which has conditioned the development of music, especially since the early Renaissance, but probably also to some extent since the classical period of Greek culture.

What the contemporary physicist tries to tell us, the general public, is that form is the foundation of all basic and scientific knowledge, for that knowledge refers to *the relations* between entities far more than to what most interests the common mind, *the substance* of these entities as perceived by our senses. We are told that we should transcend our usual way of thinking according to which "form" refers always to the form of something—the shape of some material substance—and try to think of pure relations in themselves. The substance of the world has recently become dematerialized by the physicist. The famous Einstein equation established a relation between matter and energy that allowed men, bent on conquest of self-preservation at any cost, to produce atom bombs. Matter as such has vanished. It has become a mere background for the cosmic stage on which nonsubstantial entities are seen enacting ever changing dramas of relationship. The actors have relatively little importance in themselves; what really counts is the development of their interrelationships—the dramatic plot. This development also obeys formal patterns seemingly imposed by the character of the human mind, and in many instances by the paradigms of our particular culture and its language.

At the level of the creative activity of the artist this "relationistic" approach becomes formalism. The nature and even the quality of the material used by the artist then assumes a secondary role. In music the concept of "musical note" and the formal arrangement of notes written on a two-dimensional score which can be read takes the place of the direct experience by the hearer of "living tones" whose quality or timbre are all-important.

Abstract notes vs. complex tones pulsating with magical potency—

this is an opposition which, though in practice may lose much of its absolute character, is so basic as to characterize a fundamental contrast between the music of the Orient (also of all the most developed tribal cultures) and European music.

We have already discussed such a contrast when opposing the magical to the esthetic approach to the arts. What makes such a discussion so relevant and today indeed essential is the fact that, as our traditional Euro-American culture appears slowly to disintegrate, we are confronted with the inescapable task of reintegrating these two opposing world-pictures into a new synthesis. The human attitudes which have produced them in the past can and should be seen as the two poles of a more inclusive approach to life, man and the universe. But this can be accomplished only if, first of all, we are clearly and objectively aware of the essential meaning of the two polarities and of what is the inevitable result of overemphasizing the importance of one of them at the expense of the other. In this connection music is a particularly significant field to consider because its development in the Western world has taken a totally new and striking character.

Notes versus Tones

European music is fundamentally a music of notes, rather than of tones—and interestingly enough in English the two words contain the same letters. A musical note is an abstract entity in that it theoretically has meaning primarily, and in a sense almost exclusively, in terms of its relation to other notes. The relation exists in time when one considers a note as part of a sequence, a melody. We may call such a relation horizontal for it so appears on a musical score. A vertical relationship exists when two or more notes occur simultaneously on the score, constituting a chord. A music of notes is two-dimensional; the vertical dimension introduces a factor of complexity. A modern orchestral score often displays an extremely complex organization of notes.

A musical note is like a mathematical point having neither dimension nor substance. Its relation to other notes exists in a two-dimensional outer *space*; but, at least in theory, the note itself has no *inner* space. It merely is one of many factors which, in their interrelatedness, define a form. Within that form the musical note may well play a particular function; but this functional character exists only with reference to the form. Of itself, a musical note is devoid of experienceable life-contents because it can refer to *any actual sound*. It may be performed on various instruments without losing its identity as a note and provided its relation to other notes is not altered, a note may be "transposed" to a higher or lower pitch and also retain its musical identity, thus showing that it is not fundamentally related to any particular vibratory frequency. In other words, it is essentially a black dot written on the staff of a music score. It exists primarily in the flat space of a score, and that space is essentially *empty*. Between the two succeeding notes of a melody there is nothing, only empty space—the kind of space that astronomers of the last century thought existed between planets and stars. Today, however, the astronomical picture is very different: energies and substances of various kinds fill and circulate within the space that once was considered a "pure void."

Every musical instrument produces sounds which have a characteristic timbre or quality; thus if a musical score is performed on a piano, an organ, or by a string ensemble the actual sounds being heard in every instance differ greatly. Yet the musicians say that it is *the same music* which is being performed. For them therefore music resides in the pattern of notes, not in the actual sounds (or tones) the score is supposed to represent; it is not primarily and vitally concerned with the actual sensation of sound produced by instrumentally or vocally generated air waves which strike the ears. Music essentially exists at the level of "pure forms" apprehended by the mind. As the apprehending mind of the hearer evidently affects his emotional state, the classical European music of the seventeenth and eighteenth centuries also influences the feelings of people, yet this influence operates through the mind-generated form, rather than strictly through the vibratory impact of tones releasing *tone-power*.

Sound refers to a specific kind of activity, just as does the life-force animating a living body. The Hindu philosopher names this energy of life, *prana*. Prana makes possible and sustains all the activities occurring within a "field" we call a body. Sound, in India, was considered the essential characteristic of another kind of field operating in what was called *akasha*. A "living tone" is an organism of sound, just as a human body is an organism of biological activity. For the Hindu musician the kind of sounds which can be registered as wave-motions within the atmosphere or through solid matter represents only the concrete manifestation of a finer type of motion in *akasha*. If I use the term "living tone" it is simply to indicate that a real tone has an "organic" character. It is a complex entity, a field of "sonal" activity, including a fundamental sound and many overtones. It has a particular timbre depending upon the nature of the source of its emission and the manner in which this tone has been produced.

Because it is a complex field of "sonal" activity, a tone has an *inner* space within which much can happen, just as a human body has its own multilevel inner space defining its total personality. At least in ancient times, Asiatic music dealt with tones and with groups of tones originally named in India *grama*—a word used also to speak of a village, an association of living human beings performing various definite functions. The "livingness" of these tones was implied in the accepted fact that they originally were derived from the cries of animals or in some instances from the sounds of natural elements. These tones were also believed to be the bodies of devas or nature-spirits said to ensoul and guide the growth of plants, and to control the many processes operating within the Earth's biosphere.

These processes were linked with the rhythms of seasons and days, some of which today we might call "circadian rhythms." Students of circadian rhythms affecting the daily activity and internal functions of animals and men are now aware that drugs taken at different times of the day and/or the year produce different organic effects. Likewise the traditional Hindu musician performed his *ragas* or *raginis* (primary and secondary organisms of tones) according to the time of the day or the season. To perform a dawn raga at sunset constituted a sacrilege, for such a performance would work against the over-all harmony of nature.

At no time was the musical space separating the tones of a melody (and Hindu music was essentially melodic and rhythmic) thought to be empty. The manner in which a performer *approached* a tone, perhaps gliding toward it or in some other way preparing its emission in which his entire organism was involved was—and remains today—of the greatest importance. It was important because a living and organic relationship was felt to exist between the successive tones of a melody: the instrumental or vocal approach to a tone was as significant in the melodic flow, as the quality of the approach a human being makes to another person is important in the development of their relationship. A Western musical note being in principle only a dimensionless mathematical point, it can have no *vitalistic* relationship to a succeeding note.

Euro-American melodies are discontinuous: to use Bergsonian terms, they operate in mathematical time, not in living duration. In the past when Hindu musicians first came in contact with Western music, they thought of it as a music "full of holes." Western music has an objective as well as a formalistic character, while Hindu music is essentially subjective, reflecting the "inner space" of all living organisms—the within of existence.

The performance of Western music at times includes somewhat awkward *glissandos* and especially *vibratos* modifying the rigidity of a note's insularity and pitch-purity, but these musical devices are considered by classical purists as extramusical elements. The vibrato does not belong to the musical score. It refers to an *existential* situation, the performance; not to the *essential* character of the music itself which resides in the form, thus in the score, an abstract formula of relationship. The form belongs to the realm of mind in which reason and the logic of development are supreme. The "per-formance" occurs in the "human, all too human" (Nietzsche) world of existence filled with uncertainty, errors, and compromise with the True and the Beautiful. In that existential world personal moods and emotions and sociocultural factors such as finances and politics constantly mar the majestic forms constructed by the composer's mind according to his vision of ideal order and archetypal pattrns.

The music resides therefore in the score—in the relation, not in the entities being related. It has its being in the form far more significantly than in the sounds actually heard during a performance. It is a music of mind rather than of life, a music of civilization rather than of culture. If music has experienced unparalleled development in Europe, it is because European culture is stamped with the dynamic character of the process of civilization; its restless dynamism, its constant passion for ever greater, ever more far-reaching complexity. But it is a quantitative, rather than qualitative complexity—a complexity of means and of formal structure, a technological complexity, and beyond a certain level diversity slides into a chaos of unrelatable and therefore meaningless atomized entities.

Our Euro-American culture seems to be fast reaching that level, if it has not already reached it, as avant-garde music and art may suggest. Yet chaos can always be considered also the prenatal state of a yet-to-emerge new manifestation of creative order. What is approaching death longs for the yet-unborn. He who is bound by all too familiar structures, which some deep part of his consciousness knows to be obsolete, semiconsciously aspires to a rebirth of potentiality, and very often yearns to lose his mind-identity in the intoxicating experience of unformed potentiality, the Eternal Virgin, Space. The mind can find all sorts of excuses and rationalizations to justify the yearning and the experience; it may even be lured and fooled by the exciting dream of a conquest of new planets. What it basically wants is to "jump beyond its shadow," as Nietzsche once poetically stated and to surrender its responsibility for actual rebirth to the mirage of exotic transcendence and artificial paradises or illusory nirvanas.

The Dis-Europeanization Process

In the preceding discussion the difference between *the actual experiences* of hearing Western music and, for instance, the traditional music of India may have been somewhat exaggerated, but the difference between the approaches to music, and particularly to sound, taken by the two cultures can never be too strongly emphasized. Such a difference expresses itself not only in the music itself, but in the quality of the performer's approach to the performance and to the instruments being used. We shall presently see how the performer's approach to certain instruments, when playing a type of music developed during the last hundred years, needs to be changed, if that "new" music is to be adequately performed—and this applies particularly to piano music. This new music demands that the player relate to his or her instrument in a radically different manner than that expected of the performer of classical or neoclassical Euro-American music. The reason for this is that for nearly a century at least some of the composers of the Western world—partially and often following a not too significant kind of motivation—have tried to break through the rationalistic framework of classical tonality and rigorous formalism in a more or less conscious attempt not only to produce new sounds, but to transcend the traditional approach to the *hearing* of sound.

The first pioneer may have been Erik Satie who in his youth began to sound forth on the piano sequences of "chords of ninths" for the sheer sensual joy of hearing their rich resonance.[1] He undoubtedly influenced the young Claude Debussy who was then frequenting the "soirées" at the home of the poet Mallarmé, where the avant-garde artists and writers of the day (*Symbolistes* and *Décadents*) were gathered. Debussy was also deeply impressed by the music played at the Paris World Expositions by small orchestras of Indochinese and, later, Javanese musicians, and as a result began to use what musicologists call Oriental scales—not quite realizing that scales in the Orient have (or had) quite a different meaning from scales in Europe. Thus began the dis-Europeanization of music which, in a sense Franz Liszt had also attempted within a special frame of reference when using the non-tonal scales of Hungarian gypsies.

In the field of painting, the Impressionists (Claude Monet in particular) had already sought to change the manner in which people saw the world of objects. They showed that human eyes do not actually see the real color and form of their surroundings; the eyes perceive what their cultural tradition has more or less decreed that objects — such as trees, houses, roofs, mountains—*look like*. It is the culture-conditioned mind rather than the eyes that do the seeing. The Impressionists therefore painted objects in different lights, at various times of the day, revealing how the changes in light affected *the form* which objects were supposed to have. They particularly challenged the concept of chiaroscuro — the dark-and-light syndrome, the use of muddy colors and supposedly black shadows. Optical discoveries in science stimulated their interest in color variations; but their probably unconscious intent was, at a deeper cultural level, to *dis-Europeanize painting* by freeing the direct visual sensations of the beholder from the constraints of the traditional way of perceiving the reality of the physical world, and thus responding to it emotionally.

Debussy, Ravel, and other composers inspired by them, have been called musical Impressionists; and evidently they have been influenced by the Impressionist painters. But the deeper, though largely unconscious, purpose of these men was, I believe, to free music from its bondage to European tonality and to transcend the intellectualistic approach and the scholastic formulas that rigidly conditioned the musicians' *response to sound*, any sound. It was a movement of liberation from an increasingly sclerotic culture and its paradigms.

Eventually, after World War I ended, Edward Varése in New York shocked conservative musical circles by proclaiming that "music must sound." We may think of such a statement as a self-evident truth, but the reaction of the music schools to it some fifty-five years ago plainly revealed that to traditional European musicians it was not at all obvious. For a while the neoclassical movement, which paralleled the development of Fascism in politics, triumphed because of a collective fear of Communism and all that seemed to challenge the sociocultural status quo. But World War II and the powerful influence of electronic technology upon music led to a new wave of experimentation with sounds, both by making widely available through phonograph and radios the music of all other cultures—or rather what was left of them—and by introducing the possibility of synthetic sounds through tapes and computers.

These movements of liberation of painting and music from the classical molds of the European past were followed by a similar freeing of the dance from ballet stereotypes, and of the theater from conventional topics and stage presentation; and we have also other kinds of social liberation movements, including the liberation of the human body from clothes which not only bind but forbid the skin to react to the direct influence of air and sunlight, and from the antisexual taboos imposed by Catholic and Puritan Churches. Liberation, however, can easily lead to chaos—for instance, in music, the chaos brought about by the concept of aleatory music and the atomistic juxtaposition of unrelated notes. Chaos must occur whenever there is as yet no deep feeling of some new principle of integration. Cultures fade away into empty meaninglessness; but as they gradually do so the transforming power of civilization asserts itself at the very core of the disintegrative process. It evokes the new, even as it destroys the old. The evoked images may be and in most cases are at first quite vague and pervaded with unrealistic utopianism; yet they have immense, though subtle, potency. In due time they triumph when the collective mind of a creative elite steadies its turbulence and gradually becomes a clear channel for the incorporation of the new vision into coherent forms that bring to the remains of the past a revitalized type of organic order.

In music, the Russian composer, Scriabin, was the first of the great dreamers of a new world of tones through which magical power potentially able to bring the hearers to a state of mystical ecstasy could be released. While his earlier compositions simply prolong the line of musical development initiated by Chopin, in mid-life Scriabin, deeply interested in mysticism and theosophy, became aware of the power of resonance which could be released by certain chord combinations with a gong-like character—chords featuring more particularly the superposition of sounds separated by modified intervals of fourths and producing tones rich with a vibrant inner space. He abandoned the old binding concept of tonality and used such chords as "seeds" out of which various types of melodic, harmonic and even rhythmic growths developed with a quasi-organic character. As the harmonics and beat-tones produced by his complex chords would rise, they would, as it were, polarize a descent of colors and light vibrations. A repeated use of trills and of eerie, swiftly moving and almost insubstantial wisps of sound, perhaps suggesting the motion of wings, became familiar means to achieve the specific psychic results he had in mind.

Scriabin's ideal was to bring to a state of ecstasy the men and women attending and to some extent participating in what we would today call a multimedia ritual that was to last several days. Such a ceremonial performance would revitalize at a higher level the tradition of the ancient Greek Mysteries. Music would be the soul of the ritual, releasing a magical power acting directly upon the electromagnetic fields of the participants. He even used the word, *dematerialization*, to suggest what in principle the result might be. What he meant undoubtedly was a process of total transcendence of the type of consciousness which our fundamentally materialistic culture has imposed upon us, Westerners.

The great *Mystére* Scriabin had envisioned could not be realized. World War I began, and soon after Scriabin died of a cancer of the lips; strangely enough, Debussy died nearly at the same time of rectal cancer. Scriabin was well aware of the impossibility of producing what he had conceived and before his death he wrote to an eminent Theosophist, B.

P.Wadia, that *Mystère* would have to be performed in India because only there would the spiritual ambiance be adequate for the achievement of the purpose he had in view. Before him, Richard Wagner, at a more strictly sociocultural and religious, rather than mystical, level, had envisoned "music-dramas" through which the fundamental symbols at the root of the Germanic collective consciousness, which has been basic in the development of European culture, would be powerfully reemphasized (*The Ring of the Neibelungen*), and later in *Parsifal*, the deepest symbols of Christianity would be reformulated.

Wagner's music-dramas today are commercialized and senselessly advertised as "operas," showing how little his purpose has been understood since Bayreuth ceased to be the place of pilgrimage it was before World War I. The Wagnerian music-drama represents the end-product or seed consummation of the European culture-whole—its symbolized omega state in which, ideally at least, all the arts developed in that culture were meant to come to a condition of synthesis. Scriabin's conception of his unrealized *Mystère* leads us a step further. As the cycle closes—whether at the cultural or at the strictly personal level—completion should be followed by transfiguration, religious reunification by metamorphosis and "dematerialization."

Any significant art-expression is magical in the broad sense that it implies the production of a form through which some power is released which aims to satisfy a need. But the character of that need changes as the culture develops; and in the lower type of art this need tends to be almost exclusively personal and egocentric—the need for recognition, fame, money, power—rather than collective. In many instances both the personal and the collective needs play their part in the creative process, the collective impulse and purpose operating through an egocentric artist unconscious of the true motivation, as well as of the ultimate effects produced by his creations. Church music of the medieval period satisfied the need to build a psychic aura of quasi-hypnotic devotional tranquility within the precincts of the church and the monastery. Later on, Church music came to serve a need for the shows of pomp and impressive power, and as the Courts of kings and princes centralized the cultural activity of the period, music fulfilled also the function of providing distraction to bored courtiers, or of enhancing the majesty of a king's entrance.

The Romantic music of the 19th century was essentially directed to the new bourgeois class and the remains of the old aristocracy, providing them not only with entertainment but, by proxy, with strong emotional experiences they were otherwise unable to have in their narrow "bourgeoisified" and materialistic lives. And today music beamed by all kinds of radio and television sources is asked to fill the boredom of doctor's waiting rooms, assembly lines in factories, long automobile drives, and the psychological emptiness of homes or even of the minds of students. The concept of "music therapy" is also becoming widely accepted, but when applied in mental hospitals or clinics it is usually limited to the playing of soothing or inspiring music of a cultural type. The magical power of tones is not as yet understood, or only rarely so; but, as used in mantrams it increasingly intrigues or fascinates many young people who, for various psychological reasons, are attracted to Oriental gurus and occult-magical practices. These, however, often unwillingly and unconsciously lead the unwary youth to absorption in the "astral" and psychic remains of the sects or groups having used them in the past.

The deepest need which music could fill today would be to help human beings to transcend *both* the realm of our Euro-American culture and that of physical materiality. What modern physics is attempting to accomplish (the dematerialization of matter and the transformation of the taken-for-granted concepts of our classical science), music also could do, at the level of etheric-psychic vibrations, for the purpose of breaking down emotional and psychological crystallizations and the tyranny of an ego solely concerned with its own security, bodily comfort, and personal happiness. It is to such an end that a music of what I long ago called "dissonant harmony" can be used—a music based on the complex resonance of chords releasing the power of transformation emerging from the dynamic interaction of sounds freed from the straitjacket of tonality and bondage to the formalistic patterns of our classical European culture.

Because the piano can be used as a characteristic source of such a music, and because it can be *directly and spontaneously* handled by an individual person, it has been for many decades the most significant musical instrument available for the transformation of our musical sense. Unfortunately the deeper significance of what the modern piano, since the days of Erard and Steinway some 150 years ago, offers to musicians as a potential agency for cultural and personal transformation is still not understood. By discussing the meaning of the potentialities inherent in the piano and its use in terms of "dissonant harmony" and of the magic power of tones operating according to the companionate order of relationship, we may now be able to throw new light not only on some 20th century music, especially since Scriabin, but on the way the piano should be used by the performer of such music in order to release the potency of the *sound-space* it encompasses.

The Piano as Microcosm of Musical Space

A grand piano keyboard should theoretically encompass seven octaves, thus eighty-four keys. Most of the keys—some white, some
black—are connected with three strings which, when the loud pedal is
pressed, set each other and the entire sounding board in vibration.
Powerful resonances can be aroused in the sounding board which acts
as one single vibrating sound-space, one unified field of sound encompassing practically all the normally useable sounds in music. A piano
thus is a microcosm of tones. If the field of sonal activity refers to what
in India is called akasha, then a piano potentially constitutes a unified
"akashic" field. The whole space of music exists in it in a condensed
form. This form, however, is unfortunately defined by a specific structure dividing the wholeness of that sound-space into some eighty-four
equal sections (semitones) bounded by the piano keys. Nevertheless the
sounds produced by striking, touching, caressing the keys are not
entirely isolated because they can be made to participate in the complex
resonance of the whole sounding board. One can think of them and
indeed experience them as modes of vibrations and centers of activity
interpenetrating in a higher dimension of the sound-space. The
composer-pianist pressing the keys can act somewhat as does a sculptor
when he deals with the clay which he shapes into forms he has visualized in his imagination, or forms which spontaneously and quasi-
magically arise at the touch of this fingers. Symbolically speaking, the
pianist can freely mold the vibratory substance of the sound-space. The
entire continuous and potentially unified substance of the whole space
can become "alive" under his fecundating touch; in his mind he deals
with the one sounding-board—the wholeness of it—rather than with
the separate strings and keys. The sound-space he sets vibrating is a
fullness of vibration because, while the strings and keys are separate
entities in merely physical terms, they nevertheless should be used as
means to induce the release of a power which can spread through the
whole seven-octave space of the piano. That space can be felt and
experienced as a microcosm of universal Space. The structure of that
microcosm, with its eighty-four or more divisions, can become a magical formula, which when uttered by the composer-pianist may produce
transformative results in the psyche and etheric field of those who are
able to respond to his will to transformation—his magician's will.

It is quite obvious that pianists today do not approach the playing of
their instruments in such a manner. They are taught to consider the
piano as a percussive instrument, to deal with each note separately, to
develop finger dexterity and play as fast and as clearly as possible.

Technical virtuosity is sought, and it often ends in mechanical performances so objective that they can be identically repeated, concert after concert. Such an approach does befit most classical music and those nineteenth century compositions which sought to dazzle the bourgeois public with virtuosity and showmanship; and this tradition is still strongly adherred to. Piano teaching in colleges is indeed a training in musical mummification, perpetuating the bondage to a materialistic and unimaginative image of the piano. This image reflects an equally conservative and culture-bound approach to music.

In order to play the piano in a way allowing for the magical arousal of living tones out of the resonant field of the sound-space, the pianist has to meet his instrument, not only as a sculptor handles his virgin clay, but as a lover touches and sets vibrating his beloved. A truly biological-muscular and psychic relationship has to be established between the entire body of the pianist and the piano, a magical love relationship. But this love cannot be magical—it cannot be vibrant and spontaneous—if the selection of piano keys touched by the fingers is rigidly determined by the puritanism of 17th and 18th century tonality—by the constant fear of playing wrong notes and disobeying traditional regulations concerning the way fingers should be held while playing, and notes clearly separated from each other as if they did not belong to one enveloping whole—the "auric field" of resonance surrounding the sounding board. This vibrant musical space should be considered as real and potentially as magically effective as the electromagnetic field which, we now know, exists around every living organism.

At a time when the Euro-American culture-whole is far into its "autumnal" season, piano magic—the magic attuned to the most basic psychospiritual need of human beings belonging to such a culture—will tend to assume the character of catharsis. It is most naturally the magic inherent in the dramatic conflicts, crucial problems, and tragic decisions so often found in the lives of contemporary individuals. But it is through such experiences that an individualized human being, controlled by ego patterns, is sooner or later able to free himself or herself from ancestral sociocultural stereotypes and accept the possibility of radical inner transformation. The individual has to deal with the confused and often tumultuous inner space of his own being. The basic issue is: will he be able to solve the tensions and, *through conflicts*, reach the complex harmony of the companionate order? Will he be able to become in his own inner being a chord of multidirectional energies whose resonance will call down the subliminal metapsychic light that can illumine this inner space of consciousness, upon which the power and grandeur of a greater Whole can then become focused for effective and truly magical action?

In order to fully grasp the potential meaning of the piano as a microcosm of musical space and as a catalyst to inner psychic and mental transformation, it may be valuable to compare it to the great gongs built in Asiatic countries, particularly in Java, China, and Japan. Such gongs, at the deepest level, should be understood as symbols of the principle of organization exemplified by the Buddhist Sangha (the Brotherhood of monks) and in general by similar religious or occult groups which can be consiered psychically integrated societies consecrated to a common purpose of spiritual transformation. When gently set in vibration a gong produces a tone of deep resonance, but this main tone results from the integration of a vast number of subtones, which, depending on the shape of the gong, may be more or less isolated and given relative independence. A Javanese gong with a bulging ventral knob produces a more homogenous tone than other types of gongs without such a centralizing feature; but by gently striking various parts of the instrument many subtones can still be heard. Unanimity of spirit prevails in the Brotherhood, yet individuality is still retained by its component parts.[2]

In the piano, the individuality of each note of the keyboard is far more pronounced than in a single gong, yet if large chords are struck, integrating the sounds produced by the strings of *properly distanced* keys, and the pedal is pressed allowing for total sounding board resonance, the gong-tone effect is obtained. That tone can be altered in a multitude of ways, not only by striking other keys in ever-changing melodic, harmonic, and rhythmic combinations, but according to the pianist's *touch* and *phrasing*. The piano becomes then, if handled in a truly "magical" manner and not as a pretext for finger-dexterity, a collection of gongs and even a miniaturized symphonic orchestra. Many timbres (or qualities of sound) can be produced by a pianist able to relate to the keyboard (and in a sense, to the entire piano) in ways as varied as a lover can relate to the beloved's body. What I have called *orchestral pianism* then replaces the dreary type of classical or neoclassical pianism—especially the German kind usually taught in American universities—in which mechanized fingers are made to uniformly strike insensitized keys as distinctly, separately, and rapidly as is humanly possible.

I repeat that such an insensitive and technique-oriented type of pianism may be effective when dealing with classical eighteenth century music whose origin was dance music; with the *bravoura* pieces of Romantic composers-virtuosie intent on "épater le bourgeois" (i.e. on stunning a bored bourgeois audience): and also with the physicality and crudity of many twentieth century composers of the neoclassical type. It is muscular, physical, virtuoso pianism. It has no magically psychic and transformative power; it may rouse hysterical applause or shouts because it appeals to primitive bioenergetic instincts, stifled today by the rigid behavior patterns of factory, office work, and long periods of car driving. Such a kind of pianism is totally out of place, not only in performing Scriabin's (and my own) or even Debussy's piano works; it is out of place whenever music can be regarded as a kind of nonrationalistic speech, in which tones replace words and seek either to convey a message or to release a magical transformative impact. Such music should be clearly differentiated from the kind that originally and essentially represents the complexified outgrowth of dance music, which is the case in much of our classical music.

A mechanistic pianism mirrors a mechanized society of pseudo-individuals living a spiritually isolated, alienated, and quasi-autistic existence senselessly prolonged by a symptom-removing rather than truly healing (i.e. making whole) type of medicine. But is it art's function only to reflect the vulgarization and decomposition of the values and symbols of a slowly decaying culture-whole? Is it not rather to inspire, stimulate, arouse, and impregnate our confused, yet so often expectant and at least partially ready, new generations with an eagerness to give up the role of decaying leaves and assume that of seed pregnant with a living futurity?

Today, in order to compensate for the formalism and automatism of traditional performance, and for a rigid subservience to musical scores lining up notes like starved human beings in a breadline, the value of improvisation and the concept of aleatory music have been stressed. The composer of such music only suggests to the performers what they might play, providing them with a variety of alternatives or even a merely conceptual scenario. A John Cage throws the sticks used in the oracular technique of the Chinese I Ching to determine what the new note of a melody shall be. Randomness is the keyword of the musical avant-garde. What these composers do not seem to realize is that while autumnal leaves may decay randomly when struck by cold winds, seeds embody the principle of bare functional necessity, every cell being so definitely arranged that the functions of the future life-processes can operate within a minimum of effective and truly magical inner space.

From an esthetic point of view, every part of an art-form, under the control of the artist displaying his formative power, should concur in producing an esthetic experience of order and, as the architect and philosopher, Claude Bragdon, significantly wrote of "beautiful necessity." But from the point of view of many of the socially and emotionally disenchanted and intellectualistic producers of avant-garde art—and before them of the Dadaists and Surrealists and other "ists"—art seems rather to serve the purpose of arousing the intellectual curiosity of a more or less *blasé* public or, by shocking the more conservative molds of feeling-thinking. The magically oriented artist seeks instead to fecundate open minds by projecting into them a vision and power of transformation, even if this means at first inducing a crisis in consciousness ploughing under old roots and the decaying remains of a once majestic culture.

The Performer's Function

In music the creative-transformative-artist faces the problem of performance. Music has not only to be "formed" but "per-formed." What then is the task of the performer, and what should be his/her relationship to the composer?

Contrary to the opinion prevailing in avant-garde circles, I do not believe that the performer should act as a co-creater with the composer, except in some special cases and for brief periods during which the form, as part of its planned enfoldment should open up to the possibility (always present in life) of relatively unstructured sudden revelations. As a "per-former," the pianist should act "through" a form; but this action should be attuned to the spirit that created the form, so that both the form-creator and the performer become *co-agents* for the transcendent source of the creative process whose purpose is to stir, inspire, and transform the hearers. Neither the "former" nor the performer should work merely for self-expression or ego-glorification. Instead they should strive after a vibrant and effective realization of the superpersonal purpose moving their inner beings. The performer's allegiance is not to the person who created the form, but to *that* which sought actualization *through* the creator-composer of the musical score in order to meet a collective human need.

As already stated, human needs greatly differ according to the historical phase of the sociocultural evolution in which they seek answers through the several arts, and also according to the level of consciousness of the class of people to which the art-form is more particularly addressed. There is need today for the type of personalized and heroworshipping excitement in which a bewildered and uncontrolled teen-age youth revels. There is need for jazz and songs of social protest, and sentimental popular ballads to fill radio time and relieve the boredom of middle class routine. There is need for orchestras which, as musical museums, preserve the hoary products of the cultural past and reluctantly add to the repertoire of "serious music." But it is to be hoped that the need for a music of living tones vibrant with magical, cathartic and metamorphic power will develop and grow among individuals ready to accept the now quite evident fact that they live in a transitional period pregnant with futurity.

All that our schools and music conservatories have sought to hammer into the minds of expectant and undiscriminating young students as fundamentals of music are only fundamentals of our Euro-American music; and this, mostly in terms of the last five centuries of our culture. What we call musical form is only the form which sequences of notes take in terms of the outer space. In that space they move according to rigid rules deriving from a type of order which radiates from the autocratic rule of king "Tonic" bolstered up by his Prime Minister, the "Dominant" (the note sounding a fifth above the tonic). Tonality is *theoretically* a system of law and order based on natural intonation, that is, on the already mentioned Harmonic Series of fundamental tone and overtones. But this system, like that on which modern nations jealous of their sovereign rights, and ego-controlled individuals base their feelings, thoughts and behavior, is exclusivistic. It has developed along intellectually rigid lines and at the service of a ruling class that once pivoted around a personalized central authority, but has become an all-powerful oligarchy of business and finance lacking even the glamor of religious sanction.[3]

Of course, tonal music is easy to listen to. Today it satisfies a vulgarized esthetic sense providing mass-produced satisfaction and a release of tension to persons whose nerves are battered by the conflicts of home, business, and politics. When at the close of World War II young French men and women, unemployed and nearly starving, gathered in discotheques and stifling basements to worshipfully listen to Bach, they did so because they needed the psychic and mental reassurance that ours is still fundamentally an ordered universe, whose forms are unfolding serenely along secure lines revealing the presence of Reason; and Bach's music gave them such a reassurance. This need for esthetic rationalism during an emotionally chaotic period was so crucial that it overcame the violent feeling which German conquest had created in France—a rather striking instance of how deeply music can affect the group-mentality of a generation. This also reveals how a cultural product, created at a particular time to fill a definite sociocultural function, at some later time may serve a very different and at least outwardly unrelated purpose.

Form has power. It has power over the human mind whose eminent domain is what Kabalists call "The World of Formation." But the mind, in one of its higher aspects, can also give form to the process of trans-formation. This is the paradox of mind: consciously or not the mind will seek to destroy what it has produced as soon as the *need* of any existen-tial unit of life-species has radically changed; and the change occurs because the vast planetary or cosmic cycles to which these units belong have reached a phase that call for a biological, sociocultural, or personal mutation. Then the old forms crumble. For a while, they may retain outer formal characteristics which during the period of transition are still relevant; but the *inner space* within the forms has to vibrate to new rhythms induced by the creative acts and/or magical utterances of relatively few individuals. *Through* these inwardly consecrated indi-viduals whose minds have become translucent lenses bringing to a sharp focus the release of power required for the start of a new phase of the planetary process of civilization, the culture-engendering images and symbols of the New Age take form. Around them the disintegrated and meaning-deprived remains of old cultures gather. The cycle of the new culture-whole has started.

8.
THE INTERACTION OF CIVILIZATION AND CULTURE

THE PROCESS of civilization, as defined in this book, and the development of culture-wholes coexist and interpenetrate; but we cannot truly understand either unless we realize that they constitute two fundamentally different processes belonging to two different levels of activity and operating according to different rhythms. Yet they both serve the same end purpose: the complete and perfect actualization of the complex and multilevel potentialities inherent in the archetype, Man. Philosophers of the Hermetic and Theosophical Schools tell us that Man, as an archetype embodied in a living human organism, is the microcosm of the universe, the macrocosm; Hindu seers long ago experienced in an ecstatic state the identity of *atman* (the vibrating transcendental center within the individual human being) and *brahman* (the metacosmic "Reality" ground of all existence); and the Bible tells us that Man was conceived by the Creative God in His image and likeness.

If this is so, when we contemplate the majestic and essentially nature-transcending process of civilization, and watch it operating *through* the development of culture-wholes, we are perceiving the workings, at the level of the evolution of Earth-conditioned mankind, of two movements that could also be detected within the total cosmic process. In this book, however, our attention should be primarily focused upon what happens at the level of a humanity having reached a state of development at which mind occupies a most important role. And by "mind" I mean both an organized form (or structured field) of consciousness, and the kind of activity that at first builds and forms, then seeks to experience and objectively formulate their meaning, and lastly becomes invovled in their deteriorization and disintegration when these forms become too rigid and fail to meet new human needs.

When we so define the term *mind* it seems necessary to postulate the existence of a type of activity which both transcends and acts through the mind. A power beyond, above, or within the human mind sets this mind in operation, and toward the close of a cycle of existence, affects in a cathartic or catabolic manner the forms which mind has engendered. Mind stands, as it were, between the realm of material-biological energies compulsively operating in the Earth's biosphere, and that of a transcendent supermental or transmental power which, for lack of a better word, we have to call "spirit." Spirit acts in and through minds which operate as formulating and transmitting agents. The basic purpose of such a transmental activity is to bring the materials of the Earth to a subtler and radiant state of being—thus, from our present-day point of view, to dematerialize and spiritualize matter.

If we do not accept the existence of spirit as a transphysical, transcultural, and metabiological power, the only other possible way of interpreting with some degree of consistency the obvious facts of collective and personal human existence is to adopt a materialistic approach, whether as developed by Marx or by other materialists; but such an interpretation excludes many of the most significant experiences of man. It leads to a most depressing world-view, essentially devoid of meaning and purpose. On the other hand, if the existence of spirit as a creative and transformative power is accepted, and its action in and through mind is clearly understood and adequately formulated, the material facts find their place within an all-inclusive picture of cosmic activity which takes nothing from them, but instead endows them with a transphysical and metabiological significance stimulating human beings to more conscious, sustained, and eventually more radiant endeavors.

The civilization process pertains to the activity of spirit, as spirit acts through the mind. Spirit is a vibratory power; it is *tone*. Mind deals with the forms that are inherent, but only potential or latent, within the tone. Spirit, acting through the formative agency of minds unreservedly open to its creative impulse, manifests as the Creative Word, *logos spermatikos*. "In the beginning" Spirit-in-act is the Avatar, the divine Person who impregnates the collective mind of humanity—the Earth's noosphere—with a magic power that starts the wheel of a new cycle of culture operating. As this initiatory impulse is an activity of spirit, whose essence is unitarian, it is logical to speak of one Avatar; yet, this creative activity has to sound forth through each level of organization of the planetary and the collective mind, and to take form on each of the several planes of life-manifestation in the biosphere, thus one may speak of a number of avataric personages and *avataric events*. One of these undoubtedly refers to the atomic explosions demonstrating the most material (chemical or atomic) aspect of the process of dematerialization. Not to include this atomic aspect of the avataric process—and also the type of activity referring to the improvement of biological seeds through some kind of genetic control—would reveal a narrowly *religious* understanding of the avataric process. This process represents the "descent" into the minds of human beings of a new creative-transforming impulse releasing its magic power in a variety of ways, each of which is required to meet definite collective human needs. Men and women involved in the development of such processes are the "civilizers" whose works sooner or later alter the fabric of human society and the quality of interpersonal relationships. The fact that in most cases today the civilizers are not consciously aware of what operates through their minds and of the end-results of their innovating or cathartic activity does not alter the essential process. Yet, because this activity of the civilizers operates through mind, it also has to work through the forms which, at the time, the culture makes available.

In a general sense, *culture is the carrier-wave necessary for the transmission of the creative Spirit-emanated impulse*. The mind-forms built by the culture become the vehicles for the transmission of the power that will eventually destroy them. But these mind-forms also *unavoidable* color, if not the impulse itself, at least the formulation of the message inherent in it. Because of this, an avataric and culture-transforming process must have preliminary phases. What Toynbee calls a "creative minority" of individuals has to be prepared step by step to assume its role as a civilizing agent. The steps are emotional as well as mental. They include a deep-seated dissatisfaction with the forms and institutions which the culture has built—a dissatisfaction often born of personal tragedy or of the experience of social injustice and individual mistreatment—and the development of minds able relentlessly to question the intellectual and/or moral validity of the essential premises (paradigms) constituting the framework of the collective mentality of a society having already passed its maturity.

Unfortunately the minds of such a creative minority always tend to react against the cultural patterns which have conditioned their development. Men and women seized by what has been poetically called a divine discontent come to hate the past from which they are struggling to emerge; and hate binds as much as does devotional love. These discontented and revolutionary individuals may be truly open to receive a new inspiration, a new creative impulse from the spirit; yet they receive it with minds colored by a negative attitude toward the past, and such a coloring tends to affect and (subtly or crudely) permeate the *formulations* they give to the spirit-emanated impulse. An essentially true and divine creative impulse can easily be perverted by a mind moved by an intense revulsion and passionate rebelliousness. Humanity most often proceeds by violent oscillations from one extreme to its opposite. Gautama the Buddha extolled "the Middle Way." Yet that way can also neutralize the inner dynamism of the spirit; the seemingly wise man may withdraw into the benign but static indifference of an equipoised mind refusing to be drawn into any conflict.

Conflict is inevitable because the process of civilization is one of transcendence, and transcendence implies crisis, just as the act of walking implies a fall from a position of equilibrium and a recovery. Dissatisfaction, fall, recovery are inherent in the process of civilization; and Man archetypally is the Civilizer. Man's supreme majesty is that he-she can always become greater ("majesty" comes from *major*, meaning "greater"). Not only can any individual person opt for the condition of seed and refuse to die the autumnal death of leaves; he-she can also willingly and readily accept the trauma of mutation, and the loneliness of the creative mutant bringing to the biosphere and to human society a new message of the *logos* and a new quality of livingness and relationship. Fulfillment is not enough. Nirvana is but a great dream. Man returns, even from the where that is nowhere, and from which life insists there can be no return.

Transformation is the keyword — the spiral, not the circle. But while in its own metabiological and super-existential realm civilization is a spiral process that smoothly and majestically moves through the birth-death-rebirth cycle of culture-wholes, both the individual person and the societies he builds have to experience transcendence as a "walk"—fall and recovery, death and rebirth. Man must walk on "the Path." He neither glides nor flies. He is neither earthbound nor able to soar on a current of air (*pneuma*, spirit). In order to know what it means to stand (his erect spine prolonging one of the multitudes of the radii of our globe and aiming at some as yet unknown zenith star) he must experience falling. Man does not grow like a tree, rooted solidly in the soil, a slow and sure unfoldment of seed potentiality. He walks from stance to stance by a process of radical transformation, from uprooting to self-sowing, from "dark night of the soul" to illumination.

Here it seems imperative to stress the two levels of meanings at which the word *transformation* may be understood. The process of biological growth is, in a sense, a process of transformation; yet in this context transformation refers only to the continuous unfoldment of what was latent in the initial stage. There is no essential discontinuity in strictly biological growth; one form is modified into another, and the modifying process in a natural state operates smoothly; it brings disturbances, but no crisis. The word *crisis* comes from a Greek root which means "to decide." The plant does not have to decide to bloom. The human body, biologically speaking, does not have to decide on puberty. But the human mind *can* decide to give either a positive or a negative — expansive or limiting — meaning to the experiences of the total organism which supports it. This is the crucial issue implied in the Man-archetype: the power to choose consciously. Man can choose the greater or fall into the lesser, either by refusing to choose or by deciding for the false security of the status quo—the established, the formal.

In a truly human sense, transformation means a *radical* change; and the change is radical only when freedom from the compulsive attachment to a particular set of root-ideas is obtained. Once uprooted, and the roots exposed to light and air, the plant normally dies. A plant cannot uproot itself; but man can. He can give up his reliance on the paradigms of his culture; he can deliberately change the locale of his growth. He can change his parental and culture-conditioned personal name. He may learn to act according to his "celestial Name" — the formula of his *dharma*.[1]

This is what transformation really means for a human being having inwardly accepted the burden of radical individualization: the challenge *to stand*, erect and tall, at the place and in the manner of his or her choosing. Thus the question with which this book began: where do you stand? And this means also *how* do you stand? What is the quality and significance which this stance radiates upon the human and natural environment.

Crises in our Western World

As usually understood, the term *Western civilization* refers to the development of a particular type of collective attitude of life in which two distinct trends have become combined. One of them originated in Greece, with the cultures of Crete and Asia Minor as a background; the other in Palestine, with the Egyptian and Babylonian cultures as parental influences. To say this may be considered by historians a questionable simplification, but they presumably would admit that the Greek and Hebraic currents of thought and feeling constitute the two basic influences which worked not only upon the relatively raw material of Germanic tribes, but also upon the remains of the Greco-Roman world and those of a Celtic culture of which unfortunately we know very little. Both Oswald Spengler in *The Decline of the West* and Arthur Toynbee in his monumental *Study of History* isolate two basically different culture-wholes: the present one that they both call "Western" and Spengler also characterizes as "Faustian," and the preceding one which Toynbee names "Hellenic" and Spengler "Classical." Spengler stresses the radical difference between these two culture-wholes; Toynbee sees them related somewhat as child to parent.[2]

From the point of view I am presenting here, the historical situation assumes a different aspect because what we really have to deal with is a process obeying planetary patterns which determine the rhythm of changes affecting the evolution of mankind as a whole, but which take different sociocultural forms in different geographical regions. In some of these forms the ancient rhythms of human activity and consciousness were retained, though modified in various ways concerning which we lack adequate information. Other better-known cultures reveal to us radically new mutations, especially at the mind-level, because in these regions racial groups were able to respond to the pressure of the culture-transcending process of civilization and thus to develop new concepts and a new sense of sociocultural and (to some extent) political relationship.

We are dealing with two processes: one vast planetary process of civilization, and the organic development of several culture-wholes occurring within more or less clearly defined geographical boundaries and organizing the collective life of more or less differentiatable racial stocks. Each of these processes obeys its own rhythm. Because the development of culture-wholes is fundamentally bound to and deeply conditioned (if not determined) by the telluric and climatic state of the biosphere at certain times, it obeys a kind of cycle essentially derived from one of the three basic motions of the Earth-globe: the precession of the equinoxes, the day cycle of axial rotation, and the annual revolution of the Earth around the Sun. On the other hand, the cycle of civilization, because it transcends the level of biology and physical determinants, can be significantly measured in terms of archetypal concepts essentially referring to number and ratios, yet also reflected in the cycle of relationship between the revolutions of the larger planets of the solar system. The cycle determined by the successive conjunctions of Neptune and Pluto occurring close to every 500 years is the most characteristic of these cycles.

These two types of cycles have been discussed at length in my book *Astrological Timing: The Transition to the New Age* (Harper and Row 1969), and here I shall but briefly outline their respective characteristics and the manner in which their correlation can be seen reflected in the sequence of most meaningful historical events and sociocultural changes. I shall begin with the cycle of civilization because it represents the manner in which the greater Whole, the solar system (the "heliocosm")—or rather that aspect of the heliocosm manifesting as a *transformative function*—acts upon the lesser whole, the Earth. This heliocosm is a field of energies whose radiating center is the Sun. The orbits of the planets constitute elliptic subfields. While a circle has one center, an ellipse had two foci. All planetary orbits have a common focus, the Sun; but each orbit (or subfield) has an *individual* focus symbolizing the characteristic function fulfilled by the planet within the total field of the heliocosm. In this heliocosm the most distant planets, Uranus, Neptune, and Pluto symbolize the above-mentioned transformative function. They operate as links between the solar system proper (whose *physically concrete* boundaries are symbolized by the ringed planet, Saturn) and our Galaxy, the Milky Way.

The entire heliocosm operates within an immensely vast organization of stars, a cosmic field whose spirallic structure extends over many light-years (each light-year representing a distance of 5,878, 487,289,132 miles). Our Sun is only one of the trillions of stars constituting the whole Galaxy; thus, *as a star*, it is a mere atom within the vast cosmic cell represented by our Galaxy. Yet, to us and to all that exists within the relatively small "heliocosmic" field which it animates with its immense starry energy, the Sun is the unique source of life and vibrant light. The Sun dominates its heliocosm as an all-powerful king—a king by divine right—dominates his empire or nation; but beyond the orbit of Saturn the Sun's energy (the so-called "solar wind") no longer effectively operates. The space defined by the orbital motions of Uranus, Neptune and Pluto (and probably of at least one other planet) constitutes an intermediary area between the strictly Sun-controlled space and interstellar space (i.e. galactic space).[3]

Trans-Saturnian space thus can be compared to the aura surrounding a human organism. In a sense, this aura, extending beyond the physically concrete skin, bones, and flesh of that organism, does belong to the human person; yet in another sense it is part of biospheric space. We might see it as the "no-man's land" surrounding the fortified citadel of the physical body and, at the psychological level, the castle of the personal ego claiming "I"-power. But if the fortification of the city and the castle are razed, or made translucent and with large open doors, this no-man's land becomes a zone of exchange in which the city-people meet and trade with the inhabitants of a far larger country; and through this intermingling and commerce the once narrow-minded city-dweller—and the ego-king whose castle is becoming a House of Parliament—are experiencing a radical transformation.

Thus, in a transpersonal astrology, Uranus, Neptune, and Pluto symbolize a triple power whose function it is to stir in human individuals the *will to metamorphosis* and to provide opportunities (which, most of the time, means crises) to become more than they are as biospheric human beings fundamentally controlled by biopsychic emotions and instinctual compulsions. The way to transformation is what occultists call "the Path," traditionally symbolized by the process of metamorphosis from worm to butterfly. At a planetary all-human level, this is the process of civilization; and it seems to operate essentially under the vibration 5, and in cycles of 500 years or multiples of it, for instance 10,000 years. In my early book, *The Astrology of Personality* (Epilogue: p. 490 in the Doubleday paperback edition) written in 1934-35, I mentioned such a 10,0000-year cycle and its apparent connection with the periodical stimulation of the higher mental faculties of planetary mankind. Such a stimulation in the sixth century B.C. led to at least tentative sociocultural changes in the fabric of human societies and in the quality of interpersonal relationships. It was a hesitant, only partial change at the level of everyday human existence and sociopolitical organization; yet it produced a probably irreversible transformation in the collective mentality of at least the "creative minority" (Toynbee's phrase) of mankind.

The 500-year cycle is approximated by the average 493-year cycle of the conjunctions of Neptune and Pluto; and the last of these conjunctions occurred in 1891-92 at around Gemini 8 degrees. Other cycles can be outlined by the successive conjunctions of Uranus and Pluto, and Uranus and Neptune; but the most basic seems to be that in which the motion of Neptune and Pluto are related. It is quite a striking type of relationship, and I have discussed it in the already mentioned volume *Astrological Timing* and my last book *The Sun is also a Star: the Galactic Dimension of Astrology*. Here I shall only speak, and this very briefly, of the archetypal 500-year cycle. Archetypal cycles are represented by simple figures referring to the level of pure Number and essential geometric ratios, be they of lines, surfaces, or volumes. But in the concrete existential world of existence, cycles are always more complex; and the relations between planetary cycles of motion *never* produce whole numbers, and usually are expressed as "irrational" numbers—another instance being the geometrical number *Pi*, the relation of circumference to diameter.

This fact undoubtedly refers to the infinitely complex character of existential relationships, whether at the biological or the cosmic level. For the same reason, the laws of physics are now found to be only statistically accurate. Statistics refer only to large collectivities or groups. But *individual cases*, and the relationship between two related fields of activity (cells, persons, or galaxies) can not be entirely expressed in rational, exact, or fateful terms; and in this resides the freedom of the individual. Another way of stating such a fact is to say that a factor of indeterminacy is present in most existential situations. An unexpectable release of new possibility can occur within what would seem to be the rigidly definable process of actualization of a particular set of inherent natal potentialities. Some "greater whole," theoretically at any time, might affect the well-established and expectable order of events. Yet the simple and rational archetypal structure is not to be ignored or dismissed. Somehow, at some time, the irrational *left*-oriented happening will be neutralized by an equally irrational *right*-oriented happening, and the majestic Harmony of cosmic being remains forever undistrubed in its archetypal equilibrium and meta-cosmic peace.

Coming down to the existential level of historical development, we may not find exact correlations between the starting points and culminations of 500-year cycles and crucial historical turning points, yet this 500-year pattern should help us to understand the *essential meaning* of important milestones in the process of civilization, as this process has affected and is affecting the development of the cultures with which we are most concerned as inhabitants of the Western world. We shall simply mention here the dates 600 B.C. — 100 B.C. — 400 A.D. — 900 A.D. — 1400 A.D. — 1900 A.D., and in the future 2400 A.D.; and I shall discuss these after briefly studying the other type of cycles: cycles affecting the development of culture-wholes. These cycles essentially refer to the orientation of the Earth's polar axis toward various galactic stars, and only secondarily to the movement generally known as the precession of the equinoxes.

Changes in the orientation of the Earth's polar axis (the axis around which our globe rotates during one whole day) are the result of a gyrating motion of the planet, a motion resembling that of a top in fast movement. This is the already mentioned third motion of the Earth, a slow motion taking somewhat less than 26,000 years to complete itself. During that period the poles point successively to a number of stars, called therefore in astronomy circumpolar stars. Today the polar axis is pointing to the star Polaris; and sometime next century, it will point to it as closely as it can possibly do. Some five thousand years later our pole star will be Alpha Cetei; and around 13,000 A.D. it will be Vega's turn to indicate North, unless the Earth's axis shifts considerably and the entire pattern changes in ways we cannot predict; a possibility recently popularized by several clairvoyants.

This slow change of direction of the Earth's axis seems nevertheless to be a structural feature of our globe and presumably results (at least from the materialistic point of view) from the irregular shape of the planet and the combined gravitational pull of the Sun and the Moon. What makes this cyclic change in the axial orientation of our globe so significant is the apparent importance of the polar axis in terms of geomagnetism. In *The Astrology of Personality* (p. 178) I spoke of the polar axis as the "I Am" axis of the Earth-organism — an axis which at the planetary level may have a meaning somewhat similar to that of the spinal column in a human body. At any rate, the North Pole is said to be the gate through which cosmic-galactic magnetic forces (and probably other forces of some unknown nature) pour into the interior of our globe. In other words what I have called the Great Polar Cycle should refer to basic changes in the *direct* relationship of the Earth to the Galaxy.

The Earth is part of the solar system (or heliocosm); but it also moves within the wider space of the Galaxy—a highly complex motion resulting from the combination of several movements. The Great Polar Cycle, as it were, sounds a very deep planetary tone which must affect the internal evolution of mankind in the biosphere because mankind-as-a-whole fulfills a central function in the Earth's organism, just as the cerebrospinal nervous system does in a human body. It is Man's function to bring to an objectively conscious state all the activities taking place in the biosphere and, it would now seem, even beyond it. Man, in that sense, is the planetary Mind of the Earth; and the various culture-wholes developing in the biosphere represent even finer instrumentalities for the revelation of meaning through perceptual and conceptual activities. In due time, this planetary mind is able to detach itself from biospheric compulsions. It discovers its most essential nature and experiences a process of metabiological and transphysical metamorphosis—a process which is civilization in its true character.

As the polar axis describes a circle in the nearly 26,000-year-long period, this motion reacts on the equatorial plane of the Earth which is perpendicular to it. As this equatorial plane is inclined by about twenty-three degrees to the plane in which the Earth revolves around the Sun (the ecliptic), the two planes intersect. The line of their intersection is the line of the equinoxes (from Aries 1 degree to Libra 1 degree in terms of zodiacal position). As the polar axis changes its orientation with reference to circumpolar stars, so the intersection between the equatorial plane and the plane of the ecliptic also alters its position in relation to the stars forming the traditional constellations of the zodiac. If, century after century, we refer the successive positions of the equinoxes to the constellations, we see the equinoxes moving backward in the zodiac. Practically speaking, this means that, if at the spring equinox (March 21) we prolong a line passing through the Sun and the center of the Earth until it reaches a star, that star which in 1800 A.D. was part of the constellation Pisces, will be in 2100 A.D. part of the constellation Aquarius.

Because astrology each year gives a great deal of importance to the state of the universe at the time of what it takes to be the beginning of nature's year (the vernal equinox), the position of the Sun at that equinox with reference to the *constellations* acquires a profound significance. It was especially significant in cultures that found their spiritual expression in vitalistic cosmologies, cults, and rites of fertility and the worship of the male and female polarities, because, in such cultures, the constellation represented areas of a space vibrant with cosmic life, and the abodes of creative hierarchies of gods. In those early days the year began with the Sun releasing throughout its domain the power of the Taurus Hierarchy and around 2300 B.C. of the Aries Hierarchy; then a time came when the Pisces Hierarchy began to put its creative stamp upon the spring season of the year and therefore upon whatever then emerged into a renewed life, at least in the geographical regions that had given birth to these cultures.

Thus the concept of great Precessional Ages took form; and it is still with us today when, following a renewal of interest in astrology, a planet-wide expectation of the coming of the Aquarian Age is mounting in intensity, not unlike the expectation of the end of the world throughout Europe before the Year1000. Undoubtedly *something* is to be expected; but it may well be that it will take unexpected forms, or that only one-hundredth or one-thousandth part of the population of the Earth will be aware of its happening, and even a smaller number of human beings will respond positively to whatever is released into concrete manifestation.

Even though the idea of linking the large visible stars into celestial pictures referring to sacred animals, totems, or (in the Greek period) human heroes, seems to have been held by practically all cultures of which we have remains, the celestial images and the constellations' names have greatly differed. The length of the precessional cycle and its nature may not have been known much before the sixth century B.C., at a time when, according to calculations I made some forty years ago and which have proven increasingly valid in terms of historical references, the very last phase of a complete cycle of 25,000 to 26,000 years was about to end. I place that end at about 100 B.C. The entire cycle then ending presumably saw the rise of controlled agriculture and cattle-raising, at least insofar as our present humanity is concerned; and there may have been earlier and very different types of humanity, often referred to as Atlantean and/or Lemurian. The keynote of such a long 26,000-year period can therefore be given as *Cultivation*. The keynote of the new cycle of approximately the same length—unless deep structural changes occur in the solar system—would be *Universalization*.

In the cultural forms which the aggressive Faustian spirit of our Western culture has sought to impose upon the rest of the world, either

by conquering armies or by business penetration, Christendom represents the first phase of this long process of universalization. Because of
its nature, this process has become at the biospheric sociocultural and
political level a focused expression of the transformation and metamorphic power of civilization. It was initiated by, or rather *focused through*
a few great personages who lived, thought, and taught around 600
B.C.—particularly Gautama the Buddha in India, Lao-tze in China,
Pythagoras in the Hellenic East-Mediterranean world, Zoroaster in
Persia, and others in other countries. The release of the energy of that
process was made possible because the 26,000-year-long Precessional
Cycle was then ending, thus coming to seed; or rather the time had
come for the fall of the seed into the new soil which had been slowly and
only partially cultivated and made ready to receive that seed represented by the great Civilizers of the sixth century B.C.

We might also say that at that time the "personality" of the Earth-
being, having reached a stage of crisis in organic-planetary growth, had
become at least partially open to the *reception* and the subsequent slow
assimilation of a new cosmic-galactic message or creative impulse.
Since that great moment of cosmic-galactic impregnation twenty-five
centuries have elapsed, or five 500-year cycles. This pentarhythmic
(five beats) process has manifested at the historical level as a sequence
of highly meaningful events. Studying them even most briefly with
reference to the beginning and the mid-points of these five subperiods
should give a somewhat new dimension to the well-known historical
developments in geogrpahical regions with which we are familiar.

Subperiod No. 1

(600 B.C. to 100 B.C.) The lives of Gautama the Buddha in India,
Pythagoras and Solon in Greece, Zoroaster in Persia occurred as this
first phase of the 2,500-year process began. This was also the time of the
rise of the Persian empire which, at least for our subsequent Western
culture, established and demonstrated the operation of the principle of
divine kingship and of a centralized top-bureaucracy of governor-
administrators (*satraps*) responsible for large regions. This principle
was reembodied in the Rome of the Caesars, and also much later in the
short-lived French empire of Napoleon I; it is now in evidence in
American big business with its powerful executives operating at a
multinational level through a hierarchical chain of command.

Just before 600 B.C. (586 B.C.) the Babylonian captivity deeply influenced the development of the Hebraic tradition which Europe inherited. The Kabalistic doctrines were most likely derived from the old

Chaldean wisdom-knowledge, and these deeply affected the underground occult counterculture of Europe. A couple of centuries later, the Buddhist King, Asoka, sent to Palestine Buddhist missionaries who formed groups on the shore of the Dead Sea, presumably influencing some Hebrew communities. In one of them (the Ebionites—"The Poor"), according to H. P. Blavatsky in *Isis Unveiled*, Jesus was born. Other occultists, mainly Rudolf Steiner, have stressed an even more definite occult connection between Gautama and Jesus.

Subperiod No. 2

The beginning of the first century B.C. witnessed the long and exhausting struggle between Rome and Carthage. Those Punic wars, together with the start of the westward migration of German tribes, conditioned the development of the pattern which the formation and decay of the Roman empire was to follow. The wars with Carthage led to internal revolutions, to Caesar and, through the Egyptian adventure, to the introduction of Oriental pomp and Near Eastern cults. The old idea of "universal empire" was reformulated in terms of Roman law, but with a new concept of tremendous importance inherited from the Athenian classical culture: the concept of the rational individual man. In Rome, it became the ideal of the "Roman citizen"—an ideal which recently has become reformulated in terms of "world-citizenship."

The Caesar-Image and the citizen-Image constitute the sociopolitical foundation upon which the *spiritual* concept of the Christian person could develop. Two levels of human power and consciousness are here implied, and the first has been, and needed to be, the support of the latter. Caesar and Christ are the two essential archetypal Images of our dualistic Western culture. At the root of such a culture one finds the attempt to bring into a dynamic, but also insecure and restless, state of harmonious cooperation not so much the sacred and the profane (as I have already defined these terms) as the religious and the political—or, in other words, the spiritual and the material, the quest for God and the passion for gold. Both have been basic factors in the as-yet uncompleted *first stage* of the process of universalization. This process demands the growth of a supertribal, then supernational consciousness and of a global culture sustained by some complex and inclusive type of political structure. The as yet unanswered crucial question is what this political structure so urgently needed will turn out to. Clearly, the answer depends upon the dominant state of consciousness reached by at least a creative minority of far-seeing, yet practical and realistic, individuals toward the end of the twentieth century and the beginning of the next.

Subperiod No. 3

Around 400 A.D. Rome collapsed and, as the middle point of the 500-year cycle that followed was reached, Christendom faced an ebullient and aggressive Islam. The Christian world was emerging from its formative period of childhood under the leadership of Pope Gregory and St. Benedict (founder of the Benedictine Order) whose monasteries seeded the sociocultural chaos with some of the intellectual harvest of the by then disintegrated empire. The fast conquering Arabs who had swept over North Africa and Spain finally were stopped in central France. The migrating groups were settling down.

Subperiod No. 4

By 900 A..D. the divisive patterns of European history had become more or less clearly established, with the Rhine as the basic line of cleavage. Charlemagne's empire (the root-foundation) had branched out; and with the development of the Romanesque style in architecture, the growth of new myths and heroic figures, and the spread of centers of learning and eventually universities, the great Medieval Catholic Order was taking form, after recovering from the anticipation of the "end of the world" in Year 1000. At about the mid-point of the period 900-1400 A.D. the Crusades began, and the fecundation of the European consciousness by the Near East (particularly by the Sufi movement and, through Spain, the Kabalists) took place. Alas, much of it was deliberately aborted by the combined power of the King of France and the Pope. The beautiful West-Mediterranean culture which united Provence, South-West France, and Catalonia, and gave birth to a new image of womanhood and "courtly love" was savagely destroyed, and in the North the Templars suffered the same fate.

Subperiod No. 5

With 1400 A.D. we come to the Humanistic Renascence, preceding the Classical Renaissance sparked by the exodus of Byzantine scholars when their city fell to the Turks (1453). The era of "great voyages" was beginning. European nations were formed, embodying a new spirit foreshadowed by Joan of Arc and stabilized by national languages. The Rosicrucian movement started under Christian Rosenkreutz, first as a very secret organization whose existence was only revealed nearly two centuries later. Alchemists were at work underground, while the Inquisition triumphed. At the mid-point of this 500-year cycle, the Classical period (referred to as the Baroque era, because of developments in architecture) reached its apex. After Copernicus, Galileo, and Giordano Bruno had transformed European man's vision of the universe, Francis

Bacon promoted the new scientific spirit of enquiry and empiricism; Descartes and Newton presented a world picture based on rationalism, mechanism, and the intellectual study of "natural law." Soon a totally materialistic approach to reality came to dominate the restless and progress-haunted mind of men.

Subperiod No. 6

As the twentieth century began, Roentgen, Curie, Planck, Freud, and Einstein began a revolution in thought which Karl Marx and Darwin had pioneered in their respective fields. The Industrial Revolution turned electronic, and the entire pattern of a Europe-dominated world began to crumble under the onslaughts of two World Wars and the menace of a nuclear holocaust. In 1891 Pluto and Neptune were conjunct; and the first 5,000 years of the Hindu Kali Yuga ended in 1898.

We are therefore living at the beginning of the sixth 500-year period since the "Great Mutation" of 600 B.C.— and presumably of the second half of a 10,000 year cycle which started around 8,000 B.C. when perhaps the famed Poseidonis, the island constituting the last portion of a mid-Atlantic continent, was submerged. It makes little sense to try to imagine what the future will bring, but the symbolism of numbers should give us an important clue to the potentiality of developments just ahead, provided of course that our starting point of 600 B.C. accurately refers to the beginning of a new, and probably unparalleled, focalization of the power inherent in the planetary process of civilization.

If it is a number 1 phase, the period 600 to 100 B.C. should be interpreted as one in which a new creative impulse was released, but could only affect the mind and the ideals of a small creative minority and produce only ephemeral concrete manifestations at the social or mass level—except in terms of the disintegration of older cultures. With the number 2 phase we witnessed the substantiation and implantation of the basic spiritual and social drives from which a future new order would draw its *raison d'etre*—its rationale for being—and the quality of its vitality; and we have the dualism of Caesar and Christianity. The number 3 phase completed the involutionary process of the original creative impulse, destroying what could not assimilate it and setting into operation the balance of polarized forces (Christianity vs. Islam, Germanic vs. Mediterranean Europe, West-of-the-Rhine vs. East-of-the Rhine, etc.) through which the karma of European and Near-Eastern mankind had to work.

The number 4 phase, beginning around 900 A.D., gave sociocultural form and mental formulation to the response of the gradually reorganized Western society as it began to actualize the new possibilities of human development evoked by Christianity and the Roman empire. This response was deeply influenced by the Crusades at the mid-point of that five centuries long period; yet, as it surged from the depth of the Western European "soul," it took the form of the Gothic cathedral and the sociocultural activities developing around its centralizing structure. As we shall presently see, Spengler gave to this soul the name of "*Faustian.*"

The five centuries between 900 and 1400 A.D. represent the high point of the European *culture*, with all its limitations, its narrow dogmatism, and its spirit-questing dynamism. With the Italian Renaissance, the revival of Greek ideas and forms acted as a restatement of the archetypes which the process of civilization, when focused in Athens, had sown into the mentality of the intellectual elite of Western mankind. But such a restatement had now an entirely different cultural soil in which to take form. Spengler probably overemphasized the opposition between the "static" character of the Greek (Classical) culture-whole and the "dynamic" nature of the European Faustian soul; yet this opposition characterizes the difference between the involutionary and the evolutionary halves of a subcycle of civilization, and it is important to appreciate fully the meaning of such a difference. The civilizing impulse of the sixth century B.C. "descended" into the natural, cultural collective mind of Western man; it became *involved* in human nature, mixed in with the karma of that section of humanity—and, of course, also in another way and with different results, with the character and karma of the culture-wholes of India and China.

Such an involvement almost inevitably tends to pervert the purity and to a large extent the essential quality of the civilizing impulse; nevertheless any creative impulse operating at the level of the civilizing mind (symbolized by No. 5) *needs a carrier-wave in order to operate in the biosphere.* A culture-whole constitutes such a carrier-wave; but, alas, at this time of human growth, the carrier brings in an enormous amount of distoring and confusing "static." The Promethean message of spiritual transformation is twisted, materialized, disfigured, and above all misunderstood by the large majority of individuals and groups clinging to the old concepts or attitudes and trying to make this message fit their preconceptions, emotional biases, and biopsychic appetites. This is unavoidable where the mass response of human beings is at work; yet the results can be tragic, as our Western society today characteristically reveals.

The masses never create, but they polarize the character of the creative impulse which will be the spirit's answer to their needs. These needs have first to be formulated in some manner. Religiously speaking, man must ask and pray before God can answer. There must be individuals who, becoming mouthpieces for the masses, give conscious and concrete form to the mostly unconscious needs of the people at large. These individuals, through their art, their words, and their actions, not only explicitly and vividly picture and reproduce what is actually happening in their culture-whole, but (at the highest level) they give form to the inchoate yearnings of the people. They are not only muckrakers, but revealers and formulators — "mediums" through which the collective unconscious finds words to make its demands known. They are important persons because the way in which a question is asked determines the nature of the answer. This is a principle which applies in every field, including that of scientific inquiry and laboratory experimentation.

There are also individuals who not merely set the form of the crucial questions but become agents for the formulation and enactment of the creative answers; but even they can only give answers which their own personal needs—as human beings born in and molded by a culture-whole—have brought to a conscious focus. Even though the lenses which their minds constitute may be translucent and well formed, the glass of the lens is inevitably made of the substances available to the collective mind of the culture-whole. Even the highest avatar, the God-man, is God speaking *through* a human throat, acting through human nerves, moving through human limbs; and nerves suffer illness. Avataric individuals also become ill; their illnesses may be the ransom paid to the race that bore them and to the men and women whose minds and souls they illumine—but only with the particular kind of colored light which these disciples can bear and become attuned to.

Culture, I repeat, is the carrier-wave of the process of civilization. The space of a room or a temple may be filled with waves bearing an incomprehensibly vast number of messages emanating from myriads of worlds of consciousness, but unless man develops an adequate radio-receiver within his brain-mind he cannot hear them. We all live in the space of the Galaxy; but, until a few years ago, we did not realize this. We could only think of the solar system and its spaces, perhaps only of the biosphere teeming with lives, or even merely of our small country or village, center of our narrow world of activity and consciousness. We could only think of air-waves as carriers of messages; then we found that electronic or laser waves could carry information. Now we are seeking to discover how thought may be directly transmitted. Carrier-waves are always needed as transmitters and, *through the transmission of information*, as integrators or destroyers. Because a future global culture-whole needs new carriers of information, everywhere human beings (individually and in groups) eagerly, feverishly, and confusedly work to discover what could become the new means of planetary integration. This search is the basic drive of this new 500-year period which began around 1900. It will produce the fervently hoped for New Age—unless an abortion occurs.

This new 500-year period vibrates to number 6 because 6 is the symbol of harmonization, of the union of opposites and of the love that synchronizes polarities at all levels, and by synchronizing them makes possible the emergence of the 7—the divine Child. Without the operation of this vibratory 6 the pentarhythmic process of civilization could only bring about disasters and turn self-destructive through atomization and total self-involvement; and such a self-involvment, at the cosmic level, takes the form of a "black hole" and at a personal level leads to the "black magician" who, eventually after a nightmarish series of lives, becomes a totally autistic center of ego-consciousness absolutely indifferent to anything, because absolutely unrelated.

This is why, behind all spiritual creative impulses vibrating to the 5 of civilization, there must stand the boundless compassion of a being radiating the power of vibration 6—a Buddha, a Christ, a Bodhisattva, a St. Francis. Therefore today, as we face the potential tragedies of a misdirected because misunderstood process of civilization, our greatest need is to open our whole being to the inflow of that love-*agape*, which is compassion and understanding. Such a love understands because it is willing, ready, and able to "stand under" and to sustain the present global process of alchemical purification and transmutation. We should sense that process working through our deepest being and at the core of all our crises, our catharses, our deaths and rebirths. Only then can a beautiful New Age bless our children or great-great-grandchildren; and the imprints made by our lives upon the vibrant substance of the cosmos will glow with the divine light. In us the process of *transfiguration through all-inclusive love* will have reached its fulfillment.

The Antiphony of the Gnostic and the Faustian Spirit

At the opening of the sixth chapter in the first volume of his epochal work *The Decline of the West* (p. 183), Spengler defines the essential character of what he sees as the three cultures with which our Western world has been mainly concerned, the Classical (meaning the Greco-Latin, or as Toynbee calls it, the Hellenic), the Western, and the Hebraic

CIVILIZATION AND CULTURE   123

Cultures. He speaks of the Apollonian, the Faustian, and the Magian souls. The Apollonian ideal is "the sensuously-present individual body" as the ideal type, while the prime-symbol of the Faustian soul is pure and limitless space. To him "the nude (Greek) statue is Apollonian, the art of the fugue Faustian. Apollonian are: mechanical statics, the sensuous cult of the Olympian gods, the politically individual city-states of Greece, the doom of Oedipus, and the phallus symbol. Faustian are: Galilean dynamics, Catholic and Protestant Dogmatics, the great dynasties of the Baroque era with their cabinet diplomacy, the destiny of Lear, and the Madonna-ideal from Dante's Beatrice to the last line of Faust II. The painting that defines the individual body by contour is Apollonian; that which forms space by means of light and shade is Faustian. The Apollonian existence is that of the Greek who describes his ego as *soma* and who lacks all idea of an inner development and therefore all real history, inward and outward; the Faustian is an existence which is *led* with deep consciousness and introspection of the ego, and a resolute personal culture evidenced in memoirs, reflections, retrospects and prospects and conscience." He then speaks of the magian soul of the Arabian culture, appearing "in the time of Augustus (thus after 31 B.C.) with its algebra, astrology and alchemy; its mosaics and arabesques, its caliphates and mosques, and the sacraments and scriptures of the Persian, Jewish, Christian, post-Classical and Manichaean religions."

Reacting against the traditional way of referring to our Western culture as a prolongation of what had begun in "the Antiquity" and had been interrupted by the Dark Ages, Spengler was eager, indeed over-eager, to establish the existence of a basically Germanic European culture as a completely independent historical whole. Thus he had to stress how different it was from the Mediterranean "Classical" culture. Indeed our Euro-American Society was and is different and in a very real sense the polar opposite of the Greco-Latin culture, but Spengler failed to see the meaning of such a polar opposition in terms of a larger historical whole. Arnold Toynbee recognized the parent-child relationship between these two cultures, but he may not have fully realized how (as I suggested in the preceding pages) they formed the two halves of a whole. Moreover he probably did not perceive the real meaning of the fact that in both cultures there existed a deeply significant countercultural movement. Nietzsche was aware of this movement which he identified with the Dionysian aspect of Greek culture; but did not see it prolonged throughout the European era. Spengler attempted to fit what he understood of it into the development of the Roman empire and of Christendom by relating it to a rather mysterious entity he called the

Arabian culture, even though he spoke of its existence and influence six centuries before Islam drove relatively small bands of Arabs into a frenzy of violent expansion.

Spengler and Toynbee—for understandable reasons due to their academic and empirical training as historians—failed to realize what many people today think of as the exoteric and esoteric aspects of all great religions and of the culture "ensouled" by these religions. Every Society, in Toynbee's sense of the word, has an official culture and at least a relatively submerged and unorthodox counterculture. In most cases this cultural dualism occurs because the culture-whole has been produced by the combination of two racial groups at different stages of mental development, the earlier inhabitants of a country having been conquered by a more dynamic group of tribes, usually from a Northern region, bringing with them a new type of religion; and this was the case of early Greece, in Vedic India, in Mexico. But this impregnation of an old dying culture-whole by new and perhaps relatively uncultured races always allows something else to happen: a "descent" of creative ideas which takes concrete form in terms available to and needed by the social groupings resulting from the often violent fecundation. Thus the process of civilization acts through and within the interaction of the two races.

When Toynbee asks, "Were the Mysteries of Classical Greece, like witchcraft in Modern Europe, a survival from the religion of a submerged society,"[4] he may be partially right in his assumptions, but he may be quite wrong in his implied interpretation of the spiritual movement which carried at its source the name of Orpheus. According to an occult tradition, Orpheus had come from India, after a stay in Syria, where a very ancient and once important city is named Urfa. The essential point here is that, at least since the sixth century B.C., the official aspect of any culture seems always to have been polarized by a countercultural movement. The latter may be accepted by the Establishment—as the Eleusinian Mysteries were in Greece—or it may have to go underground because of severe persecution, as was the case in medieval Europe. In either case, what most historians attention to is the official mentality that produced duly recorded public institutions and works of art and literature; they tend to play down the importance of the countercultural movements which keep existing in the background (or underground) of the official culture and may emerge only sporadically into the light of the public consciousness— just as, until Freud, psychologists dealt only with the conscious realm of the personality and ignored the unconscious or semiconscious and subliminal region of the psyche.

The correspondence between what occurs at the level of the *collective person*, which Toynbee calls a "Society" (and I speak here of this as a culture-whole), and that at which an *individual person* operates in terms of "day-consciousness" and "night-consciousness" (*Yang* and *Yin* in Chinese philosophy) is remarkably exact, if consideration is given to the principles at work rather than to literal happenings. This "night-consciousness" does not refer to what the officially *organized* religion of the culture-whole and its by-products—most forms of art—characteristically represent, but rather to the mostly submerged contents and the "occult" (i.e. hidden) activities of the people who are not entirely and *professionally* committed to the official stance of the cultural Establishment. The publicly organized, and therefore exoteric, religion, in all its often varied and even conflicting branches, may lead some of the more unusual persons practicing its deeper forms of discipline to experiences belonging to the night-consciousness of the collective soul of the culture-whole; and every great religion has its "mystics" and "saints" who constitute its transpersonal aura. But these relatively rare human beings usually are not heartily welcomed by the religious establishment; they are kept isolated and often publicly denounced or even killed, only to be beatified and sanctified after their death. They are too disturbing and irrational a challenge to the day-consciousness of the culture. Only in India was a totally "planned" and ritualized society able to set as its supreme achievement the *sannyasi*, the wandering holy man who had deliberately repudiated and transcended every form of planning, formal behavior, and rational conceptualization. The Jewish establishment, supported by the Roman governor, killed Jesus, just as, for similar reasons, the Pope and the King of France destroyed the Albigenses and the Templars. Jesus' message outwardly triumphed; but it did so only because it suffered the tragic, even if probably necessary, fate of becoming institutionalized and dogmatized almost beyond recognition.

It is this institutionalization and the attendant materialization (involving the worship of "images") that indirectly led to Mohammed's mission as a kind of early reform movement. Yet Islam, too, soon became institutionalized and made to feed an until then localized and restrained lust for power in the collective Arabian soul. However, a subsequent surge of night-consciousness ensued, producing the Sufi movement, whose roots are intertwined with those of Hebrew and Chaldean occultism, as well as with the underground aspect of the official religion of the old Persia, whose antecedents may reach far beyond the Zarathustra who flourished at the beginning of the great empire of Cyrus.

The countercultures of all these Near-Eastern regions may have been originally inspired—or rather "in-spirited"—by what, a century ago, H. P. Blavatsky and the great Southern Brahmin, Subba Row, spoke of a "the Chaldeo-Tibetan Occult Brotherhood." There seems to have been at times a strange connection between Tibet and the Near-East, presumably involving secret groups operating from the Hindu Kush mountains, which the famous Kyber Pass (the route of Mongol invasions from the North into India) separates into Himalayan-Tibetan and Afghanistan sections.[5]

While, to the east of the Pass, the Himalayas (with Mt. Everest, or rather in Sanskrit Himavat, as their sacred apex) became the Holy Mountains of the Hindu-Aryan traditions, far to the West, the massive Caucasus (with Mount Ararat) stood and still stands as the at least symbolic (and perhaps actually magnetic) source of all the sociocultural developments that occurred in the Near East, from the lands of the Medes and Persians to the Suez Canal and the Red Sea.

All these Near-Eastern developments left a spiritual or intellectual harvest that was gathered up and "spiritized" in Alexandria, as well as in some Syrian cities close to the source of the Manichaean movement and the Mithras cult which so powerfully challenged the spread of the orthodox Christianity of the Church Fathers.[6] The great library in Alexandria, symbolizing the spiritual aspect of Alexander's conquests, was destroyed several times; but the various Gnostic groups flourishing from at least 100 B.C. (for instance the Egyptian Therapeuts) to the third or fourth centuries A.D. never disappeared, although they were severely denounced and persecuted by Christianized leaders who, possibly for personal and psychological reasons, adopted the emotional and potentially more popular Pauline interpretation of Jesus' mission.

Gnosticism, in the broadest sense of the term, has represented the counterculture of the European culture-whole; and it recently spread to North America in a great variety of forms—to which we must add the considerable influence of what remained of the Medieval and Classical Japanese and now Tibetan cultures. Western man materially has conquered most of the globe. But the conquerer of land, resources, and politically advantageous regions always, to some extent, is in turn spiritually conquered by the cultures upon which he has stamped the destructive (but also in some respects regenerative) power of his ego. Underneath and at times within the official structures built by Faustian man, Gnostic ideals have exerted a constant subterranean and subconscious pressure; and periodically the pressure had burst forth into highly significant, even if seemingly defeated, surges of activity. We see in history the collectivized externalization of what often occurs in the psyche of individuals, and for this reason the kind of history Toynbee developed turns out to be a most revealing disclosure of psychological processes. The *Yang* and *Yin* trends are seen operating in the development of nations; and the supercultural process of civilization, seemingly guided by transpersonal Intelligences, makes use of the interactions of the two polar forces. The process operates, in a sense, *through* their interrelationship, at times stimulating the one, at other times, the other. Spengler's belief that a great culture is "the soul" of a people rooted in a particular land is correct, according to his concept of what "soul" represents—and today in America we speak of "soul music"! But, if culture is of the soul, the process of civilization refers to the operations of the spirit—we might say, in a Jungian sense, of "the Self"—acting *through* the mind for metamorphic purposes.

This "civilizing" activity has been particularly strong in our Western Society because the time had come for a "mutation" or change of consciousness level which, in turn, inevitably led to a collective state of generalized crisis. But at all times Gnostic forces have been active polarizing and illumining the rushing impulse of Faustian man; and it is very important for us, at this crucial juncture in the historical process, to understand the polar relationship and appreciate the antiphony of the Faustian and the Gnostic spirits, in a way freed from the cultural Germanic biases brought by Spengler to the terms Faustian and Magian.

The Faustian mind is hypnotized by material progress and physical conquest in a relentless and restless attempt to break through any *space* boundaries, but the Gnostic mind seeks to transcend the limitations imposed by *time*—that is, by the slow pattern of development of organic processes which at any time permits only the appearance of a particular form expressing a particular phase of cyclic growth. Gnostic man strives after what I have called *eonic consciousness*, the consciousness of the total process of actualization of the potential of Man in one "instant," thus in a "perfect experience" (*purna*, the experience-whole, in the Hindu Tantra). On the other hand, Faustian man has "never enough time," because his thirst for space-conquest is unquenchable and there is always more and more to know, absorb, and to transform in his own ego-image; and conquest "takes time." Gnostic man is not concerned about multiplicity—of conquests, of sensations, of accumulated data and information he has so little time to digest—because he seems to reach a state of consciousness in which he can apprehend at once all there is within his sphere of existence; and he intuitively knows that the wholeness of a small whole reflects the wholeness of the largest whole, the universe. He wants to experience the ocean in a drop of water, and he is made to realize by his illumined Teachers that the only thing standing in the way of such an experience is his emotional and intellectual attachment to the boundaries of the drop, the skin of the cell, the sense-impressions, and the logical-rational concepts of the empirical and intellectual mind centralized by his ego.

Faustian man is the extrovert in the sense that he is bound to what is outside of him, because if there were no external entities to absorb, there could be no conquest. In the same sense the master depends on having slaves, for without them he could not be a master. Faustian man depends upon conquest, or an ever-expanding G.N.P (gross national product) and bank account, because he can feel himself vividly living only when he rushes through space. Likewise, at a subtler level, he feels himself "spiritual" only when he impetuously strives in devotion to a God, pictured above, always farther, always more divine. He lives in the *living*, a process which takes him ever farther from his center. Gnostic man lives in the *being*, through an increasing awareness of all the potentialities inherent within the circumference of his existential field defined by what he essentially is.

Gnostic man also realizes that the process of freeing his consciousness from its attachment to the circumference of his total being and its constant concern with the security of all that is involved in the protection and enjoyment of that circumference requires, in all but exceptional cases, some kind of stimulus. One kind of stimulus refers to the process of organic growth which periodically produces crises of readjustment radically upsetting the interior equilibrium of the forces operating within the circle of his being. Another and potentially more frequent, and at times more drastic, kind of stimulus is the deep experience of love. By bringing two circumferences into interacting contact, love can weaken the exclusive concern of each lover with his/her own circumferential being and produce an osmotic exchange between the two circles. If the love reaches a dramatic finale, the terminal phases of the interaction can lead to an interior state of emptiness followed by a basic readjustment, which forces upon the consciousness a deeper, or at least a fresh awareness of what has been lost and (hopefully) regained.

For Faustian man love is only an adventure, a special kind of conquest or self-aggrandizement through the assimilation of external impressions, feelings, and values. The tragedy of a frustrated or harshly terminated love is a blow to the Faustian person's ego—a defeat; for the Gnostic individual it is a challenge to a more total awareness of what he or she really is. The field of personality being ploughed more deeply, latent new seeds are vitalized and mobilized. The cycle of being becomes richer, because more dynamic, more creative. The Gnostic individual is an introvert, in the true sense of this often misused term; that is, he is instinctively aware that the ultimate goal of consciousness is to live in the plenitude of being that can come only from the internal development of all the contents of the circle of one's total person. These contents—we must never forget!—exist not merely at the physical biopsychic level; they have their overtones in a transphysical and metabiological realm of consciousness—a consciousness that transcends time by fulfulling the entire process of change we call "destiny." Yet fulfullment can never be total, Yang is always ready to challenge an overdominant Yin. In the Gnostic soul plenitude inevitably vanishes in a "timeless" moment of poignant emptiness within which the Faustian voice cries its everlasting "More!" And within the hollow darkness, which may turn into a chalice, is the revelation of a new hope, a new star, a more encompassing circle of being. This revelation takes form within the mind illumined by the process of civilization that always operates at the turn of the tide, because it essentially expresses the metacosmic relationship between the potential and the actual, non-manifestation and manifestation

The real Civilizer is the man of relationship. He relates the as-yet-unknown to the known, the greater to the lesser. The pressure of the process of civilization transforms circles into spirals; yet this pressure should not be materialized into the Faustian idea of "progress" dear to the eighteenth and nineteenth century mentality. *True progress is qualitative, not quantitative.* There undoubtedly is a quantitative change and expansion of a kind when a qualitative transformation occurs, but then transformation implies a transfer, or repolarization, of consciousness from one level to another. It is not the number of *things* apprehended in space that increases, but the dimensionality of space. The "thing-ness" of the things is changed. Atoms may become stars; stars may become Souls (or "Monads"). This is the Transfiguration: the body of Jesus, son of Man, becomes the creative radiance of Christ, son of God. But Christ was potential in Jesus, in every human individual whose consciousness has become free from the boundaries of culture and personality, from concern with his circumference and the mind of exclusion—the formal mind, the mind unillumined by faith in its essential divinity.

Yet there must be circumferences, persons and things organized into culture-wholes, ideas organized into systems, emotional aspirations transmuted into philosophies. Through all of these the Promethean fire of civilization moves, shaking loose the rutted beliefs, devastating the self-complacent egos, crucifying the easily satisfied loves perpetuated in spiritually meaningless procreation. Faust is the European reflection of Prometheus. But Prometheus was moved by compassion; European man is moved by greed ambition and fear — spiritual, social, and physical. Christ's compassion but faintly flickered in obscure places during the European cycle; Buddha's compassion was chased away from India. We should reembody them in our tomorrows, if indeed there is to be a New Age.

9.

RHYTHMS OF CULTURE:
FROM THE SACRED TO THE VULGAR

BECAUSE our Western culture since Francis Bacon worships at the shrine of empiricism and is haunted by what it calls "facts," the historian considers his task to be the accumulation of data. In themselves facts are meaningless; they acquire meaning only when they cease to be unrelated atoms in a flood of events and human activities and are seen holistically within the framework of purposeful human destiny. Particular cultures can be considered symbolically like waves moved by the great wind of civilization dynamizing and transforming the inchoate masses of mankind. The wind acts upon the water, creating a trough; then to the wind's action there is a reaction. The wave rises to a crest but soon collapses, not only of its own weight, but as once more the power of the wind relentlessly presses upon the water as if to fecundate it with transcendent spirit.

Most historians can only watch the up and down motions of particles of water. Spengler realized the existence of waves but ignored the action of the wind. Toynbee became aware of this action but did not integrate it fully into the total picture of the development of his "great Societies," for he was reluctant to think in terms of cyclic processes and of the complex interaction of spirit, mind, and life. The life-span of a culture-whole, seen as a complete process, divides itself essentially into two hemicycles. The first represents the involution of spirit into matter; the second, the evolutionary response of a people gathered within a geographical field of forces (a specific environment) to the vision and energy released by the spirit operating as the creative Word.

These two movements—the descent of the new creative impulse and the ascent of the collective consciousness of a people within cultural forms answering to the spiritual message conveyed by the creative Word "in the beginning"—must be clearly defined and understood. There can be no understanding of the entire process unless one realizes that the involutionary hemicycle of a culture-whole is synchronous with the last phases in the development of a parent culture. In the yearly cycle of vegetation the plant slowly loses its vitality when the seed begins to form within the flower. In the cycle of a culture-whole when the great Civilizer appears, usually in a marginal region of its field of activity, the culture within which he has been born and to which his message of transformation is directed begins to crystallize and disintegrate.

To a historian-philosopher with a holistic vision, *the process* should be quite perceptible, but *the events* marking the workings of the process may be obscured by the interaction of forces operating *through* representative personages; and available records, documents, and between the art-forms can easily be interpreted in several ways. The conflict between the forces of past and future, operates within even the most outstanding personalities around whom the wheel often apparently fortuitous events revolves. The historian-philosopher has to be truly a "hierophant"; that is, a revealer of the sacred (hieros) nature of the process irresistibly pervading both the key-actors' personalities and their actions. True history is the transpersonal psychology of culture-wholes through which the transformative process of civilization operates.

The Involution of Spirit

The only culture-whole of which we have a really detailed knowledge is our own Western culture; but even that knowledge does not include many of the important developments related to the counter-cultural Gnostic, alchemical, and Rosicrucian movements underlying the more public and officialized culture of Europe. Nor do we really know much concerning the men through whom the original creative impulse of the cycle was focused. Nevertheless we can say that at the source of our Western culture two great Image-Symbols appeared, Caesar and Christ. The dualism which they generated has been constantly operative under various forms and impersonations.

These two symbolic personages and the contrast they created had already been prefigured before the first century B.C.; and we can relate them respectively to Cyrus and Darius, the great kings of Persia, and to Gautama the Buddha, whose disciples, during the reign of the Indian Buddhist King Asoka, journeyed to the Near East and settled on the shores of the Dead Sea. But for our present Western culture, Caesar and Christ stand as the two pillars upon which our institutions rest. They are the symbolic sources from which have flowed two rivers which, as their waters merged, vitalized the eventual building of the European culture emerging after the mid-point of the cycle around the year 1000, when the end of the world was expected. Caesar refers to the *Administrative Order* according to which the centralizing forces of social-political organization have operated at a collective level. Christ, on the other hand, is the original source of the *Creative Order* whose essential field of operation is the individual person. Both orders are implied in the process of universalization of mankind which, though heralded by the Buddha and several Greek thinkers, had its first consistent and realistic start with the Roman Empire and Christianity.

The imperial dream of a centralized society encompassing the whole of mankind undoubtedly arose after the flowering of the East Mediterranean Greek culture in Athens and its dissemination by Alexander through two decadent empires, the Egyptian and the Persian, that tried in vain to provide what was needed for the realization of the dream. It took form as the seed takes form in the flower after the crucial Punic Wars which destroyed Carthage and exhausted Rome. Yet Rome survived to implement the Caesarian principle of political centralization. Roman administrators and engineers made the ideal of *Pax Romana* a workable reality; but the reality, though it operated rather efficiently, was based on the quicksand of human slavery. Rome could *manage* the Mediterranean world; it could not *create* a new world. It could for a while contain the Barbarians to the north and the northeast; but these soon enough reached the Roman throne, and the slaves became fascinated by the Christ story whose fantastic character stirred their hopes and their vision. Though martyred for the amusement of the Roman populace and its decadent leaders, they infiltrated the aristocracy, until Constantine legalized Christianity while dividing the empire into Western and Eastern branches.

Christianity also split; but not merely because the Church found itself in different states of relationship with the political power in Rome and in Constantinople. A deeper process of division occurred as the very extensive Gnostic movement with its many groups and doctrine was cut away from the more homogenous and perhaps more ruthless religious body which the Syrian and Alexandrian "Fathers of the Church" were building. The creative impulse of Christ was still operative, though often tainted with Hellenistic intellectualism and sophistry within the Gnostic movement. It is in that movement that one must look for hierophants, "revealers of the sacred," men whose minds had been touched by the fire of Christ, the mind of transformation. And the most important of these was the personage who wrote John's Gospel and the Revelation. Whether or not he actually was Jesus' "beloved disciple" refers only to the factual aspect of the matter. What matters is that, in these writings, the Creative Order that permeated Jesus and, through him, gave a new and vibrant meaning to the Christ mythos and *potentially* to the lives of every human being, made a deep, ineradicable impress upon our Western culture. If the writer was the Apostle, then in him we see the source through which the spiritual current of counter-culture has flowed through the two millennia of the Euro-American cycle. John stands thus as the Hierophant. He was the great Poet of the involutionary half of our cycle. He not only repeated the creative utter-ances of the Avatar, the Christed Jesus, but he established their most profound meaning within the most adequate frame of reference the dying Greek culture was able to provide. He most likely was not the only one to act as Poet-hierophant, revealer of the sacred; but his theurgic words have remained, the very soul of Christianity.

In the beginning of the culture-whole the Avatar utters the words of power and enacts the life-ritual from which the great symbols of the culture will be drawn and made into concrete forms—forms that will be the foundations of religious institutions and of the art that inspirits, rather than merely reflects and mirrors, the developing culture. The Revelation occurs as the old parental culture has reached its final state of maturity and begins to crystallize and/or decay. Gradually minds which have become open to this Revelation reformulate and interpret its premises and the new vision of the divine-human relationship it evokes. They bring the creative Word down to the level of the collective pysche of the people who will become the substance of the new Society. They do this in at least two phases. During the first the new formu-lations must be such as to fascinate the discontented, the mentally bored and the socially oppressed, and to raise if need be a crop of martyrs, and in any case of apostolic men and women; this, within the pale of the dying world. Later on, after this world has collapsed, a reformulation process becomes imperative so as to provide a stabilizing but still chaotic sociopolitical situation with future-oriented goals which nevertheless do not basically surpass the mental level of the gradually converted people.

This is an *involutionary* process, because it is truly the involvement of the original impulse and power in the new and raw material now available. It is a descent of spirit into matter, and also of the sacred into the religious, the creative into the institutionalized. From the point of view of art this process is not to be forgotten, for it plays a fundamental role in the preparation of the materials which the builders of the great cultural forms will use *after* the mid-point of the cycle—thus in Europe after the year 1000. Then the *evolution* of the "art-whole," which is the exteriorization of the soul of the culture-whole, begins. Such an evo-lution proceeds at first by using as an inspiration the life deeds of some great personage and of those surrounding him; in the case of the Euro-pean culture, mainly the deeds of Charlemagne, who not only definitely stopped the northward tide of the Moors from Spain, but who defined, then divided between his sons, the field of space within which Europe was to grow through endless internecine conflicts.

The Evolution of Cultural Forms

What was then well defined before the cycle's midpoint became an intensely alive field from which a new cultural vegetation began to rise. It blossomed in the Gothic cathedral in which all arts found themselves interrelated into a meaningful Christward union, and also for a brief moment in the partially and briefly realized concept of a Rome-centered Republic, a Christiana (the Holy See, as envisioned in the eleventh century by Hildebrand who became Pope Gregory VII).

When this evolutionary phase begins, the basic issue always is the character and quality of the centralizing forces operating at the time. At the sociopolitical and religious levels, when the Papacy began to use military force to overcome its enemies, much of the fate of the European culture was decided. In its germ, the worm of militarism and political power began to sap and eventually destroyed the forces of spiritual growth. As a far-sighted Jesuit priest told me some ten years ago in Paris, the Church "began to worship a false God." As the European universities developed in the following centuries, they worshipped Aristotle rather than Plato. At the level of music a similar development occurred at about the same time when Church plainchant which had already been centralized and Romanized—at the expense of the Syrian, Mozarabic, and Ambrosian schools of plainchant—became further frozen into set melodic patterns and a rigid style of intoning by the adoption of the musical staff and musical notes, after Guido D'Arezzo. When in the fourteenth century, Flemish composers built up their polyphonic structures of musical notes and a new concept of music grew to an imposing stature, this concept stressed formalism and an intellectualistic esthetical approach completely repudiating the magical, and as well the sacred element. What came to be known as "sacred music" is not in the least sacred; it exteriorizes in powerful, yet magically inoperative, organization of notes—but not of real vibrant tones — the soul of a religion that had become also rigidly formalistic and intellectually dogmatic.

Against this cold and politically oriented religious, but not spiritual, consciousness a new psychic wind blew, giving rise to the art of the people. The Christ-spirit was reflected in the soul of St. Francis of Assisi who stands as the symbol, not only of all that tried to regenerate from within a gradually corrupted and money-conscious Church, but of the incarnation of the purest Christ-love in the medieval European personality. The spiritual beginning of the cycle always in some manner seeks to reflect itself in the mid-phase of the cycle; for each cycle has three great moments which can be symbolized by the Greek letters, *alpha*, *mu*, and *omega*. In the Bhagavad Gita, Krishna, the embodied Supreme Spirit, states that he is the beginning, the middle, and the end of all cycles—while, unfortunately perhaps, the Gnostic Christ in John's writings says only that he is the alpha and the omega, thus evoking Christianity's actual emphasis on transcendence rather than on immanence. Yet such an immanence of the Divine in the human was the essence of Jesus' message to a future culture-whole in which an ever greater number of individualizing persons would be torn by the conflict between, on the one hand, a religiosified and intellectual cult of the ego and of the mind of reason and, on the other hand, an essentially sacred realization of the Christ within—a realization that, as it implies rebirth (a new beginning) and an eventually total transformation of all the implications of existence, is therefore "sacred."

The new mind that pervaded the religious structures of the early Middle Ages came, in the one hand, from the old Celtic culture and its love of nature and natural forms, and on the other, from the Sufi and related movements whose ideals were carried back to France by the crusaders and the troubadours. This love of nature can be seen as the inspiration of many of the sculptured decorations of Gothic cathedrals and also in the beautiful illumined manuscripts devotedly written and painted in monasteries many of which had been founded since Charlemagne's reign by Irish men with latinized names.[1] This love most likely did not spring from the Germanic temperament; nor was it the heritage of a Romanized Mediterranean world. It blended with the mystical influences of Near-Eastern Sufis and Gnostics, influences that Dante felt in his spiritualized glorification of love and the "eternal feminine"; it radiated from Abelard's tragic experiences and his challenge to the lifeless rationalism of Scholasticism; and it found their beautiful, yet so little-known, expression in the culture of Southern France. That culture—encompassing South-western France around Toulouse and Albi, the Provence and the French Alps, and Spain's Catalonia once conquered by the Visigoths—was ruthlessly destroyed by the power-greedy king of France, Philipp Augustus (1180-1223) with the asistance of Popes who proclaimed the tragic Crusade against the Albigenses and began the Inquisition (1203-1229). But it was in Southern France that the ideal of "courtly love" grew and an entirely new approach to womanhood developed which inspired some of the greatest cultural productions of Europe—later to be reformulated by the spirit of nineteenth century Romanticism.

In music, the combined influences of Celtic and Arabic-Syrian songs forced upon the followers of an emasculated and intellectualized Pythagorean tradition the adoption of the musical interval of "natural third," which was considered dissonant and unusable by the Pythagoreans. Popular songs invaded the Church services; as polyphony grew, the profane melodies mingled with the old traditional plainchant, and a Pope condemned in typical terms the *Ars Nova* of the early fifteenth century. As Gothic art lost its simplicity and baroque style churches were built, especially in the Latin countries and later in the newly discovered American continent, Humanism and the early Renaissance produced a strong reaction against the medieval religious consciousness. Individualism triumphed, together with scientific empiricism: Luther and Francis Bacon. A new picture of the universe was outlined by Copernicus, Galileo, Kepler—its heliocentricism matching the development of centralized nations ruled by powerful Kings-by-divine-right—Sun-kings.

It was at this turning point that Shakespeare's dramas appeared, giving to the drama a new form and establishing it as the most significant cultural manifestation of the Renaissance and Classical spirit, thus of the *evolutionary* hemicycle of the development of the culture-whole. Drama played a powerful role during the *involutionary* half of the cycle; but it was the sacred drama of redemption, God's drama as He projected His personified spirit-power into the human material of the disintegrating Greco-Latin culture-whole. This drama in its most essential form was the Catholic Mass, forever reenacting in "sacred time" and within the consecrated place of meeting of the *Ekklesia*—the group of Christ's apostolic servants and devotees—the divine Act of sacrifice at Golgotha, the Mount of the Skull, the human mind.

All Church-dramas are ritualistic reenactments of the sacrifice of the Divine into the human, and at times—because Medieval man is still very close to the biopsychic rhythms of nature and vegetation—the sacrifice of the germinating seed into the new plant. These dramas have thus originally a sacred character; yet, as the Church became a social and political factor with mundane ambitions for power, rulership, and wealth, the sacred faded out into the religious. *The sacred creates; the religious binds.* The dramas of the Church bind together the faithful; but, as the evolutionary power of the people develops—and it inevitably develops in the midst of, and through interpersonal and intergroup conflicts—the profane or secular drama appears in a new role. It brings to a focus and seeks to give meaning to human crises and human decisions or indecision. The *mu* type of psychological drama supersedes the *alpha* type.

In the future an omega type may appear if our culture-whole does not commit nuclear suicide or irrevocably poison the biosphere before the omega consciousness of this Euro-American cycle can manifest in more than a few dreamers. Scriabin's Mystére, which could not possibly have been produced in the period of two World Wars actually representing the Civil War of a global humanity, was a dream vision of the theurgic drama of the cycle's end. As to Wagner's Parsifal, one might call it a prefiguration of the omega dream, but it closed the cycle of the European religious tradition rather than being the first manifestation of the sacred, in which end meets rebeginning: the consecrated seed of the culture-whole in process of germination.

Shakespeare, or whoever was operating through his mind, brought to a focus the dramas of human personages past the middle phase of the cultural cycle. But before the Dramatist, the Poet always appears. Aeschylus and Sophocles follow Homer—and before Homer, Orpheus, the utterer of the magical words. Shakespeare follows the poets of the Chansons de Geste and Dante, these poets narrating, on the one hand, the deeds of the culture-Hero and, on the other, the spiritward ascent of the symbolic person who, after the midpoint of his life, repolarizes his consciousness along the path of religious initiation. Later on, in an America trying to develop a relatively autonomous collective consciousness while focusing on the building of a continental empire, Walt Whitman, the poet, magnificently extolled the great vision which the magical words of Thomas Paine's Common Sense, Jefferson's Declaration of Independence, and the deeds of the Founders of the Republic had made viable; but the reality of the dream in our modern cities finds itself expressed in the plays of Eugene O'Neill, the American Shakespeare, and of a few other playwrights baring the greed, the neuroses, and the soul-emptiness of modern men and women.

The Six Levels of Art-Activity

At this point and in order to clarify the character and meaning of the various levels of development through which the art-whole passes as it exteriorizes the successive phases of the collective consciousness of a Society during its life-span, it seems important to define six basic levels at which art operates, or can operate. At each level we can speak of a positive and a negative type of manifestation.

1. *Art as release of power through magical forms.*

I have already discussed the main characteristics of the magical approach to art, and I defined magic as "a purposeful release of focalized power through an effective form in answer to a need." At the primitive level of human evolution, this need is primarily biological and historians speak of natural magic, which includes control over forces in man's environment and healing, or the destruction of enemies and competitors in love, war, or business. The life-will, and later on the ego-will, are the power-releasing factors. What we call so often and carelessly "primitive art" is essentially a means for magical action. The statue of a god, masks worn in rituals and all instruments used in magical ceremonies are not meant to be "beautiful"; their form and substance are selected because they will most effectively focus and release magic power. *Magical objects have a functional character.*

Today in our industrialized city-centered life, political propaganda through repeated slogans and business advertising are magical forms of mass-directed activity dedicated to the acquisition of social-political power and wealth by individual egos or organized groups. In a very real sense, American life is primitive living in the jungles of cities, where competitors can be as dangerous as wild beasts. These jungles have a biosociological character and, though the instrumentalities for the release of the wilful cravings of intellectualized and ego-centric minds differ from the tools, charms and statues of tribal cults used by shamans or medicine-men, our modern business and political rituals (from Wall Street to political conventions), both types have similar functions. The business executive of a big firm is not interested in the literary character of advertising slogans, but only in whether or not they work and increase sales. The political leader likewise uses his slogans for the emotional effect they produce at mass-meetings, or in multimedia presentations.

For the same reasons, the machines built by engineers do not originally aim at being beautiful, but only at the best possible utilization of energy in the performance of work. If, later on, concern with shape and decoration intrudes and combines with engineering efficacy it is because competition for social prestige and the attention of prospective buyers enters the picture. The decorative concept of art then comes into play.

The negative aspect of magic is its basic resistance to change. A tradition takes form which develops enormous inertia. Old magical practices remain in use after the human and social situations which gave rise to them have become radically altered. Business, political, and also scientific and laboratory practices resist transformation as long as they possibly can—until a competitor demonstrates the spectacular validity of a new technique and new attention-focusing forms or ego-titillating gadgets.

2. Art as decorative enhancement of value

When the primitive swordmaker begins to carve on the hilts of his products images of gods or elementals which no longer are meant only to enable the sword to kill better, but also which display the wealth and taste of their owner and the outstanding skill of the maker, decorative art appears. Soon the term *art* takes on a meaning of its own, an esthetic meaning divorced from the concept of utility or even of function. A beautiful object acquires a value simply because it is beautiful. But what then is meant by "beauty?"

What is beautiful for people of a particular culture may not be considered so by men of another culture. Until fairly recently in Europe and America the music of China, Africa, and even India was characterized as barbaric and mere noise. African idols and carvings seemed ugly to Europeans until Picasso and other artists glorified their forms. The appreciation of "primitive art" is of very recent origin. Male animals display what we call beauty in order to attract the females' attention; but these displays of colors, dance gestures and songs, are magical expressions of the life-will. Beauty as such is mainly a sociocultural factor, especially when an esthetic valuation is placed on the beautiful object. Nature always undergirds culture; yet the conscious human act of embellishment, even if used for biological purposes, surpasses this factor. The biological "survival of the fittest" is a magical process in which the life-will operates; but decorative art (musical as well as plastic) is used, consciously or not, to exalt cultural values and to benefit the groups, cities, or provinces acquiring fame and perhaps wealth for their special ability to produce a new style of wares.

Competition in the development of ever more intricate decorative forms leads from the baroque to the rococco style, to preciosity or intellectual stratagems drying up the flow of inspiration. It also produces virtuosity and the glorification of technical *tours de force* to charm a cultural elite, or even (at a less artistic level) a crowd easily impressed by the display of a spectacular skill in action which they are too lazy or unimaginative to obtain for themselves. Action still speaks louder than words for human beings whose consciousness is embedded in the biosphere and who value muscular achievements far more than the discovery of meaning.

3. Art as esthetic enjoyment of cultural forms

This level of art-activity is closely linked with the preceding one, but it becomes differentiated when the work of art is at least theoretically able to reveal to particularly aware and sensitive human beings a principle of order and proportion which gives to their consciousness a sense of peace and psychomental security, or an exalted feeling of participation in a transpersonal or even transcultural reality. At this level one can even speak of a "religion of art," because such art-experiences "bind together" (re-*ligere*) the mind-feelings of a cultural minority.

Many books have been written in an attempt to define the precise nature of the *esthetic experience*. All that seems necessary to state here is that the pure esthetic experience, detached from all biological and sociocultural elements so often involved in it, is based on the intuitive, mental, and/or emotional awareness of the harmoniously ordered (or meaningfully disordered and dynamic) relationship between all the component parts of a whole confronting us. The experience has a holistic character. It is an experience of archetypal form and order conveyed to our consciousness by an existential combination of lines and spaces, of colors or sound vibrations. We may speak of a *transmorphic* experience, because the apparent shape or color of an object, the sequential relationship between the tones of a melody or the events of a scene linking several actors—be they men or natural entities—are perceived only as translucent means for the revealing of a principle of order and harmony at work in the universe. If we had no awareness at all of such a principle our own experience and the world's existence would make little or no sense. A beautiful object or scene fascinates us because through it we come to feel or intuitively apprehend the ordered play of natural or supernatural forces in the cosmos, be it microcosm or macrocosm.

In a preceding chapter I spoke of the extraordinary attraction Bach's music had for young people in Paris after World War II, when its tragedies and tortures had ended, even though it was music made by a hated German and indeed filled with the peculiar abstract intellectuality of a Nordic culture. We all need to feel that ours is an ordered universe, a universe of balanced and meaningfully distributed and evolving relationships. If this feeling is taken away from us we slowly disintegrate. Order calls to order. If the organic within does not find an integrating response to a cosmic without, catabolic forces begin to operate within the organism deprived of external cosmic support. The belief in an absurd universe makes a neurotic of the believer, just as a suddenly lowered air pressure around a tightly closed room will make the glass windows explode. One can think of order-pressure just as one thinks of atmospheric presure. A people having lost its sense of order and meaning will blindly follow a leader who, at least for a moment, becomes the embodied symbol of order.[2]

Order has charisma. Art likewise has charisma whenever it fills the need for a convincing restatement of ordered relationship. A tragic crisis can be endured if a new order is promised or expected beyond it. A bitter interpersonal relationship can be accepted if given the transpersonal meaning of rebirth. In classical music the composer can use harsh dissonances if these are resolved into a consonant chord. But recently a new type of art has been born, presenting dissonances (musical or interpersonal) which the hearer or spectator himself is expected to resolve into harmony; he is meant to be a participant in a total creative process reaching beyond the esthetic, which therefore can be called "transesthetic."

The strictly esthetic approach to art has its negative aspect in "estheticism" and the snobbery of art-critics hypnotized by form and insensitive to contents. The concept of "Art for Art's sake" dehumanizes the creative process. The *how* of art drives away the *Why*; form-analysis destroys meaning; scholasticism and academism stifle spontaneity.

4.   *Art as personal expression*

Before we speak of the transesthetic experience we must consider a type of art which has dominated the cultural scene in the West since the beginning of the Romantic reaction to the Classical period: art as a form of personal self-expression. The title of a recent composition by the one-time *enfant terrible* of modern music, Leo Ornstein "Autobiography in the form of a Sonata," brings the issue involved in this type of art to its clearest focalization, but during the last 150 years all fields of art have been involved in one type or another of autobiographical expression. In a society featuring the ideal of individualism and giving most of its attention to personal relationships, problems, or conflicts, and to the development of a complex, integrated and independent personality whose fulfillment is the supreme purpose of living, the artistic aspect of self-expression was bound to gain an extraordinary importance.

Creativity, however, does not need to be equated with *personal* self-expression. A creative process can operate through a person whose mind and organs of action (and the muscles involved in that action) are servants of a transpersonal downflow of energy and revelatory consciousness. The actions of an Avatar are, I repeat, transpersonal rather than personal; and so are the creations of a great genius through whose mind new archetypes and a wider vision of future potentialities take existential forms conditioned by a collective sociocultural need. The personal aspect of self-expression dominates when the creative release is determined by ego needs and an individualistic or even autistic approach to the challenges of everyday existence. When such an approach prevails almost exclusively, the form taken by the intellectual-emotional release of energy appears meaningless to other individuals.

The psychological pressures, the states of consciousness, and the personal experiences of the artist are uncommunicable to the degree that they do not use, or distort beyond recognition, the basic symbols of the culture-whole. Every culture has its collectively understandable languages for words, forms, gestures, and tone-relationships. As long as the artist accepts the limitations and structures of those various languages he or she can communicate his feelings, his joys or torments, his intellectual vision and concepts to his people. Through his creations the people of his culture may experience, by proxy, states of wider consciousness and more intense feelings than are normally parts of everyday living. The artist is then a catalyst to greater living. He spreads his intensity as a contagion of enhanced supernormal responsiveness to events and inner psychic changes to which most persons can only feebly react. The artist is an intensifier of emotions, working with the chiaroscuro of joy and pain, of ecstasy or the dark night of the soul.

This is the Romantic ideal of art. It is a cultural ideal to the extent that the artist still uses the language, the great symbols, the religious or musical ideals of his culture. When the artist finds these images inadequate for the expression of what he feels or experiences and tries to build his own language of (to him) symbolic forms, he enters an a-cultural realm in which interpersonal communication becomes difficult, if not impossible. Other artists, witnessing or involved in the upheavals of a culture in crisis, begin to distort the syntax of their art-language, to relate what no one else normally relates except in dreams or hallucinations caused by drugs or psychotic states, and to build fantastic, irrational structures. Then we have Expressionism, Surrealism, and the many varieties of "Fantastic Art."

These manifestations can be considered the negative aspect of the art of personal expression, but they also belong to at least the initial stages of a new type of art. Romanticism has its most characteristic shadow-aspect in sentimentality and uncontrolled vapid or formless emotionalism. Self-indulgence may turn into masochism and overextended lyrical or downbeat statements.

5. *Art as catharsis and mantram of rebirth.*

A culture in a state of radical crisis calls from its collective human depth artists who act as cathartic or catabolic agents. These develop numerous forms of *catesthetics*: antiart, antinovel, purposefully discordant music or congeries of atomistic notes related to each other only by police-like systems of totalitarian control. The most characteristic exemplar of such a trend was Arnold Schoenberg who began as a post-Wagnerian lyricist and soon developed as a symbol of reaction against the chaotic disintegration of his natal land, the Austro-Hungarian empire. A famous American critic once wittily said that he was a "decomposer" rather than a composer. This is only partially true. It is valid only in the sense that Schoenberg's Twelve-Tone-System is a quasi-desperate attempt to force the decomposing materials of European tonality into a rigid intellectualistic structure holding the now unrelated atonal notes, as people who no longer have faith or respect for the old order may be relentlessly held together by a police force. Schoenberg's pupil Anton Webern pushed an atomistic approach to music to the extreme. The movement has been sweeping Europe and America since World War II; it is an answer to the disintegration of the entire Western culture. Toward the close of the evolutionary half of the cultural cycle, it represents also a symmetrical repetition, at another level, of the formalism and the intellectual games the Flemish composers of the fourteenth and fifteenth centuries played with the new musical material of *Ars Nova*.

As I see it, this Schoenbergian Neoscholastic movement and the synchronously developing Neoclassicism of Stravinsky are both expressions of inwardly insecure and culturally frightened personalities. The Bolshevik Revolution of 1917 shocked Stravinsky, who had become seduced by the intellectualism of the "Cerebrist Movement" in Paris, then art captial of the Western world.[3] He seems also to have been frightened by the power he had let loose in the *Sacre du Printemps*, whose tumultuous first performance in Paris during *La Grande Saison* of May 1913 both prefigured and symbolized at the level of culture the shock produced a year later by a World War which neither the general public nor the intellectual elite expected. The return to the Classical seventeenth century formalism—even if the old forms were to be filled with a fermenting new tonal substance—constituted, like the parallel development of Fascism, a hopeless or panicky return to the security of the Western culture at its moment of late flowering, a psychological "return to the Mother." Neoclassicism in the twenties invaded America, where, after Guggenheim Foundation-subsidized trips to Paris overshadowed by the matriarchal mind of Nadia Boulanger, young composers sought to prove to themselves and to the world that they too could write "serious" music equalling in technical virtuosity the best Europe had to offer.

Underneath these returns to the past, and working through the outer garment of an expanded tonal system or through attempts at pantonality or polytonality, we can see developing, mostly unconsciously, a cathartic approach to the arts. We find it hidden under a fascination with exotic art (whether African sculpture, or Hindu and Balinese music) as an unconscious or unclear endeavor to de-Europeanize the arts. We see it manifesting in the Neoprimitivism of the *Sacre du*

Printemps and Prokofiev's *Scythian Suite* and in the Surrealistic cult of the irrational. It is shown in its crudest form in Erik Satie's spoofing and Dadaism, but also in the repeated attempts of artists to extend the ability to hear, see, and feel in people still clinging to, while fighting against, the tenacious ghosts of Puritanism and Victorian morality and racial-cultural elitism. What underlies all these disparate and confused endeavors is a tense and often tragic will to free men and women of our culture from the ancestral past, indeed to shock them into freedom, including of course, since Freud's day, sexual freedom.

The return to European Classicism was based on *fear*. The return to the primitive, to nature and natural functions, to all that human beings have in common and can experience in an open togetherness of feelings, has been fundamentally an expression of *hope*. The early Hippie movement was a naive but beautiful song of hope. At another level, Scriabin's music and his dream of *Mystère* were also songs of culture-transcending hope, haunted by the possibility of collective transhuman ecstasy. In a cultural world breaking down, cathartic art—whether in music, painting, poetry, writing, theatrical dramas—strives to accelerate the breaking down by forcing more and more people to consciously experience, even if only by the proxy of art, the inevitability of the collapse of the sociocultural structures in which they have grown to consciousness, or at least to habitual behavior.

The inevitability of collective death as a redeemer—this is what the hydrogen bomb thunders forth to our self-complacently deaf ears! But do we believe that this collective death can act "as a redeemer"? This is the essential issue. Henry Miller wrote a small book entitled *Murder the Murderer!* But in real life can two negatives make a positive? What kind of culture has the Russian Revolution produced besides a mass return to bourgeois ballet and pompous proletarian art? Can a disintegrating culture transubstantiate itself? Could the future-oriented passion of a self-sacrificing band of men and women, whose materialistic gospel was the product of minds steeped in a Hebrew and European past, blossom out as total faith in a New Order that is really new, creative, releasing of as yet unenvisioned possibilities?

People try to escape the confrontation with their latent creativity—their potentiality of rebirth—by dreaming of flying saucers, Space benefactors, the Second Coming of Christ. But alas, most of the time this is only an escape, an ego-subterfuge to avoid translating collective crisis and imminent chaos into personal catharsis powered by faith in the inevitability of rebirth, a self-made, willed, consciously assumed, joyous inevitability.

It is such an inevitability of rebirth that art today *could* proclaim. Yet what is it doing? The despondent, confused, anemic mind of so many artists escapes into intellectual concepts and vague metaphysical-scientific discussions of *intent*. But, as an old proverb stated: The road to Hell is paved with good intentions. What count are deeds, creative, self-transforming, others-arousing acts moved by an irreducible faith and all-human compassion. It is for individuals and groups of individuals to chant themselves into seedhood, accepting at the same time the inevitable sacred act of germination. It is for individuals to live as mantrams of dawn, as living *Gayatris*. This alone is creativity.

6. *Art as Hierophany*

We can envision such an art. We cannot produce it at this time of history, except perhaps as an uncompletable sketch, an evocation of possibilities pregnant with irrevocable futurity. At this level we are dealing with the mythopoetic function of art, the art of revelation. What today is called "conceptual" art is at best the precursory shadow of such an art. But who among the mainly confused intellectuals playing with concepts is able to create new myths, or even really understand their function as *transcultural* factors emanating from the vast planetary and all-human process of civilization?

Art as revelation is, like the seed, both end and beginning, *alpha* and *omega*. The creation of myths occurs before the end of the cycle of a culture-whole *through* the Avatar and the apostolic beings who extend and give to his life-deeds and words their initial rapturous formulation. These men are the hierophants, the revealers of the sacred. What they reveal is clothed in the words, concepts, and images provided for them by their culture; but they only "re-veal"; they present "new veils" for the ineffable Truth, the Avatar's sacred performance of dharma—the dharma of the culture-whole still only a potentiality in the mind-womb of the parental Society. They release the seed of the future myths of the new culture. This seed will germinate during the *alpha* phase of the development of this culture-whole. It will evolve into the great stories and dramas of a still distant future.

This mythopoetic seed-art is not art in the current sense of the term. Yet its creations are tremendously powerful, if not in themselves, then in what they will accomplish. The art-hierophants project into the planetary psyche of mankind such images as those of the Solar Hero known by a myriad of names, of his death and resurrection, the images of the meditating Buddha, the crucified Christ flanked by the two thiefs, Baha'u'llah (last century's Persian Avatar) thrown into an old cistern transformed into a dungeon and reached by three steps, chained with criminals, and there receiving his illumination in the form of a celestial

Maiden. They reveal the lineaments of the myths which future generations will transform into religious ceremonies, sacred Mysteries in which the elect few or the faithful at large will participate. In music, the hierophantic spirit has revealed itself in the mantrams of India, the sacred incantations of Gnostic Brotherhoods, the chants accompanying communal meals partaken in the memory of the Last Supper. These chants and hymns, with a change of words, were stolen wholesale by the Fathers of the official Church, who, after changing the words, made of them the earliest forms of religious plainchant. The ecclesiastic chants in turn were transformed by the peoples of the developing early culture-whole into what appear to be "folksongs."

Bela Bartok's studies of the popular music of the Balkans clearly showed that most of what was long considered the "spontaneous" creations of the people were in fact derived from Church plainchant. Similarly, Negro slaves in our southern states produced "spirituals" from models provided by Church hymns. "The people" do not create; they only react to bio-emotional urges which are actually procreative, not creative. Life procreates *through* polarized human organisms; Spirit creates *through* the great Civilizers and those disciples whose minds catch fire at the flame of their transfigured consciousness and their hieratic, sacramental lives.

In their most often confused and egocentric way the artists of recent years who have dreamt of conceptual art realized that our Euro-American culture has reached a dead end; that no living substance can be drawn out of the old culture. Art can no longer be a collective celebration of values because the sources of all cultural values—the old myths—have dried up, their meanings are perverted, and their revelations have become something to joke about or dismiss as children's tales since the irreverent and cynical mind of a pseudo-science tore down the veils and sullied the figuration of the Divine in man. What then remains for the artist? *To think*—to translate his or her neurosis and frustration into dream-fantasies, abstract metaphysical-occult escapes, or in the most significant cases to lead *individuals* (or small groups of individuals) to experience meaning and tone in a precultural, prenatal way.

These are almost desperate attempts at *revirginizing* the sense-responses of people seeking to evade the octopus-like arms of industrialized, citified, and police-controlled living, either by making them involved participants in "catesthetic" experiences glorifying modern conflicts to a point of collapse of rational faculties, or by educating them like children through "happenings" aiming at de-education, and hopefully leading them to a naive, quasi-primitive return to natural nondiscriminating experiences of sound, color, form, and interpersonal relationships.

At the fountainhead of the present Western phase of the process of civilization we see the great figure of Pythagoras, the Civilizer of music, bringing to the Mediterranean world the great concepts of Number, Proportion and Form, and raising them to a cosmic level through the profound myth of the Music of the Spheres. Such a myth was an answer to the Orphic Mysteries celebrating the birth-death-rebirth cycle of the Solar Hero, the heliocentric God also worshipped by the visionary Pharaoh, Akhenaten. It was an attempt to de-personify the Divine and to substitute an impersonal vision of cosmic Harmony and essential Order for the worship of deified Beings. At the same time Gautama the Buddha, by propounding the *anatma* doctrine, was seeking to "disegoize" human beings entranced by their sense of individuality and the ecstatic identification of *atman* (the individual self) with *brahman* (the universal Self).

Pythagoras's revelation of the cosmic archetypal Mind assuredly did not want to glorify rationality *per se*, as a function independent of all biopsychic functions. His teachings were transrational, transformal, transintellectual. He used his visionary metabiological experience of the dynamic Harmony of the cosmos as a means of healing, of making whole, of integrating personalities rising uncertainly from the tribal to the individualistic state of consciousness. The Pythagorean *gamut* (badly understood as merely a "scale" of notes) was a dynamic mandala of tones, each of which had magic power. The Church music of the late Roman empire, and especially of the Middle Ages, took out of the Pythagorean harmony the magic which at least some Gnostic communities had retained, and soon the Flemish polyphonists began to build patterns of notes from which all livingness, as well as cosmic sense of harmony, had gone, though a few theoreticians still talked about abstractly cosmic principles.

Since Schoenberg, the conceptual and mathematical emphasis that characterized the formalistic Nordic music of five centuries ago—and, with Bach, of two centuries ago—began to be revived in a new mode. Picasso also gave to the incipient movement the shape of Cubism. After various esthetic adventures and hairpin turns, the road of modern art has led to the art of concepts. For the conceptual artist it is not the performance that matters, but the formative concept—not what one does, but what one conceives. Alas, the conception most often seems to be but a blind striving *away* from the past, not *toward* a future, partly because any future today seems so dismal, potentially catastrophic, and hopeless. A culture chapter is closing in the long Book of Civilization; and as the writer faces the chaotic and neurotic present, he or she disdainfully procures antinovels whose unbound pages can be read in any order whatsoever. The composer writes scores suggesting only a variety of possibilities to be actualized according to the mood of performers-improvisers. The painter-sculptor builds long trenches in the desert to no particular purpose or tries to balloon a mountain in some enormous plastic bag. And, at least in the conceptual-statistical minds of Rand specialists, the Pentagon plays dice with its Russian counterpart in a futurity game whose pawns are millions of underfed and hopeless human beings. Heirophany has become Thanatophany, the Middle Ages' Dance of Death magnified in a planetary *Marche Funébre* in which the whole biosphere is involved.

Yet the presence of death is necessary for rebirth. As Castenada makes Don Juan say in *Tales of Power* (p. 147) "Without an awareness of the presence of our death there is no power, no mystery." In the everyday banality of living, an individual is only what he is; with death as his companion he can become more than he is. Looking back is now useless. The will of the potentially creative spirit in man has to give to the entropic psalmody of the dying culture the antiphonic answer of culture-free creativity. He has to create new myths in counterpoint to the process of vulgarizaton cacophonically spelling the decay of cultural values. The creation of myths is the only valid answer to vulgarity. *Vulga* means the crowd. In tribal societies, in medieval villages or towns, there were no crowds. The crowd and all its products constitute the triumph of sociocultural entropy. The crowd is the dark shadow of civilization. The old Babylon or the modern megalopolis is the shadow of the Holy City, the New Jerusalem.

Rebirth requires both the light and the shadow. Power and Mystery emerge from their antiphony; and what is human life without power or mystery? What is man without the myths he creates to give meaning to his world?

10.

OLD MYTHS, NEW MYTHS AND
THE CREATION OF A NEW CULTURE

MAN'S senses convey to his brain the impressions they receive. These are the raw data of knowledge. Once the brain decodes and correlates these signals we can speak of them as "in-formation"; they acquire a preliminary form as percepts. Working further upon these percepts and relating them to similar or opposite ones received in the past, the human mind builds concepts. Through the process of building concepts the mind reifies or "entitizes" the raw sense data. To reify is to organize a set of sensations into the concept of a "thing" (in Latin, *res*, from which the word, *"reality"*, is derived). If we attribute to a thing a more or less independent and autonomous character, we think of it as an entity and, when this character is further emphasized, as a being or even an organism.

When all apparently normal members of a human community agree in their conceptualizing of a set of sense data into a thing, an entity, or a special sequence of events, we speak of "facts." The common consent of the group to the existence of a thing makes it a fact. What does not elicit this common consent is only an individual experience. It has a subjective character. Facts are objective; they have reality. The subjective experiences of an individual may be called either illusions, hallucinations, or suppositions by the other members of his community; or they may be tentatively accepted as possible facts if the experiencer is considered sane and known to possess either unusually developed sense perceptions or the intuitive ability to discover relationships between what normally are considered separate objects or concepts.

All living organisms have in varying degrees the ability to perceive an external objective reality and to integrate the percepts into conceptualized things and entities; their existence in a specific environment depends on such an ability. However, as every class of organism has its own way of perceiving—its own kind of senses and brain centers—it seems evident that the facts perceived and the way in which these facts are organized into conceptual entities must be very different from ours.

A further and most characteristic difference arises, as far as we know, from the apparent fact that man alone has a mind capable of going one step further than conception; the human mind can give *meaning* to its concepts. Man attributes meaning to the relationships between events, and he gives names to what he has reified or "entitized"—names which reveal the character and meaning of the entity whose presence and description have been accepted as a fact by his community or at least by his peers in the field of a specialized knowledge, a science.

In the second chapter of Genesis, Adam is said to have "named" all that he perceived in the Garden of Eden (the symbolic realm of embodied prototypes); and God accepted these names as relevant characterizations. The story is profoundly significant. God creates; but man's role in the divine creation or Play (or *lila*) is to formulate the *meaning* of the Play. God releases a vast amount of energy in the Creative Act, then that energy unfolds its latent structural potentiality of form according to the character of the creative impulse behind the release. It is man's function to give a formal meaning to the relations evolving out of the process of differentiation of the complex original energy-release. Though the creative Word "in the beginning," of which John's Gospel speaks, is a unity, it is nevertheless composed of a myriad of "Letters"; and all the potentialities latent in this original and originating Word can be actualized only if every one of these trillions and trillions of Letters relates itself to all others. The result of this incomprehensibly vast process of interrelationships is what man calls the universe or cosmos.

To use the word universe or cosmos is to interpret and synthesize the multitude of facts which human minds, operating within the psychomental boundaries of a culture-whole, perceive and agree to call "real." To speak of *a* universe is an interpretation of sequential and spatial relations between the perceived facts of existence. Such an interpretation gives to the immense variety of human sense-experiences and inner feelings the *meaning of unity*—thus, the "divine" meaning of having been created by, and revealing the Presence of, one God.

Man's most essential function as he operates within the field of some vaster whole, planetary or cosmic, is to give meaning to all his experiences. To give meaning implies being *conscious* of the many aspects of the reality to which meaning is given. Of all living organisms, man is the most adaptable and the best able to experience the immense variety of conditions and relationships existing in the Earth's biosphere, and beyond it in interplanetary space. This ability to experience, then to give meaning to experience, is seemingly unique.

To give meaning is to create a myth. Essentially, a myth is a meaningful interpretation of the conceptualized data of human experience. More precisely, it is a meaningful interpretation which at a particular time in human history fills a definite collective purpose because it is *a convincing and power-releasing answer to the collective need of a cultural group, a culture-whole, or even of humanity as a whole*. Man is above all a myth-maker.

The capacity to create myths is the mythopoetic (or mythopoeic) function. In an unpublished and mostly discarded book written in 1940, *Man Maker of Universes*, I spoke of this capacity as the "cosmogenic" function, because any meaningful and purposeful field (or organized system) of interrelated and interdependent activities having an autonomous, self-sufficient, dynamically balanced and inherently "beautiful" (i.e. harmonic) character constitutes a *cosmos*. Whether such a system is described as small or large (a microcosm or macrocosm) does not alter its essential meaning. I repeat, God creates the facts of existence, but man gives meaning to these facts by interpreting them. Human interpretations differ greatly, but their difference does not invalidate them. It simply reveals the inherent complexity of man's environment and the ambivalence or multivalence of all facts of experience.

To say that "God creates the facts of human experience" is, of course an interpretation. It is a myth, the Myth of Deity. By means of that myth, human beings who accept it as a valid, or even incontrovertible and self-evident, fact can give to at least certain aspects of their existence and to some inner feeling-intuition of centrality (the I-feeling), a fundamental character generating a sense of security, of acceptance, equanimity, and indestructible inner peace. For them this myth fills a basic existential need. Thus it has "value."

Validity is what counts at the level of existential facts. If one speaks of "truth" one has to state at once that every phase of existence has its own truths. What an existent *needs* to believe so as to insure optimal conditions of survival, growth, and eventual fulfillment is "true" for that existent. Because what applies to an individual organism applies as well (at least in basic structural terms) to a collective organism such as a culture-whole, we indeed find that each culture-whole has its own "truths"—the paradigms, the Prime Symbols, the great myths of that culture. As long as the collective mentality of the people of the culture *needs* these myths to provide sociocultural security and psychospiritual stability, the myths are meaningful and valid. Once the meaning fades away and the myths no longer provide an answer to growth and to the longing for fulfillment through significant action, the validity of the myth and of all the so-long-taken-for-granted assumptions on which it is built, either gradually fades away or is violently challenged and denied.

Because we are now living in a period of history when most of the myths of ancient culture-wholes now still in existence have all but lost their power of psycho-spiritual sustainment and creative mental stimulation it is imperative for us to understand what is implied in the mythopoetic function and to know where we can find it in operation, *if* it still operates anywhere! If it should not operate at all, we should still try to discover how it might be once more stimulated and made effectual; for without it there can be no "New Age."

Can there be truly a New Age? Has it already begun? Do we understand its present and future implications? Today these are crucial questions for our society. They should be straightforwardly faced by every individual whose psyche is consciously or semiconsciously disturbed by sociocultural uncertainty or tortured by a sense of alienation, emptiness, and futility. This is especially true for those seeking in drugs, outlandish experiences, or perhaps catabolic relationships and perverted forms of magic a soul-satisfying revelation of meaning to stabilize their consciousness and their emotional lives. But first of all we should inquire as penetratingly as possible into the nature of the myths our Euro-American culture has lived by, and of those as yet tentative and largely unformulated or misunderstood myths which could become stabilizing foundations for a new culture.

The Myth of Reality

A man in deep meditation, or stirred by a peak experience of communion with his beloved or his guru, may become aware of motions, shapes, entities transcending his ordinary perceptions; he may feel ecstasy, bliss, or extraordinary pain; his mind may be vibrant with as yet unthought ideas no words seem able to formulate. All these are subjective experiences. They do not fit into the normal frame of reference his culture has built within his consciousness to contain, localize, and give meaning to the everyday flow of his experiences—experiences of separate entities; objective things, or classifiable beings. This does not mean that the man's peak experiences and extraordinary feelings are not "facts" *for him*. If, however, he finds that other human beings have or have had unusual experiences which seem to closely resemble his own, and that these experiences are expectably and consistently linked with certain practices or chains of events which can be summoned more or less at will or under special but repeatable conditions, then the subjective experiences acquire the character of objective facts. The substance of the visions, the words heard, the stirring emotions felt are "real." Somehow, sooner or later, man will be able to relate them to a wider frame of reference and thus give them a meaning on par with the meaning attributed to the entities, things, or inner events once considered normal for the men of his particular culture and possibly, once a global culture is formed, for all men. If, however, the person of the group of persons who have experienced the supersensible, superintense facts reacts to the experience by stating and teaching to others that *only* these experiences are real and the normal ones of his culture are illusory, then he may be creating a myth—the Myth of Reality.

The individual person or the group creates that myth if it is felt to fill a definite purpose in answer to a vital or essential need, be it personal or collective. It may be a *personal* myth, if the need it fills is not shared by a number of other individuals; and the person creating it may be called a psychotic, building a schizophrenic world of reality having value only to himself. But it is a *collective*, sociocultural, and potentially religious myth, if it turns out to be a constructive or regenerative answer to a collective need, even if only a few members of the community at first are fully conscious of having such a need.

A typical example is Plato's allegory of the cave: men chained at the entrance of a dark cave able only to watch on the cave's walls the shadows of other beings moving freely in front of the cave and thus behind their backs. According to this allegory, the spiritually unaware mind is like the chained men able to see only shadows; if these men could turn their bodies and face the world outside (the world of light) they would perceive the "real" world.

What Plato presented to his fellow Athenians was a myth of Reality. It was a myth because the Athenians (and those of us, Western individuals, who have inherited their particular intellectual and sense-bound consciousness) needed to be spurred into seeing the world of existence in a new way. They needed to have their conceptual world devaluated. For this reason that world was presented to them as a world of intellectual shadows. Nevertheless the experience of shadow on the cave's walls is *as real* to the chained men at the entrance of the cave as the outside world is real to the supposedly free people walking in the light. Free in relation to what? A "real" world with reference to what?

All that can be said is that because a person walking in the lighted world in front of the cave's entrance is able to see *both* his three dimensional body and its two-dimensional shadow he has a more *inclusive* frame of reference, a wider sense of meaning—the meaning of shadows and of being chained adding itself to what, to him, is the meaning of solid being in a world flooded with light. But this world of light is not without shadows either! To call the outside world Reality (with a capital) and the world of shadows in the cave "illusion" is to formulate a myth. If the world of shadows is a consistent frame of reference for the experiences of the chained men, it is for them as real as any other world is for other persons for whom their own world is also a consistent frame of reference. Both worlds are equally valid for their respective inhabitants.

The world of shadows ceases to be valid only when some of the chained men have come to understand that the chains can be broken. Then those men find themselves in a crisis situation. They are challenged to move, to stand, to experience the three-dimensional reality of bodies in the light-world. If, after they have been "liberated", they return to those with whom they had shared bondage and tell them of the new experiences, the story they tell will be for the chained men a myth—a new interpretation of reality, a revelation of new and more encompassing meaning. In this myth the shadow world will be devaluated as "mere illusion"; it will be devaluated in order that the still chained people may experience a sense of hollow emptiness, of tragic discontent, of the futility of living as they always have been living. It is a transformative, cathartic purpose, filled with the hope that the tragic experience may arouse in the people an irresistible desire to break their chains and turn to the world of light. The fact remains that the shadow is as "real" as the body casting it; samsara is as real as nirvana, except when the moment of crisis has come, when the liberating, chain-breaking, turn-back act is not only possible, but necessary.

The Creation Myth and the Myth of Conscious Plenitude of Being

The self-conscious human mind feeds on centrifugal energy. Biological instinct is unitive; but the individualizing consciousness of men stirring within the psychic unanimity of the tribe is driven by a will to differentiation whose aim is to reach a state of individual uniqueness. Such a centrifugal will obviously tends to disrupt the wholeness of any community, even at the primitive tribal level. Tribal unity has therefore to be at least periodically re-emphasized; and this is the role religious rituals, tribal festivities, and public sports are meant to fulfill. Religion is essentially an attempt to turn back the attention of differentiating and individualizing tribesmen to the experience of a primal unity from which they all arose; it is to re-evoke the great Cosmic Event which propelled the myriad of existential entities into existence, the Act of Creation.

Of course, no medicine man actually knows the facts relating to the Creative Act or, at a later more civilized stage of sociocultural development, to the utterance of the Creative Word, the Logos. Neither do astronomers today know what their postulated Big Bang that started the universe actually consisted of. All creation myths are extrapolations *backward*. In religious societies these myths were meant to be magical evocations of the unitarian release of power in which all differentiated entities had their common origin.

A common origin, a common center: in occult numerology (or "arithmosophy") this refers to number 1. At the spiritual level of energy release, this number 1 operates by adding itself to itself *ad infinitum*. At the level of "life", number 2 incessantly multiplies itself by geometrical progression through the process of self-division (mitosis). Then number 3—the union of the One and the Two, of spirit and substance—manifests as Mind, or what Blavatsky's *Secret Doctrine* calls "cosmic Ideation". Number 4 symbolizes the emodied Idea, the Archetype becomes a Person; 5, the power of transformation which number 6 can and should illumine. Number 7 recenters what has been transformed and illumined; with it we reach the omega state with which the alpha unites; and number 8 is the symbol of "eternity", the serpent swallowing its tail, re-infinitizing the process of Creation into the transcendent plenitude of ineffable "be-ness", while transcendentalizing all that remains into the Prima Materia (*Mulaprakriti*).

At the universal level of Number (and leaving aside for simplicity's sake such irrational numbers as $\sqrt{1}$ and *Pi*) this is the Creation Myth. But in tribal days the myth most often evoked mysterious cosmic animals, perhaps the spider, master geometrician, or the primordial Man and Woman; and, as monistic religions took form, God the Creator was seen as the personification of number 1—yet a 1 holding within Its incomprehensible essence the potentiality of all numbers. India has her Brahma, the Creator emerging periodically out of the ineffable timeless and spaceless (or rather time-transcending and space-transcending) Brahman. In our Western Creation Myth, the Creative Act is performed by Elohim, but Elohim is a plural noun; it is unity pregnant with multiplicity; or is it not rather the multiunity of the unanimous group of Perfected Beings at the omega state of a previous universe (a "cyclocosm") reappearing as the unified alpha condition of the new cycle?

Why should the Myth not be a *Cyclocosmic Myth* rather than a Creation Myth? Is not the beginning dependent upon and, what is more, implied in the cycle's end? Must the consciousness of differentiated and still centrifugal human beings *only* be drawn back to the alpha-beginning? Why not also to the omega-end, as these individualized human beings struggle through the conflicts and dramas of the mu state, the mid-period of the cycle? Is mankind not ready for a new myth spelled in its existential as well as in its essential totality—not merely the Ouroboros Myth of the serpent swallowing its own tail, but the

Spiral Myth with its concomitant infinitude of potentialities of existence?[1]

The Creation Myth binds to the past, the great Ancestor, the one Creator-God, number 1. But beyond, yet within number 1, is the *principle* of integration and individual existence, ONE! the principle of cyclicity within all cycles; yet not an exclusive principle, not a binding cause-and-effect sequence, because there are also irrational numbers. Every circle begins with a 1, an energy-radiating center; yet the relation of the creative power of radiation—the radius of the circle—to the circumference that sets boundaries to the centrifugal radiation is an irrational number with a never-ending series of decimals. The omega state is irrationally related to the alpha of creation, perhaps because an infinite number of possible radii are bounded by the circumference, and all of them are interrelated and interacting within the two dimensional wholeness of the circle—a fullness of space, of relationship and *therefore* of consciousness, because consciousness is the expression of relatedness embodied in harmoniously balanced form.[2]

We therefore should be able today to formulate a cyclcocosmic myth, the Myth of Conscious Plenitude of Being, to supersede the old Creation Myths. Greater than the mind whose strength is its rootedness in an Act of Origin located in a collectively re-evokable and experienceable past, is the holistic ("eonic") mind whose vision encompasses beginning, middle, and end, yet is not bound by the repetitiveness of circularity (Nietzsche's tragic picture of an Eternal Return). It is not bound because, as it accepts and is open to the irrationality of total relatedness to all there is within its life-field, it transforms circles into multidimensional spirals.

To the development of such a mind of plenitude of being the New Age, for which so many persons today are longing, should consecrate its spiritual power as well as its transpersonalized life-energies.

The Myth of the Free Individual

Our Western Society worships the individual and glorifies individual freedom, or what passes as such. The free individual is a myth; the concept of individuality is a magic carrot held in front of the instinct-bound, soil-conditioned, culture-emprisoned mind of tribal man. It is the glamor driving him toward taking the next step in his evolution; it is a myth because it is a visionary answer to the evolutionary need of mankind at a particular stage of its development. Man needs glamor. At the biological level the glamor of love-making insures the perpetuation of the species. At the social level the glamor of wealth and power goads human beings to spectacular efforts in business or in war, and the process of civilization uses these efforts and their inharmonic results to destroy and transform. At the psychological level men and women lured by the fetish of individual freedom, or of "liberation," find the cathartic strength to break down biopsychic tribal or sociocultural chains binding their consciousness.

Of course freedom can be "proven" to exist as a fact by the apparent actions of the rugged individualist or of the vehement crusader for social rights or women's liberation. What our senses perceive and our brain-mind reifies takes the form of a factual sequence of events, measureable and classifiable. But what is freedor₁ for? What happens at the level of the consciousness of "liberated" individuals? Are they really "in-divisible" and unique? Does not "man's common humanity" undertone and sustain all the acts of self-styled individuals, often wildly gesturing in order to prove their originality to themselves as well as to others? Yet in a world of change and step-by-step unfoldment, would-be individuals must be given the courage to take the next step, to "walk on,"—inevitable falls making possible the necessary recoveries. In order to learn to realize and give sustained attention to "the One-within" (the center of the mandala of personality) man had to believe himself indivisible, thus, an individual. When the centrifugal drive toward ever-renewed differentiations and the restlessness of the analytical atom-splitting mind dominate a phase of human evolution, and when the possibility of interpersonal relationships is immensely multiplied generating traumatic confusion in the mind, it becomes necessary to emphasize the uniqueness of individual souls and the constancy of monadic being. The myth of the free and responsible individual acts then as a catalyst to the process of differentiation, giving it a steady direction and centralizing its many and varied by-products. It is formulated by great Civilizers. The visions it evokes pervade the entire culture-whole, rousing the spirit of free enterprise, but also generating the crises of selfishness and ambition.

The Man of Reason and the Compassionate God-man

The mythic figure of the Man of Reason living a balanced and harmonious life in a well-proportioned world of beautiful things is the greatest contribution of the classical Greek culture. The Man of Reason emerged out of the matriarchial field of the *polis*, the city-state. He is the "civilized" man able to transcend the biopsychic conditioning of the tribal community and its vitalistic cults, yet accepting as a psychic background the birth-death-rebirth cycle featured in the ancient Mysteries. The ideal of the Man of Reason, before it became intellectualized and argued about, drew root strength from the Mysteries, but he rose above their horizontal circularity as the upward reaching germ rises from the dark soil fertilized by decay to the clear light of the sun-drenched Mediterranean atmosphere. This clear light is the light of Reason. Logic, clarity, reliance upon numbers and measures, a sense of proportion and, summing all these, the worship of Form superseding the cults of fertility glorifying life and its passionate embraces: these are the basic elements of the new myth Athens bequeathed to Rome and thus to our Euro-American culture.

It was a myth, the vision a few clear minds evoked in the hope of transforming a culture still based on slavery and retributive violence. It brought little peace to the city-state where it shone most admirably; the pressure of the world of material things and the personal ambitions of men whose egos at times drove them to emotionally unstable activities, while at others they became lost in the sophistry of intellectual argu-ments, made a sham of the emergent potentialities appearing during the sixth century B.C. The Roman empire translated reason into political order. The Middle Ages placed the sanctified mask of Thomas Aquinas upon the mummified countenance of Aristotle. Later on, Cartesian philosophy replaced reason with rationalism; the Pythagorean experi-ences of the Music of the Spheres were replaced with French logic, and Greek prosodic rhythms with the pompous, even if at times majestic, flow of twelve-syllable *Alexandrins* verses.

Myths do degenerate as human beings try to incarnate the vision they seek to communicate in the quicksand of cultural materialism and individual mediocrity. Yet in some way, at least partially, they serve their purpose, even if it should only be by stimulating the birth of their spiritual complements, which at first appear to be opposites. Greek intellectualism and mental cleverness in building concepts out of per-cepts called forth the downpour of the supramental light of love through the skylight of Jesus' soul; and in the same manner, the Mosaic "I AM" myth, once enthroned in the tribal citadel of the collective ego of the Elect People, when starvation for spiritual food became too intense, aroused the incarnation through Christ of the ideal of sublime compassion. Compassion also became the substance of the myth of Bodhisattvas renouncing the time-transcending and ego-extinguishing state of Nirvana for eons of compassionate service to last until all sentient creatures would have crossed to "the other shore" of the river of time and cosmic manifestation.

In the West the traumatic nature of the sense of guilt gnawing at the soul of the Hebrew culture forced upon the Christ incarnation the mythopoetic mask of "the Man of Sorrow". Compassion became divine atonement through suffering. But, in Asia, where the sense of guilt is not a socio-psychological issue, compassion took the form of translucent waiting—the immeasureably long waiting of noble souls through which the boundless light of the clear Mind, beyond form and name, would be able to illumine the as yet hesitant and unsure rise of humanity out of the biopsychic darkness of the mass-mind. Radiant myths which, when created, can stir human beings into taking a new step in their evolution and fulfilling a new collective dharma, soon become formalized and dessicated in the hands of men who can think only of institutionalizing them into dogmatic religions. Then new ones are needed.

Civilization is the celebration of the birth of new myths, revelations of always new possibilities of response to the immensely varied challenges of transformation the universe presents to mankind.

The Myth of Democracy

The ringing slogan of the eighteenth century revolutionary spirit, "Liberté, Egalité, Fraternité", is perhaps the most ambiguous of all mythical pronouncements. It was nevertheless a necessary correlate to the spreading tide of individualism, once this tide had reached the rocky shore of the political life. That shore, famous for recent shipwrecks, is now called democracy. On this shore every grain of sand, rock or cliff carries a number. Quantity is king and statistics the Law of the realm. It is a mythical realm. On the map it looks wonderful; it calls all the ships at sea to its harbor; but when the passengers debark, they soon become feverish with the ego disease which magnifies everything out of natural proportions, changing reason into rationalism, and latent capacities into vocal demands for immediate actualization and public recognition.

This is the dark side of liberty which can also, but does not need to, mean freedom. The English language is blessed with two words which unfortunately are so often, and senselessly used interchangeably. When Patrick Henry proclaimed "Give me liberty or give me death," he clearly referred to the *objective* state of affairs, liberty, which is the opposite of tyranny or authoritarian rule. Freedom, on the other hand, should refer to a *subjective* state of individual consciousness and being. Freedom from fear, anxiety, or sense of guilt, refers to a subjective condition. Unfortunately the possible discrimination allowed by the two words, liberty and freedom, between objective facts and subjective realizations, is usually ignored. For the French, however, there is only *liberté*; for the German, *freiheit*, which implies that French people have been specifically chafing under authoritarian rulers and yearning for the ability to act as they individually please, while German people are more specifically concerned about overcoming an inner state of binding acquiescence to traditions and biopsychic feelings of conformity.

What most Americans call freedom is the ability to act as they please, to go where they want, to read or see what (for no special reason) they personally feel like reading or seeing. This is liberty, rather than a subjective condition of freedom—freedom from whatever *within them* binds them to Puritan traditions, to a craving for money, social prestige, and "being liked," or simply to fashion. Likewise what is meant by sexual freedom is the capacity to *make* love, to act in ways individually decided upon; but the unasked question is: why the decision? That question refers not to action, but to what in a person makes or fails to make significant decisions—significant solely in the sense that they are signs or symbols of what the person *is* as an individual.

No one thinks or longs for liberty unless he or she is experiencing external constraints. The tribesman of ancient times would not have understood what liberty meant as long as he lived in his own tribe. The word would have had meaning only if he had been enslaved by another tribe. Archaic tribal taboos did not bind—any more than having to breathe binds—simply because in either case there is no sense of bondage. The yearning for liberty presupposes external restrictions against which a person's own nature rebels. *Of itself* such a yearning has no meaning or value. The situation is different where inner freedom is concerned, for such a freedom essentially implies the ability to transform oneself personally when the time for transformation has come. Such an ability can be partially or totally restricted by outer pressures and binding situations, in which case liberty is curtailed. Its manifestation within the personality can also be stifled or perverted by psychic and mental laziness or physical inertia; in which case the individual is not free, even if nothing is there socially to curtail his liberty. He can act as he pleases, but it does not please him to act!

When destiny demands of the individual that he open himself freely to a process of transformation, yet his mind and feelings cling to the status quo, this individual is not free, however permissive his environment. The permissive educaton experienced by young Americans now in their teens, twenties, or thirties gave them liberty, but not freedom. A permissive society allowing ugly and love-perverting pornographic movies to be produced and widely advertised provides liberty, but by creating a binding fashion may in fact curtail the freedom to love naturally, spontaneously, and meaningfully. To put it in a different way, it is not the freedom *from* fear caused by lurking external danger, or from hunger caused by outer scarcity, which is most important; it is the ability to significantly decide what freedom is *for*. Providing the outer freedom (liberty) to do anything at any time, yet at the same time confusing the mind with so many doubtful or unconvincing alternatives that the will to decide on a personally significant course of action is not aroused, can lead to countless spiritual miscarriages. If the child is not provided with anything *against which* he can develop an individualized will; if he is not held within a matriarchal structure from which he can emerge only by an act of conscious and self-directed exertion, this child may lack the incentive to operate as a truly free individual save in exceptional cases and within a very special community.

The concept of equality is as ambiguous and ambivalent as that of liberty. Does it refer to a quantitative or a qualitative value? Is *majority rule* the panacea that will cure all social ills, or will *functional adequacy* (if not excellence) define social position and condition the character of a person's participation in the sociopolitical process?

These are crucial questions. They have been answered in our Western democracy in a rationalistic rather than in a reasonable way. The answer has been abstract and theoretical, rather than existential and functional or organic. It has led our society to unrealistic make-believe and officialized hypocrisy. Majority rule makes no sense unless the voter is considered not merely an abstract number, but first of all an operative whole functionally able to make significant decisions. Yet what are the alternatives in a society based on the premises of individualism, self-determination, and personal responsibility? There are, *as of today*, no more valid alternatives.

What this means is that mankind is in a situation of crisis of transformation. It is experiencing such a radical crisis because the premises on which the democratic ideal can only meaningfully operate have in most instances not consciously accepted validity in the lives of the people of officially democratic societies. They are abstract concepts, founded on quantity, not on organic quality. There is no available majority of self-determined, self-reliant, functionally effective individuals totally ready and willing to assume personal responsibility for their decisions and the eventual results of their actions; therefore democracy is only an ideal.

It is also a myth, according to the meaning I give to this word, because at this stage of human evolution the ideal is a necessary answer to an all-human evolutionary need. Yet, necessary as it is, as we usually understand and attempt to formulate in practical terms the meaning of the myth, the actual results represent a perverted form of the myth. We are dealing with abstract quantity, with intellectualized and analytical numbers, and *not* with what the great civilizer, Pythagoras, experienced as Numbers referring to essential, archetypal *qualities* or modes of formation. We juggle with numbers, or get caught in the spider-webs of complex instrumental measurements abstractedly extended to n-dimensional intellectual frames of reference; we worship statistics giving us an insecure hold on a world of existence reified by the common consent of scientific minds hypnotized by an empirical methodology. We rarely experience with mind open to the subtlety of qualitative changes, to the polyphonic interweaving of dynamic currents of energy whose rhythmic and melodic interactions form the warp and woof of life-experiences. For instance, we build at high cost and with strenuous intellectual efforts "computer music" presented by an incredible array of taped numbers instead of listening within us to the qualitative Music of the Spheres.

As to the third element in the myth of democracy, fraternity, how unrealistic it too can be in our society based on acquisitiveness, competition, and the violence, overt or covert, of ego-structured power-motives! We should realize now the difference between an ancestor-worshipping tribal order totally rooted in the past, and the companion-ate order harmonizing distinct, consciously aware, and self-determined individuals into a communion of consciousness founded on their unanimous consecration to an envisioned purpose. Of course we can imagine the ideal case of a family-group in which the companionate order would operate in the linking of cohabitating children, parents, and grandparents. We can dream of such a type of family relationship and see it superseding the type of interplay which has so far existed in biologically united and culture-bound families. If humanity *needed* now such an ideal type of family, we could try to evoke a new family myth, the myth of the companionate family. But is it really what the evolution of human consciousness demands today? At today's level of consciousness, is it possible, except in the rarest cases, that such strong biopsychic compulsions still exist?

An "occult Brotherhood" always seems to be bound to the past in terms of ancient rules and traditions, which accounts for the sociopolitical conservatism of the great majority of people deeply involved in occult contacts and in the philosophy they derive from these. But as mankind passes the mid-point of its planetary evolution, is it not time for individuals who have experienced a birth in spiritual freedom to reorient their consciousness futureward rather than pastward, to think of themselves as Companions rather than as Brothers and Sisters, especially when family relationships today are so filled with tensions, conflicts and unsolvable problems of personality relationship? The old Church speaks to us of Father and Brothers; but in Free Masonry, the terms are Apprentices, Companions (or Fellows), and Masters, and the goal is the common dedication of each participant in the Lodge's activity of the building of the Temple of Man. Originally, Masonry was to be a workshop for the development of a democratic consciousness based on the efficient functional workings of the Companionate Order, through rituals revealing the archetypal essence of the process leading from the mid-point (mu) state of consciousness to the omega completion of the Temple of Man, a temple built, not by material hands, but by consecrated minds illumined by all-encompassing love. But, like the various fraternal Orders, developing from its trunk as rather spiritually fruitless offshoots, Free Masonry has retained the forms and lost the spirit.

The slogan of democracy has now a hollow sound. Yet the myth it betrayed by its ambivalence and ambiguity could yet experience a rebirth of meaning, together with another myth to which it has clung for support, the Myth of Empirical Knowledge.[3]

The Myth of Empirical Knowledge

The statement "The sun rises in the east" may seem self-evident, yet it implies a number of assumptions which could be replaced or superseded by others. To speak of "the sun" is to express a concept; it does not refer to a simple sensation. The sensation of light on the retina, when transferred to and reified by the brain according to cultural patterns of thinking, is interpreted as "the sun"; but such an interpretation can only be reached in its inception by many steps of perception and conceptualization shared and discussed by many human beings. The words "rise" and "east" are also simplistic; they imply a peculiar conception of "the sky," an ambiguous feeling of verticality (if "sky" is interpreted as a celestial sphere) and an abstract concept of "east" which a series of successive experiences actually would deny, as sunrise occurs at the exact east only at the two equinoxes.

I have already referred to the character of "facts"—and the word fact comes from the Latin factum which means "having been made." Man builds the facts of which he speaks when he develops the concept of empirical knowledge. Empirical knowledge, built on facts not only perceived by man's senses but reified by man's conceptual and cultured mind, is only one type of knowledge, resulting from one mode of "knowingness." To say that it is the only valid mode, or even the most basic and valid, mode is a form of mental myopia or cultural provincialism. Yet at a certain time in man's historical evolution the nearly exclusive value of empiricism and of the modern scientific method of objective observation, aided and abetted by machines refining man's physical capacity for measurement and recognition, was undoubtedly an answer to a collective human need. The validity of the method had to be assumed and conveniently left unquestioned because our Western society was meant to develop a kind of knowingness enabling it in the long run to perform highly meaningful deeds: to circumfly the Earth-globe, to overcome the Earth-binding pull of gravitation, and directly or indirectly to bring every human being in contact with all other human beings, thus establishing an evidential basis for the belief in the unity of all men living within a finite "spaceship Earth" with equally finite resources.

Therefore, after the Renaissance, the medieval approach to knowledge could not have produced these results required at the present stage of human evolution because it was a scholastic and dogmatic interpretation of the Aristotelian world-view, which in turn led to the materialization of the great vision of Pythagoras and probably of a few of the Greek minds of the sixth century B.C. Moreover, the Mind of Reason, once divorced from cosmic supersensory experiences, had to become the empirical mind; "pure relations' need some kind of substantial contents and experienceable facts, at one level or another, in order to have communicable materials to work on—just as automated factories need raw materials to process. The European intelligensia of the sixteenth, seventeenth, and eighteenth centuries had therefore to be fascinated, even seduced, by the Myth of Empirical Knowledge in order to deal with something it could experience concretely and with which it could build. The descendants of these intellectuals, in the nineteenth century, realizing how far man had advanced, reacted by excitedly describing a new myth: the Myth of Science, source of unchallengeable Progress.

Francis Bacon, the Civilizer, had impregnated the collective mind of his epoch and of the succeeding century with his empirical method; Descartes and Newton, each in his own way, then stressed concepts which buttressed the citadel of empirical knowledge. Yet the last decade of the nineteenth century and those of our present century have revealed that the magnificent building was not earthquake-proof. Thus a new myth, having the power to gain the allegiance of deconditioned and adventurous minds, is now necessary. It has to become a new frame of reference for a transfactual knowingness, a new revelation unerringly pointing to a new dimension of experience. In terms of such a transcendent, because more inclusive, dimensional frame of reference, the old principle of exclusion and other paradigmatic concepts of a gradually more obsolescent methodology have become unapplicable; they are far too crude and simplistic for a mind able to experience the interpenetration of all the facts and entities it had in the past laboriously conceptualized as isolated and independent of each other. Holism, at a new level of experience and realization, will have to supersede, *though not negate*, the relative value of atomism. The principle of holarchy, relating hierarchical levels of experience to each other, will have to be taken as a foundation for the development of a New Age type of knowledge. On that foundation new myths are bound to arise. A very ancient one is now experiencing a crisis of potential transformation and, what is more, of transfiguration. I am speaking of astrology.

The Myth of Astrology

When in 1933 and 1934 I began to write articles for the first popular astrology magazine *American Astrology*, just started by Paul Clancy in New York, and when, in 1936, my book *The Astrology of Personality* was published by the Lucis Press at the instigation of Alice Bailey, astrology attracted only a limited public, mostly interested in fortune telling. Evangeline Adams in New York had pioneered a rebirth of astrological practice and won a well-publicized court action. Max Heindel in California had written *The Message of the Stars*; Alan Leo in England had for some years attempted a theosophical interpretation of classical European astrology, also undertaken at a more occult and kabalistic level by Sepharial; and Marc Edmund Jones had begun to write for his Sabian Assembly twelve mimeographed lessons on astrology. These lessons marked a basic departure, for they dealt with ancient astrological concepts on the basis of a profound and utterly consistent type of philosophical conceptualization.

It was Marc Jones' presentation which made me aware of the potential of psychological revelation inherent in astrology, if astrology were reformulated in terms of the then newly developed schools of depth-psychology, particularly that of Carl Jung. Thus the holistic, harmonic, and (as I called it much later) humanistic movement in astrology began and is now widely spreading. It is especially spreading among the youths of today; they are longing for new paths to personality integration and are wide open to ideals of transcendence and to the possibility of death-rebirth, a possibility more or less effectively and healthfully revealed to them by ancient Asiatic techniques and the use of ecstasy-inducing drugs. Following the lead given by "Third Force" psychologists—since Jung and, later, Maslow, Anthony Sutich, and many others—*humanistic* astrology is now being reoriented and, in many recent works, reformulated along *transpersonal* lines.

As I have conceived and presented it, astrology should be considered a powerful myth, perhaps one of the most powerful New Age myths.

Indeed the very concept of a New Age, the Aquarian Age, has an astrological basis. It is a myth because it is, at least potentially, a consistent, well-organized and all-inclusive answer to personal human needs, collective as well as individual. These needs today *must be met*. A sense of organic wholeness and significant relatedness must be re-established in minds deprived of the support of now repudiated classical frames of reference and deeply confused by a multitude of possible alternatives, while these minds search for transcendence and hope for rebirth in a new social and cultural world that would be attuned to the superpersonal rhythms of the cosmos.

The keyword here is *attuned*. The most dynamic and restless members of today's youth, and many of their elders, poignantly feel "out of tune." Their entire society appears to them a discordant magma of wrong notes. By shrieking their out-of-tuneness louder than anyone else, they dare an essentially inert middle class, drugged by the gloss of suburban comfort and slick materialism, to face the horrendous possibility that their agitated and empty living is actually a magnified medieval "dance of death." In the past, the mythical violinist-leader of the dance was a skeleton; now, as more and more people begin to believe, it is the Pentagon and CIA, and their counterparts in other nations, that play the nuclear tune, while big business beats the drum.

This apocalyptic vision seems increasingly to take on the massive character of reality. The jungles of the biosphere, where small tribes of men once eeked out a difficult death-haunted existence, have become equally dangerous megalopoles of cement and asphalt scarring the once beautiful earth. Death or rape may still wait at the corner; neurosis is as endemic as malaria in tropical swamps. Primitive man looked to the starry sky and studied the movements of the Moon and the Sun because there, in the "Above," they could see the *magic of order* at work. The sky was indeed magical, a revelation of transcendent divine harmony to which man and his society could attune their cultural endeavors as well as their agriculture, because man essentially belonged to that Above. Was it not his task and responsibility to make of the earthly "Below" a reflected image of the celestial Order? So indeed thought the old Chinese philosophers and emperors, and the Hindu seers, raising their consciousness to a point not only of response but of identification with the Above.

Astrology then was the supreme Myth of Order and Being. Primitive men needed that celestial answer to their earth-bound insecurity, their fears of the unknown, their yearning to commune with whatever they visualized as anticipations of a future godlike state of humanness. We need just as poignantly today an answer to our modern insecurity, our fears of personal disintegration under the pressures of city-life, of business passion for power, and of the menace of nuclear war or ecological disaster. Where can we find such an answer? Only a new myth can provide it for us, a myth relating our seemingly incoherent and tragically out-of-tune social and psychological movements to an all-encompassing and universally acceptable frame of reference whose vastness can absorb conflicts and redeem them into harmony.

How could such a "redemption" be possible? It can be possible only if the collective consciousness of Western people realizes the crucial need for a change of frame of reference. As Count Keyserling (the great German philosopher and culture-interpreter) once said: No basic conflict can be solved; it can only be transcended. By reaching a position in consciousness above the opposites, we may realize that both polarities are valid; both have something essential to contribute; both are essential participants in the counterpoint of life, not to be rejected but to be understood and, through understanding, harmonized.

The myth of the sky should give form to the as yet mostly inchoate and insecure feelings that, essentially, harmony prevails in the universe, once that universe is perceived and understood in its totality. We are blind to it because our perceptions are only partial and biased by emotional reactions, and particularly by our fears. Yet everything is related to everything else in a polyphony of interdependent and interpenetrating activities. If we lose this sense of relatedness—which is also love—everything falls apart within us, and our world collapses into meaninglessness. We must regain that sense of relatedness. We may achieve this through astrology, but it is not the only way.

Astrology can be, and has been at least tentatively, reformulated as a myth that could inspire and, here and there, has already inspired distraught human individuals to see within the magic mirror of their birth-charts the revelation of their truth-of-being, their dharma. If truly understood as a power of transpersonal revelation of order within—a mandala of archetypal selfhood and destiny—it is not a religion. It does not "bind back" to an external source to be worshipped. Yet it can reveal the outline of the process of growth gradually evolving on the foundation of the persistent and never-silent AUM-tone of individual selfhood, sustaining all that we are and can potentially become. It is guidance, not subjection; companionship with our greater celestial Self, not worship of an absolute Other, called God.

In my recent book The Sun is also a Star (Dutton and Co., N.Y. 1975) I spoke of "the Galactic Dimension of Astrology." We are in the Galaxy. We have not to go elsewhere to reach our galactic form or fulfill our galactic destiny. Galactic space pervades and illumines every cell of our body, every circuit of our thinking brain. If we are willing and ready to abandon our subjection to the dictates of an autocratic Sun, ruling over our personalities with the compulsive power of biological drives and psychic emotions; if we are willing to surrender our dependence upon the ego-Sun and see ourselves as one small star in the immense choir of galactic centers of radiant light, then our voice may rise above the apparent discords of interplanetary relationships, symbols of our social and personal limitations. Our life may then become a mythopoetic expression of trust in the harmony of the universe and of "that" out of which universes are born, then die and are reborn. In this realization our problems may fade into peace. We may learn who we are, where we stand, and how best we can fulfill our role in the cosmos.

This is evidently not what, for most people, astrology means today, or has meant in Western cultures since Athens, Alexandria, Rome, and classical Europe. But it is what it can mean to individuals who take seriously—and intelligently attempt to formulate by their actions—the real, yet so rarely understood significance and purpose of our recently emerging counterculture. The problem our Western society faces is to give stability, meaning, and validity to that counterculture; it is to give to it a mythopoetic character. It should be able to give birth to new myths, or at least to do for the new myths in process of revelation what the Mediterranean "proletariat" of the Hellenistic and Roman world (to use Toynbee's term) did with the Christ-myth propagated by the seed-sacrifice of a few illumined and courageous men and women.

The New Age Myth

If one asks: Does the idea of a New Age now beginning, or about to begin, correspond to actual, concrete, expectable facts, or is it merely an illusion, a dream-like utopia? The only possible answer is that the need for a radically new departure in human affairs is evident. What is much less evident is whether mankind's response to that need will be sufficiently strong, lucid, and sustained to produce a new and viable global culture encompassing the whole of humanity within some complex form of sociopolitical organization.

The astrological fan may exclaim: "But don't you believe we are at the beginning of the Aquarian Age?" The answer is that it is man who makes the Aquarian Age. Man perceives certain facts, such as the precession of the equinoxes mentioned in a previous chapter; he organizes these facts of experience into a conceptual picture by using the symbolism of Number, because he believes in cosmic laws and the invariance of the basic motions of our Earth and in general of all celestial bodies. He speaks of twelve precessional Ages dividing the assumed length of the cycle of precession; he studies what he knows of past history and establishes correlations between historical changes of major significance and the divisions of the precessional cycle his use of numbers has produced. And as these correlations release into his consciousness a deep and illuminating source of meaning, the astrologer states that we are at or near the threshold of the Aquarian Age.

Such a statement is a concept, because it takes for granted what could also be interpreted (i.e. given meaning to) in other ways. The most basic statements made by astronomers are also concepts based on theories which evidently depend on the scope of perception of man's senses and the machines his particular type of intellect has built to assist him in a particular type of endeavor dictated by the particular mentality of our Western culture. In spite of what the Declaration of Independence proclaims, no statement should be called an absolutely "self-evident truth." What is evident is that at a certain time the need for taking a particular statement as self-evident arises. The asserted proposition answers the need, and therefore it acquires the validity and power of a great myth.

Only a naive and unhistorical mind can think that facts are more powerful than myths. All radical changes in human history are the results of the spread of a myth that, in a totally convincing manner, answers a crucially experienced need during a period of crisis. When, in the defeated and chaotic Russia of the fall of 1917, Lenin gained power by his mantram-like repetition of the slogan "Peace, Bread, Land," he formulated the myth that answered the traumatic need of the mass of the people. What immediately followed was neither peace, nor much bread, nor privately owned land. Yet what Lenin started and Trotsky's army was able to defend led, in an extraordinarily short time, a huge backward country to a position of world-influence equalled only by the United States.

Lenin created a myth giving a totally unexpected form to Karl Marx's dream-vision. The myth triumphed over the facts and over the interpretation which anyone in 1917 would have given to them. A band of Christians likewise triumphed over the massive administrative machinery of the Roman empire which the facts had proven to be eminently successful in its ability to bring order to a collection of disintegrating culture-wholes.

These myths won the day because they aroused in a few individuals an ineradicable and irrefutable faith in the validity of the answer they gave to the collective need of a large collectivity of human beings, and the contagious power of that faith proved irresistible. Yet there was blindness in that faith, and it led to a basic perversion of the ideal vision. The faith of the early American pioneers in total self-reliance and individualistic freedom of action also led to the robber-barons and the widespread murder of Indians during the westward rush toward more land and gold. The "American dream" was also a myth, answering to the need of oppressed classes in Europe; alas, it has come to the disillusion of the Vietnam war and Watergate.

The Aquarian Age concept is a myth in the sense that mankind today needs to believe in not only the possibility but the inevitability of a rebirth of culture, however delayed it might be and however much man may cling to the old. Most people have to believe in a renewed descent of divinely transforming power and Wisdom. Because Western man has lost faith in the ability of political and religious leaders (and increasingly of late even in the ability of scientists and technologists) to reshape our chaotic society in terms of obsolescent, if not actually obsolete, traditional values and concepts, he *has to* create new myths or his world will crumble, if not physically and ecologically, then spiritually. Whoever creates the convincing myth that truly will answer the crucial need of men, women, and children will prove to be the agent of the potential of ever-renewed transformation inherent in Man.

All great transforming myths are backed by facts; but we should now realize that these facts are also made by the same historical and evolutionary forces which generated the need to which the myth is an answer. The validity of the myth of an astrological New Age depends on the ability Western man has displayed to invent telescopes, photographic and electronic mechanisms, and also mathematical formulas to organize and conceptualize in a plethora of new sense-data. On the other hand, it is this intellectual ability which has been responsible for the Industrial and Electronic Revolutions and the attendant disorganization of culture-wholes all over the globe. This is the periodically repeated paradox. Science and technology *at the same time* gave rise to the present world-wide human need, and to the facts on which a mythopoetic creation could base new symbols evoking a potent creative answer to that need. This answer is based on a precise calculation of the cycle of precession, on the discovery of Uranus, Neptune, and Pluto, and the realization of the nature of the ordered multitude of stars we call a galaxy.

The great astrological New Age myth is the Galaxy Myth, for the symbols man has to use in order to conceptualize his basic sense of belonging to a greater Whole no longer have to take a transcendentally superexistential character. Man does not have to say that in Christ he "lives, moves and has his being," as the New Testament asserts; because *now* the new facts of astronomy tell him that he lives, moves, and has his being in the Galaxy. Galactic space pervades every cell of evey human being's body. We all are as much galactic beings as fishes are organizations of sea-water. Yet we do not normally realize this is son. We need a new, powerful myth to entice our minds into vividly, indisputably, unforgettably experiencing that fact. We need a myth which *at the same time* will transform on the one hand our human sense of physicality and on the other the ancient concepts of the solar system, the constellations, and the Milky Way. In the past such concepts made of the sky a celestial abode for celestial Hierarchies of gods (the old vitalistic myth), or else pictured it as a black emptiness in which stars separated by incomprehensibly vast distances shine in lonely isolation (the nineteenth century materialistic myth).

Both types of concepts no longer answer to the intellectual, or even the emotional, needs of modern man. A new galactic myth should now rephrase the message of the sky and give it a new meaning in terms of a newly experienced manifestation of cosmic order. It seems probable that the creators of the myth of the New Age will evoke in the minds of the new generation a "cosmophanic" rather than a theophanic vision of the wholeness of existence. God would not be displaced by the new cosmic realizations, but rather made integral with a cosmos irradiated through and through by the divine Presence. Without such a cosmic revelation as a background, and by merely basing our hope for a New Age on the vague ideas of Aquarius being an "air sign," succeeding the watery devotionalsim of Pisces, the fervently longed for New Age could well be a deceptive dream, a utopia without factual consistency.

The statement that we are entering the Aquarian Age because at the vernal equinox an infinitely prolonged line passing from the Sun to the Earth is reaching, or will soon reach, the space designated as the constellation Aquarius is an accurate astrological deduction. But it is deduced from the old picture of the sky which we have inherited from now disintegrated and mostly unknown cultures reconstructed from only fragmentary records by archaeologists lacking really adequate data. These cultures "made' the constellations and gave them characteristics represented by names whose symbolical meaning for modern man has lost its experienceability. The meanings of the elements Fire, Earth, Water, and Air have to be carefully explained to and memorized by students of astrology. Other cultures used other names. If there is to be a really New Age (and we have to believe in that possibility if we are to retain our spiritual sanity and our will to create) we must find within ourselves the answer to the need for its formation. And first of all we must, as individuals, experience the incontrovertible pressure of that need and an inner spiritual compulsion to allow the universe's answer to take form within our open and expectant mind.

What we have to watch for is the tendency of our minds to follow the line of least effort, and thus to use the immediately available and easiest way of giving form to this inner creative answer, the way that is already encumbered with familiar words and stereotypes. The first characteristic of the creative mythopoetic individual is his courage, his determination not to follow the easy path. I have repeated elsewhere the statement made by Erik Johnson during World War II "Beaten paths are for beaten men." In the realm of mind nothing beats a path as effectively as the indiscriminate use of old names into which small minds try to pour new meanings. Surely we cannot impulsively break away from all past formulas, lest we have eventually to return to them as supplicants for sanity. But we need not be rooted in the form the gradual rise of mankind has taken in more or less recent culture-wholes; we may allow ourselves to be *drawn into* the very flow of the great river of civilization while remaining conscious of its distant source and aware of its eventual merging with the cosmic ocean.

The New Age is to be created with new symbols, not manufactured by the use of reclaimed mental materials which once substantiated the creative impulse that gave birth to what then was some other culture's New Age. Astrology in its traditional form can point the way by showing us how the order of the sky, in contrast to the chaos of earthly jungles, can provide for us the substance of mythopoetic creations ensouling the efforts of material builders. The soul has to have a body; it is the new astronomy which is providing us with the body of new myths whose messages can be deciphered in the sky. Astronomy challenges us to write new poems of creation to give meaning to the new facts it has obtained.

There will be a New Age if and when we create it. We will find in us a readiness and the will to create when, having attuned ourselves to the rhythms of the Galaxy, we can let the immense Company of the Stars project upon our minds the hieroglyphs of the New Age. Why should they necessarily be the words of a latinized Chaldean-Greek tradition? We had to start with these words as scaffoldings; but let the Temple rise!

There is a schedule for its completion. We have to believe there is, in order to challenge, every morning, the laziness of our minds and the weariness of our spirit deafened by the noise and chaos of the building process. That there is such a schedule is what constitutes the myth of an impending New Age. This myth is an answer to our impatience, but also to our innate demand for ordered processes of growth. We accept the myth; yet need be neither bound nor haunted by our concern for its implementation. *The New Age is our creating it.*

11.
CREATIVITY AND THE INDIVIDUAL'S
ROLE IN A CRISIS SITUATION

THERE have been many recent research projects dealing with what is defined as creativity or the creative process. Because our contemporary Western Society is mainly concerned with individuals—their rights, their development, and the myriad of techniques devised to assist and normalize the actualization of their innate potentialities—these studies of creativity are almost always focused upon the root-causes, the necessary or optimal conditioning and the modes of operation of the creative process in individuals. These studies are motivated by the hope that when the process is better understood it will make it possible for a greater number of persons to release effectively and harmoniously the creativity now assumed to be latent in every human being.

Whether or not such an assumption is correct and whether it would serve humanity's essential destiny to arouse in every person an emotional eagerness to create something, whatever it be and for whatever purpose, is not the main issue. It can be stated nevertheless that such an emphasis placed upon the value of individual creativity, and the popularization of analyses of the creative process in personalities today regarded as especially creative, are developments related to the apparent fact that our Western culture-whole has reached the last phases of its cycle; these developments are typical symptoms of the vulgarization process always accompanying the closing period of any culture-whole. We would easily understand the reason for this if we realized that the state of the culture and the approach to creativity are definitely interrelated. It should be fairly evident that discussing the creative process in individuals without much reference to the state of the culture-whole in which these individuals are "being creative," and also to the character of their relationship—conscious or unconscious—to the culture and the social processes it features, makes very little sense. What essentially matters is *the two-way relationship* between the individual and his or her society. To consider the individual alone, as if he operated in an environmental vacuum, is as fundamentally meaningless as to discuss social, cultural, economic, and political processes with no regard to the individual human beings affected by these processes who, to a large extent, give them a conscious direction by formulating goals and means.

To be creative in twentieth century America is to a large extent different from being creative in the Europe of the seventeenth century. What the individual does and how he feels about it acquires its basic meaning from what his society *needs* and can accept at the time he is living and creating. As an individual, he may think of his activities as creative, yet if there is no cultural need for them, he will either not be able, for a variety of reasons, to bring his creative activity to completion, or else what he somehow completes will remain unrecognized and ineffectual; perhaps (in rare instances) he may be discovered much later and interpreted as a premature prophetic vision. Victor Hugo once stated that nothing is more powerful than an idea whose time has come. What he actually meant was that nothing is more effective and transformative than a creative activity (however it manifests) that fulfills the then operative need of a culture-whole toward which it is directed.

In other words, if we want to deal significantly with the creative process we have to consider the implied cultural need it is meant to fulfill. Whether or not the "creator" is fully aware of that need, is certainly not the main issue. Neither is what the process of "creating" does to the psychology of the individual in whom it operates the most important factor in the evaluation of the process. The essential value of the creative process, as I see it, is in the answer it gives to the collective need of a culture and a society, or of a special group or subculture within this society. It should be an eminently convincing answer, arousing in the people coming in contact with it not only the urge, but also the power to transform themselves in terms suggested by this creative answer.

To create is to transform; but the basic issue is what is being transformed. It may be raw materials (clay, wood, words, pigments, or the patterns of social behavior) to which a more integrated and meaning-releasing form is given; but it also could be the consciousness of human beings and their capacity to respond effectively to the challenge of a greater life.

In the first instance, one is dealing with what should more accurately be called *productivity*. The tribal artisan making beautiful pots or rugs, according to traditional models existing as prototypes in the collective unconscious of his people, is a "producer" rather than a "creator." He transforms the raw materials he uses into objects having, to him or his community, both a character of utility (whether he uses or sells them as articrafts) and an esthetic value. The artisan may modify the traditional forms and this may give him a feeling of exaltation or pride, especially if his community praises him rightly for what he has produced. Such a feeling is similar in nature to the emotional stimulation and the sense of increased power which a person receives from an especially successful sportive or even sexual performance. The organism-as-a-whole and its functions may be stimulated, but above all it is the performer's ego that is enhanced by a feeling of achievement. Because, in the performance, his biopsychic energies have reached a condition of greater fulfillment the artist-producer is *more fully what he is*.

On the other hand, in the above-mentioned second instance, when what is transformed is consciousness rather than materials of one kind or another, the creative individual, as he creates, becomes *more than what he was*. He has been moved by a power that is transcultural as well as transpersonal. Through him this power is able to evoke in others the desire, or perhaps the will, also to become more than they are, provided they open their consciousness and/or their feeling-responses to the magic of the creative act.

The dualism of creativity vs. productivity parallels that of magical will vs. esthetic pleasure. In the first case, a transpersonal power operates *through* the creator, or we should rather say the creative agent; in the second, the productive activity flows *from* the artist who produces objects or gives performances that meet the demands of the people of his culture, and perhaps in some instances of mankind as a whole. The *demands* of the culture-whole for objects of beauty or excellence should be clearly differentiated from the *need* of that culture for a radical transformation of its sense of value and its paradigms when a time of transition has come. When such a time comes it manifests outwardly in a "crisis," which (etymologically at least) means the opportunity for making a decision.[1]

A transition is a "going through"; what one goes through are boundaries. It is a passage from the know and the familiar to the as-yet-unknown. It implies a necessary process of "defamiliarization," and this refers to the disruptive, catabolic and "catesthetic" aspect of the truly creative process. *All creative processes have their shadow aspect*, but there need be no shadow in productivity, or (at the biological level) in procreation and in the various forms of procreatively oriented sexual activity. However, the creative-transformative (i.e., alchemical and re-generative) use of the sex-force has its shadow aspect; and this applies also to the now popularized process of the "raising of Kundalini."

The fundamental theme of this book is that our Western culture-whole—and by extension the whole of humanity subjected to its pervasive and catabolic influence—is, and has been for at least two centuries, in a situation of crisis. The crisis was brought about by the development of a new faculty, the analytical power of the intellectual mind, whose most fruitful field of operation is the world of physical matter, because all physical entities are infinitely divisible. This faculty in turn developed as the result of the general process of individualization of consciousness required for the fulfillment of Man's place and function on the planet, Earth.

Man, as the Individual, is intended to act as the conscious intermediary linking, through many and varied forms, the realm of spirit and the world of matter. Man is essentially Mind; but Mind is both "former" and "transformer." In its purest aspect Mind is the formative principle of the universe; but it contains within itself the power to destroy forms that have outlived *their usefulness as alchemical vessels within which the "marriage" of spirit and matter can be performed.* When the time has come for a new phase in the cyclic (or cyclocosmic) relationship between spirit and matter, this new relationship calls for a new type of "marriage" and this in turn requires a new type of forms within which *the quality* of the new relationships can come to maturity, as an embryo matures within a womb. Once matured this new quality of being and relating can radiate through the form's boundaries and bring a new inspiration to whatever it touches.

As soon as the evolutionary need for the new quality of humanness is felt, the old forms begin to break apart and to reveal their obsolescence. Then the crisis begins; it may be called catharsis at the psychopersonal level, or revolution at the sociopolitical level. At the telluric planetary level it may refer to a glacial period and an alteration of the direction of the polar axis. When the crisis begins, the relation of a significant group of individuals particularly sensitive and mentally alert to their society's needs takes on, at least potentially, a new character. A new role presents itself to them—a creative, transformative role.

If these individuals, consciously or only half-consciously, respond to the potentiality of assuming such a role, this response involves a twofold relation which to some extent is bound to affect their lives: a relation to the source of the creative activity, the character of which they may not be consciously or fully aware; and a new kind of relationship to the environment, group or society which is eventually to be transformed by that creative activity. This transformation may be *interpreted* by the people of the obsolescent cultural institutions as destructive or constructive, and to some extent it is both at the same time. The way it is interpreted could be considered of no great importance to the truly dedicated creative agent; yet what this interpretation does to the collective mentality of the new generation which will be most radically affected by the forms it takes can have a crucial importance. What is even more a determining factor is the *quality* of the relationship which the creative agent is able to sustain toward both the source of his or her creativity and the people to whom it is addressed. The creative agent should be able to understand both what it is he is *tuning to*, and the character of the need his culture has for his creative activity. He should understand his place and function in the whole process of evolution of his particular culture-whole.

Without such an at least intuitive understanding, the creative agent's relationship to either his source of inspiration or his culture (and most likely to *both*) tends to be inadequate because vitiated or distorted by egocentric reactions and mental or emotional confusion. The formulation of such an understanding may be difficult for the creative agent, for it inevitably implies a philosophical and historically aware mind; and such a mind need not be fully developed in the creative agent, or developed along the traditional lines of the old culture, which might be worse than not developed at all. Yet, in some way, the creative agent should be aware of what is taking place within him and at least of the ultimate purpose of his creative process. If he is not aware of being *an instrumentality through which a creative power takes form* this most likely (and perhaps always) means that the creative process working through him has only a catabolic or catesthetic character, even though he may feel during the creative act the same personal emotional exaltation as that experienced by a creative agent consciously and transpersonally dedicated to a purpose of collective transformation.

If the men and women of our present-day culture are fascinated by technique, always eager to know the "how to" of every doing, and intent on producing *more* of "bigger and better" things, it is because they consider and value almost everything in terms of how an individual person feels about it. If some type of activity feels good to a person, and it increases his or her material and psychological welfare and productivity, then—it is believed—everybody should learn how to act in the same or a basically similar manner; thus psychologists study the "successful" artist or business executive and attempt to extract from such a study "recipes for success."

This is a spiritually meaningless endeavor. Its results add to the process of vulgarizationdominating the last period of the life-span of a culture-whole. Everybody must create so as to feel better, it seems! But the results are not really "creative." More things are produced, more canvases painted, more novels written, more of everything to glut the psychomental environment of people, each of whom has to feel what "successful people" are supposed to feel as they produce more and more and, in many cases, useless ego-titillating objects, including what passes as "works of art."

Productivity, even in the field of art, is not what should be called creativity. One may experience a real thrill at giving birth to forms, integrating pigments, chunks of clay, words or musical notes into forms which may or may not relate to the actual shapes or sounds of our physical experience or to the traditional conceptualizations of the culture in which one has been born and educated. But, in the sense I am using the term, this is no more creativity than is giving birth to a baby reproducing the generic pattern of biological integration long established by the human species. To give birth to an entity or object organized by a formative power replicating its blue-prints *ad infinitum* according to a standardized procedure is to produce, not to create. Creation implies transformation, a definite act of radical reorganization by, or if it is a truly significant creative act, *through* a mind dynamized by spirit—the power said to forever "make everything new."

Spirit creates, culture reproduces. Spirit releases a new creative impulse which the creative-formative mind then objectivizes as *archetypes*. Spirit sounds forth the Tone, the AUM of a new cycle—or it may be a subcycle or sub-subcycle; mind concretizes the Tone into "forms of power." When personified by the Avatar, or the Hero whose great deeds anchor the ideal archetypal structure of the emergent new cycle, these magical forms become *prototypes*. These prototypal realities of the world of collective existence are then seized upon by the poet. His inspirited mind makes them into myths; and upon these myths (prime symbols which in turn become paradigms in the hands of concept-builders and institution-builders) a culture-whole is formed. Once formed, the culture gives birth to men and women who produce the immense number of objects and systems multiplying the original prototypes. This multiplying operation is productivity; whether in the field of what we call art or in terms of the production of an ever increasing variety of wares.

To be productive is of course a highly satisfying personal activity for the producer. Productivity has ample room for what we call originality, because an individual person can be *a new variation on an original theme*. The producer's mind can succeed in integrating new elements provided by his individual (and therefore relatively unique) experience into the basic forms established by the traditional prototypes. It can extend the scope of operation of a prototype—let us say, in music, a sonata form—by incorporating it into new element abstracted from his experience; and obviously the personal experiences of individual human beings gradually changes as the culture-whole evolves from infancy to maturity and eventual death.

This basic cycle of organic unfoldment is not the only one to consider. Within it subcycles and sub-subcycles operate. When these smaller cycles reach the seed-condition of their own life-span, new prototypes—outstanding personages—appear personifying in every field the essential character of new subcycles and revealing the new quality of living, feeling, and thinking to be demonstrated during their limited span of operation. New symbols and a new style of life are "sung" by poets and given generalized meanings by philosophers. These seed-men become the origins of new subsidiary developments, of variations on the primordial themes of the culture-whole.

Within the range of the periods of the culture's development which their activity has inspired, these seed-men are indeed "creative," but from the point of view of the culture-whole, their creativity is less characteristically different from the productivity of the rank and file of intelligent and mentally effective members of the culture, because it is less radically transformativve. It produces variations on themes already existing within the culture's field of concepts and symbols. They did not create the themes, they only developed one or another of their inherent potentialities. Such a process of development does not necessitate a catabolic form-destroying prelude, because a new variation on a theme does not do away with the theme's basic identity.

Thus one can say that there are several levels of creativity. Because all human cultures can be seen as successive variations on the great planetary theme, Man, the life-span of a culture-whole may be interpreted as a subcycle within the much vaster planetary cycle of the evolution of mankind. And if we wished to envision still larger cycles, we could speak of the evolution of the Earth as a planetary organism, of the solar system as a whole, of the galaxy. But then we would no longer deal with human creativity; we would have to think of divine creativity. The typically human organism and the human mind are able not merely to perceive, but to experience. Man, moreover, not only can experience a multitude of conditions and situations, he is able to communicate the meaning and value of what he has experienced. This can be done only through symbols which can most easily be transferred and developed. Myths are organizations of symbols. Algebra is a myth as much as is any religious cosmogony. Without man's mythopoetic capacity, there would be no human culture-whole.

In an advanced culture-whole the mythopoetic capacity takes on an extreme variety of forms, and once the process of individualization of human beings started in earnest, taking public sociopolitical and religious forms, a new factor began deeply to accept the human condition. The focusing of man's attention upon the individual, and the recently intensified concern of individuals and of society as a whole with the problems resulting from living and functioning as an individual are now producing very drastic stresses and strain within our Western culture and all that remains of ancient cultures. Tensions are generated which must be solved. They can be solved only by a reformulation, and indeed a radical transformation of "the Myth of the Individual" which has dominated our Western culture.

The Myth of the Individual

To use Spengler's symbolic statement, this myth has for centuries in Europe and America taken the form of the "Faustian man," and I have already outlined the main characteristics of what Spengler meant in formulating the type. Faustian man has led us to experience spectacular trips to the moon and the transformation of atomic matter into energy and deadly fall-out. He has spread his inventive genius all over the globe; but in so doing he has poisoned the Earth's biosphere. He has achieved these extraordinary feats by allowing every individual to pursue his anarchistic egocentric interests and his uncontrolled cravings for ever-increasing power and productivity. This has been done in the name of *laissez faire* and of a freedom whose scope man's ego was supposed to be able to define and justify. In principle the ego definitions were supposed to obey much talked about religious and ethical directives; but in fact these have turned out to be enforced only as window-dressing and mainly in order to keep a power-elite in control.

The global crisis we all are facing is a struggle between myths. Mankind is struggling to build a new Myth of the Individual. Mankind is in a prolonged crisis of parturition; and the odds for miscarriage are still high. It needs great poets to name and sanctify a new image of the individual—and perhaps first of all an Avatar to give to the slowly emerging ideal of the "new man" a substantiality which only a fascinating personification can give to an ideal. It must be "fascinating," because what is needed is a concentration of human energies upon one single image that for a time blots out all other images, as in the case of hypnotic trance.

The early Christians won over the might of Rome because their consciousness was hypnotized by the Christ myth: the most precious Son of God dying a horrible death out of incomprehensible love for each human being without distinction; thus "for me also." By this sacrificial love, I, you, every human being became sacralized, made valuable, made equal. What a vision, what a dream! In recent years the Baha'is who believe the Persian Prophet, Baha'u'llah, to be the Manifestation of God, Avatar for the New Age, have shown a similar faith which can truly be called "fascination." At all levels, the charismatic personages fascinate those who come in touch with them. If their charisma is not merely based on extraordinary vitality or personal radiance, if indeed it proves to be the manifestation of a transpersonal flow of creative power and not merely a passing answer to a superficial need of the people or of those who dictate collective fashions for personal gain, the charismatic personage and his or her deeds and words may become the foundations of a myth. But the foundations are not the entire building. On the foundations embodied in the Avatar's or the great Hero's life, the poet builds the visible and effectual form of the myth, while the philosopher seeks to convey its meaning to the community.

In nineteenth century America, Walt Whitman most closely filled the role of myth-creating poet for the ideal "New World" which fascinated millions of European immigrants. Jefferson, Lincoln, and many others contributed to the creation of the myth; the great millionaires of last century also brought living material to the formation and dissemination of the "American success story," a myth of great power to which millions of egos all over the world responded. Every historical period—every subcycle within the cycle of development of our Western culture and of the Greco-Latin and Hebraic cultures which not only preceded it but form with it a large coupling—has produced characteristic modifications and variations on the theme of "the individual." Some of these variations have ended in violent discords, others in strenuous and ineffectual modulations; and today we are faced with the awesome problem of dealing with the highly toxic products released into both the biosphere and the noosphere by the negative aspect of the forms Europe and America have given to the Myth of the Individual.

It seems unnecessary to restate here what has been said so many times concerning what these toxic results of our Western culture brand of individualism are. Our air, our homes, our cities, our newspapers, radios, and T.V. sets are so filled with them that for many people it is at times hard not to give up any attempt at creative transformation, so oppressed does one feel by a sense of futility and powerlessness. But this is precisely what one must not do or feel in a time of radical crisis and sociocultural catharsis. Carl Jung has vividly spoken of overcoming the "cramp in the conscious"; but there are other kinds of cramps to endure and allow to dissipate—spiritual cramps and gut-reactions. What today is essential for any potentially creative person (certainly a limited number, yet larger than one might think) is to stimulate in oneself the courage to see oneself and to act, in whatever way it might be, as myth-maker, as one of the small groups of individuals who are cocreating the new image of the individual.

How does one become cocreator of the new myth? Always at first by the individual manner in which one straightforwardly meets one's own crises within the context of the collective crisis of Western man. The myth-maker does not meet his crises in terms of strictly personal circumstances and idiosyncrasies; he sees in them symbols; he expands their meaning until they begin not merely to reflect, but bring to a personal focus, the crisis of his culture and, perhaps in the larger sense, of humanity. He lives a symbolic life. But it is the kind of symbolic life that fits in and gives meaning to a crisis situation; it is therefore a life of transformation, an alchemical life, a hierophanic life, revealing of the sacred nature of the world crisis.

Our world-crisis is "sacred" because it is a rite of passage and all rites of passage have a sacramental character. They contain, pulsating at their core, the power to make a new beginning—the power to re-create oneself, not as an isolated, lonely, and frustrated ego, but together with those who also have the vision, the lucidity of will, and the gut-strength to begin again, and by so doing to cocreate a new Image of Man, a new Myth of the Individual. This great myth is central to the development of mankind at least for the last twenty-five centuries. Every human advance, every new faculty human beings have developed, every spiritual realization, every truly heroic and creative act or pronouncement has revolved around and contributed, positively or negatively, to form the Myth of the Individual. Everything revolves around the meaning we give to the individual. If our Western world is in a state of potentially tragic crisis it is because our culture as a whole has not been able to sustain the image of individual selfhood and of autonomous self-reliant and responsible "parenthood" which had been rather imprecisely and only partially outlined by the spiritual and intellectual leaders of our Greco-Hebraic tradition. Many of these leaders failed to understand the possibilities and the problems inherent in the glorification of the individual and all its by-products at our present stage of human evolution. They either did not provide sufficiently strong and precise safeguards, or else they tried to force the nascent realization of individual autonomy and rational mind-power into the straitjackets of religious dogma and intellectual dependence upon an already perverted or misunderstood Aristotelian empiricism.

Therefore our task is to illumine and reformulate the image of the individual, to understand how and when it took form, and in terms of man's place and function on our planet) for what purpose we must disengage it from the ruts of a materialistic and egocentric Western tradition. By seeing the individual in a new and challenging light, as the lightnings of the present historical storm strike our collective consciousness, we may give it a new philosophical and cosmic, as well as practical and psychosocial meaning. Thus in the very midst of the crisis we may receive the revelation, and as poets we may incorporate it into the new myth for which an incipient New Age is waiting.

How then can we formulate, or at least evoke the new image? What is, essentially, the individual?

The Principle of Integration, ONE

In the "cyclocosmic" philosophy I have outlined in my already-mentioned book *The Planetarization of Consciousness*, I have used the all-capitalized term, ONE, to represent that universal principle and power responsible for the fact that energy is released discontinuously in *quanta* (or units of energy) and that existence is to be conceived in terms of *wholes*, of units of existence we call entities. We have seen that existence is cyclic. It operates within a defined and structured field of activity, whether this be microcosmic or macrocosmic, an atom, a human organism, a planet, or a galaxy. A cycle of existence begins with a creative Impulse, a creative Word or *Logos* which releases a limited set of potentialities, immense perhaps, yet limited. These potentialities will be gradually actualized through a process whose life-span is also limited.

But why should there be existence and cycles of existence? The fairly obvious answer is that potentiality implies the urge to become actualized. We can however, express this in various ways. We can speak of a metacosmic, ineffable God "desiring" to manifest the infinite potentialities of His nature, a difficult concept to picture except in the anthropormorphic image of a glorious Being who forever creates new universes as a human artist produces many works, all of which do not exhaust his creative capacity. We can also imagine some kind of "infinite Ocean of potentiality," out of which periodically (and perhaps also simultaneously) universes of concrete substance emerge, objectivizing immense spurts of energy and, after passing through long cycles of growth and transformation, collapsing and returning to the undifferentiated metacosmic state of potentiality.

If we think of a series of such universes, we cannot avoid conceiving the process as endless, and there could be no reason to think of an *absolute* beginning or end. The series is endless because every release of new potentiality should be thought to operate in both a positive and negative manner; there will be some entities who will succeed in perfectly actualizing the potentiality being released in the beginning of the cycle, others who will fail to do so and will drop by the wayside and decay as waste products. And our human experience makes it possible for us to see how in theory the process can work out, as any new discovery or cultural advance seems inevitably to lead to both positive-constructive and negative-destructive results. The very fact of existence implies a dualism of results: success and failure, seed-perfection and decay. Therefore, a new cycle of existence is periodically needed to give to the decayed elements—the humus of disintegrated leaves—a new chance to experience the state of *organic integration*.

What does organic integration mean if not the joining together of two factors: the power of integration we usually call "life" and the mass of earth substances taken from the soil as foodstuff? In metaphysical terms we speak therefore of spirit and matter. Existence manifests as fields of activities within which spirit and matter are in the process of being integrated. This process needs a structure of some sort to make it effective and to give it form, at whatever level of activity it might be. This form is the product of mind. *Spirit acting through mind integrates matter within the boundaries of structural fields of activity*: this not merely at the physical level, but at other levels of subtler or coarser types of matter. What we call the cosmos is such a structured field of activity; so is the planet Earth, the atom, and the human organism.[2]

A human person is a structured field of activity operating at several interrelated and interacting levels. In popular terminology one speaks of body, mind and soul, the word *soul* being given a rather ambiguous and uncertain meaning. At the level of the physical organism, the human body, we can distinguish *material elements* (or chemical substances) being organically integrated by a principle of integration, *life*, acting through *a structural web of lines of force* to which esoteric philosophy usually refers as the "etheric" (and in some cases the "astral") *field*—unfortunately also spoken of as a "body." Thus the three basic above-mentioned factors of "spirit, mind, and matter" are present, but they manifest in the special manner pertaining to the realm of "physicality"; and the "matter" factor plays a dominant role which colors the whole level of physical activity.

A human person operates also at a level to which we generally refer as that of mental activity. According to the esoteric concepts developed in all advanced cultures, but particularly known today in their Hindu formulation popularized by the Theosophical Movement, and later on by Hindu swamis and yogis, the mind-field of activity is also basically threefold. It has a spiritual integrating factor, a structure through which this factor works, and a substantial base which manifests as a kind of "mind-stuff," as yet mostly unperceived by modern scientists and investigators. At that level of mental activity the spiritual integrating factor is no longer "life" (as we know it at the physical level), but a power that sustains and unifies all mental activity. It is the power responsible for what we call "individuality" or the *I am*-realization. (I have referred to it in the past as individual Identity, or as the "individual soul," and to the field of mental activity as "the ideity field."). It is individual because "indivisible." If what we call in psychological terms a breakdown of the mind, split personality, or schizophrenia occurs in a human being, this does *not* mean that this principle of individuality becomes "divided," but rather that it ceases to be effective. What breaks down is the mental *structure* through which it operates, the breakdown of the structure either renders this operation impossible, or at least partially or temporarily suspends it. What we call psychological complexes, innate tendencies and, at a more collective or generic level, archetypes, refers to the structural aspect of the mind-field (or ideity field).

As to the level at which the Spirit-factor of the above-mentioned metaphysical trinity operates in a most central and dominant manner, we today know very little about its existence *per se*. We refer to it in a metacosmic sense as the three aspects of the Deity, of the three persons of the Catholic and the popular Hindu Trinity: Father, Son, and Holy Spirit, or Brahma, Vishnu, and Shiva. By so doing however, we only create a myth, the Deity Myth, which probably obscures rather than elucidates the operation of whatever it is that is responsible for the process of cosmic existence.

In the symbolic language of modern Theosophy and in relation to man's being, the trinity of principles at the level of activity dominated by spirit is that of Atma, Buddhi, and Manas. Atma refers to pure unconditioned Spirit; a "mere breath" without substance or identity (wrote H. P. Blavatsky) perhaps therefore pure Motion or rhythm. Buddhi gives to this rhythmic activity a substantial foundation—its involutionary aspect is divine creative energy; its evolutionary aspect is divine wisdom. Manas refers to the conditioning and particularizing principle of structure, and therefore can be related to—and, in a sense but not exactly, identified with—what at the level of the ideity-field is "individuality." In terms of the process of involution one may speak of it as the primordial desire to manifest. At the close of the evolutionary arc of the cycle it is the desire for individual existence which is the last obstacle to be overcome by the "individual soul" (and the mind it operates in) before reaching liberation or nirvana, the extinguishing of *all* desires.

What then do I mean by "the individual" with reference to the planetary crisis mankind is now experiencing and to the need for a new Image of Man?

The individual is the human being operating as mind integrated by the principle of individuality (the I-am principle)—ideally, mind in a harmoniously structured fullness of mental substance. But in order to understand the *function* such a mind and the principle of individuality operating at the center of its mandala-field are meant to fill in the total scheme of unfoldment of planetary existence, we should first of all consider the *place* they occupy in the scheme. Man, the individual, stands at the mid-point of existence. He occupies the "middle realm." He is essentially the intermediary and the mediator. His function is to bring together, to connect, correlate, and integrate spirit and matter.

What we have next to realize is that at the core of the three basic levels of cosmic activity—spirit, mind, and matter—the principle of integration, ONE, operates. It operates as pure, undifferentiated spirit, the Atman, in the transcendent field of spiritual activity; it operates as the I-am principle (the individuality or individual identity) at the level of mind; it operates as "life" at the level of organization of physical or chemical particles. It is the same principle at all three levels, a principle endowed with power. This power is irreducible and undefeatable; yet it may be challenged for long ages by solely mental beings who have cut their individualized will from the Spirit and are "all-ego." But these beings of total spiritual darkness inevitably face dissolution at the close of a more or less vast cycle of existence.

Individuality is power; it is the power of integration, ONE, operating through mind. But being in the middle of the dualism of spirit and matter, mind can be attracted by either pole. The I-am power centralizing the mind's activity can be so attracted, so fascinated by either spirit or matter, that it loses the sense of its essential function, which is to bring together, to firmly link and (eventually) to completely integrate these two poles of existence. The individual can become spirit-mad or matter-mad; and because at this time of racial evolution on our planet the forces of materiality are stronger than those of spirituality, it is far easier for the individual to be fascinated by the exciting play of material-biological energies than by the rarefied atmosphere of spiritual ecstasies and insubstantial bliss.

In the vitalistic age of tribal development during which human beings normally operated at the biopsychic level of activity and seed-multiplication (agriculture and cattle-raising), the human mind had mostly to be the servant of the power of life. But once the process of individualization began to affect the collective or public consciousness of mankind, especially in the Western world, what used to be bio-spheric norm: the real meaning of "fate" began to take a new character. The mentality of the whole culture became "materialistic" in a new, *conscious and individualized* way—in a destructive way. Mind, aware of its place in the universal scheme, turned away from it. Materialism became the betrayal of the individual's function.

The beginning of the process of individualization, which emphasized activity at the level of the mind, occurred long before our Western culture and the preceding Hellenic or Greco-Latin culture took form. The coming of the Promethean host had given to mankind *the possibility* of experiencing the mysterious fire of I-am-ness and of developing a structural capacity for "reflective" self-consciousness. But this possibility could only be realized under very rigid safeguards and within the precincts of sanctuaries; thus, in relatively rare cases, through initiations implying a transfer of function (and not merely power) from *Initiator* to long-tested disciples. But since the day of Buddha, and even more Christ, the process of individualization has begun to operate publicly and on a large scale. This is, twenty-five centuries later, the essential cause of the unrest our Euro-American culture has brought to the world and of the entire crisis man is facing. Unless this cause is understood, there can be no lasting solution to humanity's problems, to man's crisis of growth and, shall we say, to our *global menopause?*

Mankind is indeed facing a crisis similar to the "change of life" experienced by individual men and women in their forties or fifties. It is a biological and a psychosocial turning point. Both the individual person and the organizational character of human society are confronted with a radical change. This change has a truly planetary character. It implies the need for a fundamental reorientation of consciousness and a repolarization of human activity at the level of mind-activity; and the central problem is a re-evaluation of the meaning and function of individuality. The *feeling of being I-myself* must be given a new meaning. And perhaps the only way to consciously grasp this new meaning is to realize that the individual experiencing this I-feeling stands at the mid-point between spirit and matter. The very fact that we can say consciously and deliberately "I am" should reveal to us that Man, the individual, stands at the crossroads of existence, mediator between spirit and matter.

If we clearly and powerfully realize the character and meaning of this stand, we are potentially able to create a new Myth of the Individual. We can anchor the new myth in a metaphysical understanding of what this cosmic place of the individual entails. We can "see" Man as the archetypal manifestation of the crossroads of existence, and of the function of intermediary between spirit and matter belonging to whoever assumes such a position. If our "seeing" is clear and penetrating, we can deduce a wealth of images and symbols from such an experience in consciousness. These in their togetherness constitute the Myth of the Individual.

Gautama the Buddha extolled the Middle Way. Jesus presented himself as Son of Man and Son of God—thus as the point of convergence of the human and the divine fields of existence. In the Christ-Individual the two currents meet. This meeting is the substance of the Myth of the Individual. The new Image of Man is revealed in that meeting at the crossroads of existence. It *is* that meeting, which should lead to a merging. The philosopher may speak of the meeting of opposites, *la réconciliation des contraires*. The mystic may glory in the dialogue of I and Thou. The individual is the meeting, the dialogue that eventually may merge into the unison of the silence of a realization beyond all conceivable words and symbols. He is the symbol to end all symbols, because the individual is a lens through which, if the lens is clear and well-formed, ONE can operate. Man, as the individual, is ONE in its most complete, most integrating focalization; because, in the individual the wholeness of existence can be integrated and focused *in work*. This work is an activity that encompasses both the realm of spirit and the realm of matter. Through this activity compassion takes form.

Many, names have been offered to characterize the new Image of Man that is rising in the consciousness and in the heart of future-oriented creative persons in search of a focalizing concept for the work of transformation. What such a name should evoke is the deepest, most characteristic and most sublime function of Man—Man standing at the center of the cosmic interplay of spirit and matter, focusing through his translucent mind the universal Presence of ONE, the Integrator; Man, the Compassionate Individual, in whose plenitude all the polarities of existence are reconciled and merge in a magic Tone, whose vibrations stir in all beings, whether in heaven or earth, the will to transformation and to ever more encompassing wholeness.

12.

THE WORK OF CIVILIZATION

THROUGHOUT this book the contrast between culture and civilization has been stressed. Yet it should also have become clear that all cultures are carrier-waves for the vast, planetary, all-human process of civilization. Culture operates fundamentally at the level of life; civilization at the level of mind. Archaic cultures were almost entirely the product of a human type of biospheric activity in which mind played the devoted servant role. With the extensive and precisely controlled use of fire, a new type of culture developed. The focus of mental activity gradually shifted away from a state of total subservience to biological and emotional needs. As the mind sought, at first hesitantly, then more deliberately, to free itself and to operate at its own level, internal conflicts began to develop.

After the sixth century B.C. a new stress was placed on the Mind of Reason and intellectual processes structured by logic. The Greek culture came to extoll internal consistency in a type of rationalistic thinking rooted no longer in biology or personal psychology, but derived from universally valid principles of abstraction, generalization and classification. Later on, as minds long oppressed by dogmatic religion discovered in physical matter a most convenient field for the analytical activity of the mind, our Western culture, reaching its maturity, glorified the empirical and rationalistic methodology of modern science. This Faustian culture has been so pervaded with the restless spirit of civilization that it became utterly fascinated by research, invention, change at all cost, and even by a policy of planned obsolescence for its ever-multiplying products, a striking homage to the death instinct developing when the organic life-impulse begins definitely to deteriorate.

To clearly understand the character of the forms which the process of civilization takes as it affects the character and the development of culture-wholes, we have to realize that the patterns controlling bio-cultural activities are essentially static; they have a high degree of inertia, thus of resistance to change. Tribal life has a basic *solidity* that matches the massive strength of mountains, the ponderousness of earth, the unvarying ascent of redwoods and pines—a regular, unchanging kind of coherency and consistency. Cultural inertia manifests as the stubborn will to retain, on the basis of genetic exclusivism and in a specific land-area, a collective structure befitting a more or less definite group of people. We have also to realize that at the level of spirit a similar type of resistance to change operates; only there instead of "solidity" we should speak of "solidarity."

The term *spirit* has a variety of meanings. When I speak of the realm of spirit, differentiated from that of mind and of matter, I speak of a level of existential activity, not of some abstraction without form or substance. A cosmic cycle begins with *a release of spirit*. What is released operates as power, form, and substance. Similarly a vegetable seed is a mass of substance having a definite outer form and an internal structure—the potentiality of the future plant—and is animated by an at least latent power of life ready to operate according to a generic plan. The seed must protect itself from anything that could destroy its integrity or induce from the outside a mutation; the seed has inertia. So does the *alpha* stage of a cyclic process. It must retain its identity, unchanging and inviolate, so that at the end of the cycle it may become the glowing center around which the *omega* stage of the process will crystallize, as the symbolic perfect Diamond of fulfilled being; the Occult Brotherhood of which the Theosophist speaks; the Church triumphant (or Communion of the Saints) of the Catholic doctrine.

The "realm of spirit" is both *alpha* and *omega*; but it can also reflect itself at the middle-stage of human evolution (the *mu* stage) in the Avatar who, as Krishna states in the *Bhagavad Gita*, comes *to restate the original dharma* of this particular cycle of existence. Whoever exemplifies in his consciousness and inner being that original dharma (or seed-truth) lives in a state of solidarity with all those who have been and are in the same condition. "Solidarity" comes from the Greek word meaning companion. A true "Companion of the Spirit" is protected by the solidarity of each and all participants in the divine Companionship or Communion in the realm of spirit.

There is a profound difference between *earth solidity* and *spirit -solidarity*; but in a sense, at both levels an intense resistance to change operates. H. P. Blavatsky spoke of "inertia of spirit." At the tribal biospheric level, *blood* is the potent symbol of psychosocial solidity; at the level of spirit-activity, *light* is the symbol of solidarity—for light operates as a wave, even if, when that wave encounters matter, it can be seen operating as a myriad of particles.

In the preceding chapter I stated that mind, as it stands "in the middle" charged with the task of relating spirit to matter, can easily become so entranced by *either* matter or spirit that it forgets, and thus fails in its function of mediator and integrator. In that statement the term *mind* is meant to refer to the whole realm of mental activity; but there is also a kind of mind which, operating at the level of matter, is entirely subservient to the power of life. This life-serving mind is not the autonomous mind that can be a steady intermediary between spirit and matter. The mediator-mind must be impervious to the fascination which life-energies can exert upon it. It is the *mind of the civilizer*, of the individual who has reached at least a basic degree of independence from the biopsychic and psychosocial patterns—the paradigms and taboos—of the culture in which he or she was born and educated.

What differentiates "civilization man" from "culture man" is the actual development of the form of the civilizer's mind. This mind bases his thinking processes on fundamental principles and universal or archetypal truths. From these principles and truths civilization-man *deduces* the framework he needs for consistent and integrating thinking. On the other hand, culture-man stresses *inductive* procedures, for his mind is solidly, and often ineradicably rooted in facts of everyday experience. Both deduction and induction are valid for civilization-man, because he stands in-between spirit-born principles and matter-born sensations; his task is to correlate and integrate both. But—and this is a crucial point—the mind of the true civilizer is always open to the fecundation of the spirit; *Spirit in him takes the initiative*.

If his senses provide him with raw materials with which he has to deal in his life-work as an individual person, he seeks first of all to *orient his consciousness* toward the realm of spirit. He allows the revelatory power of spirit (what Sri Aurobindo calls the Supermind) to take form within his mind. That form could be an image or vision, a voice seemingly speaking inaudible words, or an irresistible impulse to act in response to whatever the situation requires; but if it is any of these, it should also carry the "signature" of the spirit within, otherwise what takes place would have to be considered a "psychic message," a *reflection of* spirit, not a *fecundation by* spirit. The clarity, purity, and reliability of a "reflection" depends entirely upon the quality of the reflecting surface; and in most cases this surface is usually only the type of mind operating mainly, if not solely, in the realm of matter. This is the realm where we usually find at work a personality not yet liberated from the pull of bio-psychological energies and from the pressures exerted by an ego whose inertia is matched only by its possessiveness and its passion for exclusive power.

What therefore differentiates civilization-man from culture-man is the nature, character, and operation of their minds. The mind of culture-man is "solid" but bound by the resistance to change of instinctual or traditional modes of biosocial activity, unless it is challenged by external forces and intertribal relationships. On the contrary, the mind of civilization-man is essentially dynamic, eager for transformative experiences, usually restless and at times scattered by a multiplicity of envisioned possibilities. In the civilizer's mind potentiality constantly (or at least periodically) presses upon actualized mental formations, impelling them to open themselves to the as-yet-unknown. This pressure manifests as the capacity for *creative ideation*.

This word, ideation, today is little used, but it is an essential symbol for the creative process of transformation of the human mind that so easily becomes set and enamored of his own past creations. This mental narcissism is responsible for the formation of schools of thought, set patterns of behavior, artistic *cènacles* or coteries, and indeed organized religions. Culture seizes the new ideas civilizaton creates and erects them into systems and truths endowed with permanent value. The civilizer "plays with" ideas; this is the *lila* (or Play) of the creator. His mind experiences ideas; while usually culture-man merely *thinks*. The civilizer's mind "sees"; the culture-man's mind cogitates and endlessly argues pros and cons. To see and experience at the level where ideas are spontaneously arising formations of "mind-stuff" requires inner freedom; the inertia of both the realm of spirit and the world of matter has to be overcome. The typical civilizer often is convinced that everything is possible, that he can produce miracles. This conviction differs from the belief of the God-trusting devotee (or mystic) who has an emotional faith that "*with* God everything is possible" because the inherently creative civilizer, in whose consciousness the fiery realizaton of a "mission" burns, *experiences his individuality as an Act of God through his person*. He *is* the possibility of creation of everything, but actually only of the things that are *needed* for the accomplishment of his mission. To him the spiritual life can be defined as thinking only the necessary thoughts, feeling only the necessary feelings, performing only the necessary deeds. He *is* that necessity. He is ONE in operation; but ONE is simply the everlasting, ever present, and protean answer to every need for integration. Where every duality exists ONE is at work; and all existence is duality.

This is what is meant in Mahayana Buddhism by the Bodhisattva's pledge of renouncing the final liberation of nirvana until "every sentient creature" reaches that liberated state. As long as anything exists, there is the bondage of duality—of spirit and matter. The Bodhisattva refuses to *identify himself* totally and irrevocably with spirit, for if he did so a mind of absolute materiality would inevitably have to balance his identification, and an at least relatively unresolvable dualism would be created opposing pure matter to pure spirit. The Bodhisattva refuses identification with pure spirit, but he accepts being an ever-open, ever-ready channel for the integrative operation of ONE. He is, however, no longer *a* particular individual, because he has become *the* archetypal Individual.

It has been said that the Buddha, having experienced the reality of nirvana, "returned" to teach mankind the truth that could liberate. But what returned was not Gautama, but Buddhahood in the form that had been built by an individual who had been given the name of Gautama. Even at levels of lesser perfection the civilizer nevertheless always *is* his work. To separate him from his work is to reduce him to the condition of culture-man, to make of him a worshipable personage, a "reverent." It is to force him into the framework of an ego, when the only framework that really befits him is the archetypal structure of the work he performed in answer to a collective need. He had first to experience that need within his culture-bound consciousness in order to be able to identify himself with the answer ONE is providing to that need; but if he is a true civilizer he has become totally and irrevocably that answer. He is no longer a culture-bound individual person; he is a person through whom the Individual, ONE, freely operates. He is the process of civilization at work in a particular place and at a particular time. Upon all he touches he bestows the potentiality of self-transformation; and this bestowal implies as well, for whomever has been touched, the *responsibility* of actualizing the revealed potentiality in the world of persons and cultural relationships.

It should be a conscious, deliberate, and unswerving response; and such a response demands courage and the mobilization of will. It demands action, clear and well focused action. And there can be action at other levels than that of muscular physical activity, even though all activity—even that of thinking—involves physical and to some extent muscular processes. The civilizer is a man of action. He is a "warrior" even though his weapons may be only ideas and art-forms, plus the contagion of faith and vision he may focus upon those he attracts by the light and warmth of the fire of ONE burning within his compassionate mind. He is the true Noble Man ever ready to fulfill his function and his responsibility to whomever is attracted to his realm of consciousness and the charismatic emanation of his being—because he *is* that function, whatever the character of the function may be.

The function of the civilizer may have any character, because an answer must be as varied as the needs of the many types of human beings in the world of culture. Always, however, it implies *piercing through* the conditions characterizing either the biopsychological or the psychosocial realms of human existence. Such a breakthrough demands both a lucid mind and a well-tempered and effective will. Will alone cannot produce the needed results, because it is only an instrument. It is like a sword; it will cut or pierce only in the direction given by the hand holding it and the mind controlling the hand. A hand uncontrolled by an enlightened mind and obeying only the impulses of emotions, however inspiring and beautiful these may be, cannot be a true civilizer's hand. It will fail even if it calls upon what men call "love" to overcome the will of ego-dominated and ruthless individuals who represent the shadow aspect of civilization and are always ready to materialize the vision of the light-radiating civilizer and confuse or seduce his followers.

The enlightened mind is the mind that fully and irrevocably accepts the function of agent of ONE, the universal power of integration. It pierces through duality by accepting the inevitability of opposite polarities, the chiaroscuro of existence. It uses light and dark to produce forms into which it instills the quintessence of meaning whence arises the revelation of purpose. But meaning and purpose can take an expressible and operative form only if realized within an all-encompassing frame of reference. The essential function of the civilizer is to present such a frame of reference in relation to which the individual person may discover *where* he or she stands. Such a discovery may then lead to a significant and effective realization of *who* is standing, and for what purpose, thus, *why* there is at that place *a* being, rather than nothing.

Thus, as we conclude this volume, we return to the questions with which it began: Where do we stand, now, in relation to our culture? Who are we, and why are we here standing—or perhaps reclining in doped semi-slumber, dreaming of the beyond of existence and of illusory nirvanas?

It is our relation to our culture that will define for us our concept of civilization, whether we see civilization as a Spenglerian nightmare, or as the New Jerusalem, the Holy City, in which the perfectly formed Mind finds a cosmic and hieratic manifestation. As is our understanding, so will be our acts—and thoughts are potentialities of action.

If we accept the ordinary way of life characterizing the megalopolis as the only possibility of determining our individual responses to human existence and interpersonal relationships within the deteriorating field of our culture-whole, we will inevitably open ourselves wholly, even if reluctantly, to the poisons of city-living; slowly or rapidly we will die from them, divorced from the reality of spirit, even if lulled to comfortable dying by the drugs of success or of religious respectability and naive faith. On the other hand, if we react emotionally and blindly against megalopolitan values we have come to hate, we may escape from their miasmas only to see our individuality dissolve into various types of return to Mother Nature, or fall asleep while holding the illusory hope that some day we shall be reawakened by some new "second Coming" leading us to a Promised Land of milk and honey. History, past and present, should make us wise about Promised Lands and what happens in them, but it is easier to bounce along unconcernedly and refuse to know the past!

We can nevertheless so clearly understand the state of our culture, and realize the potentiality of development and action inherent in our living, now and at the very place where we are standing, that we may see ourselves as agents through whom a vaster rhythm of existence could and would operate if we were not merely open and ready, but, what is more, steady in our willingness *to let it operate*. This vaster rhythm is the planetary all-human process of civilization. The existence of such a process does not deny or impair the validity of culture, any more than mind denies the validity of life. Culture is, I repeat, the carrier-wave of civilization; and life establishes the foundation upon which mind is able to operate in human beings.

At every level and in every mode of existence, mind is formative power. But the forms created by mind may be filled by the binding and dark energies of life or illumined by spirit. Human relationships may operate according to the biological, organic and tribal order, or they may unfold their potentialities of harmony and meaning according to the companionate order. Mind may give form to the pure unitive activity of spirit, or to the compulsive drives of instinct-driven and emotionally blind human beings. The creative artist may attune his or her power of visualization and intonation to the universal rhythms of the Music of the Spheres; or as servant of men who at any particular time constitute the ruling aristocracy of the culture-whole, he may be satisfied to produce the repetitive forms glorifying the particular style of the century or even the fast changing fashion of the year—and by so doing acquire fame and in some cases wealth.

To face at all times two basic alternatives is man's inherent destiny. Because of this, human life (when it ceases to be totally and unconsciously controlled by biological energies playing their fateful drama of birth, growth, copulation, and death) is a life of crises that can be resolved only by consciously meeting them and making of them catharses leading to creative transformation and reorganization at a higher—because more encompassing—level of consciousness, meaning, and purpose. Through crises courageously accepted and lucidly understood within the framework of some larger process, culture-man proves his creative stature to himself and to his world. He emerges as civilizer and myth-maker. His whole individualized being may become a poem celebrating Man's essential function as integrator and revealer of meaning.

REFERENCES AND NOTES

2. Culture-Wholes and the Process of Civilization

1. On pages 209 and 210 of the Abridgement of *A Study of History* (Oxford University Press, 1947) Toynbee discusses the two "stock answers" to the question of "the relation in which societies and individuals stand to each other." One of the answers is "that the individual is a reality which is capable of existing and of being apprehended by itself and that a society is nothing but an aggregate of atomic individuals. The other is that the reality is the society; that a society is a perfect and intelligible whole, while the individual is simply a part of this whole which cannot exist or be conceived as existing in any other capacity or setting." And he finds that "neither of these views will bear examination." He dismisses the "atomic way of life" attributed by Homer to the Cyclops on the basis that "in fact no human beings have ever lived Cyclops-fashion, for man is essentially a social animal inasmuch as social life is a condition which the evolution of man out of sub-man presupposes and without which that evolution could not possibly have taken shape." Toynbee rejects also Oswald Spengler's concept of *Kultur* (a term which he translates as "civilization" thereby missing an essential point) as an organic form born out of the formless primitive psychic conditions of an undifferentiated humanity, as a mighty soul which comes to flower on the soil of a country with precise boundaries, to which it remains attached like a plant. He rejects this "organic" concept as he dismisses as "myth-making or fictional infirmity of the historical mind . . . the tendency to personify and label groups or institutions—'Britain,' 'France,' 'the Church,' 'the Press' . . . and so on—and to treat these abstractions as persons." He adds that "it is sufficiently evident that the representation of a society as a personality or organism offers us no adequate expression of the society's relation to its individual members" (p. 211). He sees a society as "the product of the relations between individuals, and these relations of theirs arise from the coincidence of their individual fields of action. This coincidence combines the individual fields into a common ground, and this common ground is what we call society . . . Society is a 'field of action' but the source of all action is in the individuals composing it."

We shall return to the relationship between individuals and their society in a later chapter, but it seemed valuable to point out early in this book what I shall call the *Myth of the Individual*—the individual person considered as a starting point, a source *from* which creative activity flows. The Creative individual of course is a source, as the French philosopher Bergson indicated in a passage quoted by Toynbee in support of his ideas. But while the source is the starting point of a river, the water flows *through* it rather than *from* it. This water in most cases comes from an underground reservoir, lake, or water-table. The source and the river constitute only specific phases of the vast *planetary cycle of water*—ocean, clouds, rain, underground water, source, river, and ocean.

Toynbee, Bergson, and the personalist Ian Smuts (whose book *Holism and Evolution* popularized the words *holism* and *holistic*, yet is hardly ever mentioned by the persons now using those terms) are modern exponents of the type of *empirical and rationalistic individualism* characterizing European culture and leading to the glorification of the genius—or of a "creative minority"—in a *personal* sense. In the approach I am presenting here, the creative person—whether individual or collective (as an "aristocracy")—is understood to be a source *through* which the answer to an existential human need given by a metabiological and transpersonal Power (in whatever way it is precisely conceived) takes a focused and formed external manifestation. That answer-releasing and activity-inspiring Power is *not* an abstraction; nor is it a personification. It is the very real spiritually fecundating principle at work in the process of planetary and human evolution. Humanity itself, in its global totality, is an "organ" of the planet Earth, which in turn belongs to the solar system (the "heliocosm"), itself but one small constituent in the immense cosmic cell, our Galaxy.

This is the holistic view of the universe and of Man. A "holarchic" principle infuses all experience. The universe is a hierarchy of wholes, of structured systems or fields of activity, operating at several levels. Before such a world-picture the naive classical Greco-European concept of "the individual" pales into insignificance. It reflects the empiricism of a Renaissance, reacting violently against the rationalism of the Scholastics, and the dogmatic exclusivism of the medieval Church whose real character was revealed by the Papacy's dependence upon military force and by the Inquisition.

There is nevertheless a sense in which Toynbee and his supporters are right in denying to a human society or culture the character of an "organism." A living organism originates in one single cell—a seed or a fecundated ovum. The organism develops through *mitosis*—the process of division of each cell into two new ones. Thus each of the billions of cells of a human body is directly related to the one original ovum in the mother's womb. This biological process of self-multiplication operates at the level of *physical* matter.

It is quite evident that a society does not develop in such a manner, in spite of the Adam-Eve myth according to which all human beings would have a common ancestry. Yet it is also clear that the members of a tribe, operating within a fairly narrow environment and increasing in size through intermarriage and the conquest of other tribes, come to have common genetic characteristics as well as common social features derived from common experiences in that special environment. Moreover, from my point of view, it is *the culture-whole, rather than the group of socially related human bodies*, which constitute an organic field of activity; and at the root of this culture-whole—that is, of a complex system of symbols, ideas, feeling-responses, and institutions—we could find one and usually two fundamental psychospiritual impulses which act as "parents" of the culture.

One can of course insist that the word, organism, should be kept to characterize *physical* organizations of cells issued from two male-female parental cells.

One could object to the vitalistic use of terms such as "the One Life" when referring to the dualistic Yin-Yang principle animating or ensouling the entire cosmos. Yet when science tends to accept the "Big Bang theory" to account for the origin and development of the universe, it does not seem too far-fetched to think of this universe as an "organism" originating in one sudden release of energy-substance. I therefore am using the term *organism* to mean a structurally self-regulating system of interrelated and interdependent activities operating at any level.

2. cf. particularly *Modern Man's Conflicts: The Creative Challenge of a Global Society* (Philosophical Library, N.Y. 1948, but written in 1945-46 and before that in my book, *Art as Release of Power* (1928-29) the chapters "the Cycle of Culture and Sacrifice" and "The Individual and the Work of Civilization"; also several essays (particularly *Toward the Unanimistic State*) and the unpublished large volume *The Age of Plenitude* (1941-42).

3. Biblical scholars explain what superficially seems to be two "Creation myths" by saying that each came from a different cultural-religious background. Such an explanation satisfies the empirical and factual approach dogmatically pursued by our factories of data-processing which we call institutions of learning. It is of no real importance when one tries to uncover the *meaning* of human existence and evolution. It is such a meaning that the Sacred Books of any culture "re-veal," presenting it "under the veil" of myths *essentializing* the existential historical facts. Events of themselves are meaningless. Man gives them meaning by establishing relationships in depth between them. A myth is a series of deliberately interrelated facts, which, in their holistic coherence and "organicity" evoke in the open and ready mind a complex and basically transformative meaning. This meaning satisfies a vital emotional or intellectual need.

The first two chapters of Genesis, as all occultists should know, reveal their meaning through a consideration of the Kabalistic values of letters of the Hebrew alphabet and of their combinations in words whose significance differs according to the level at which they are read and understood. This is a highly complex study, and Kabalistic interpretations may greatly differ in substance, though based on the same principles. In my book *Fire Out of the Stone: A Reinterpretation of the Basic Images of the Christian Tradition* (Servire Publications, Wassenaar, 1963), and in the chapter "Creation and Evolution" I discussed at length the relation between the two stories narrated in Genesis 1 and Genesis 2. The first chapter tells us about what occurs at the level of *organization of creative thought* in the mind of the Creator. When the creative process being considered refers to the creation of a cosmos by the Divine Mind, what is spoken of are Archetypes, or we might say "models" defining the essential proportions and qualities of the factors of which the evolving concrete and physical universe will become a gradually more perfect manifestation.

A "creation in *mind*" always, consciously or not, precedes a "creation in *life*." The latter reflects perfectly in theory, but in practice only embodies more or less accurately, the elements of the former. The second chapter of Genesis refers solely to the creative process as it occurs within the Earth's biosphere. This process operates at a material biological level; it deals with the "dust of the ground" and the "breath of life" which Yahweh breathes into man's nostrils. Man becomes a *living soul*; but as such he is only a passive reflection of divine Nature, which at that level is Life itself. Yahweh is the god of Life, ruling over all biopsychic processes.

In the center of the Garden of Eden *two* trees grow, the Tree of Life and the Tree of the Knowledge of Good and Evil. By partaking of the fruit of the latter, Man, who by that time has become the dualistic entity Adam-Eve (or more significantly Ish-Isha), enters the world of existential duality—the world of choice between alternatives and of personal responsibility. He-she are on their way to the state of individuality, later symbolized in its absolute supercosmic aspect as I AM THAT I AM, the Name of the Creative Principle operating at the level of personality-integration and (in Jungian terms) of individuation.

4.   The original end-purpose of yoga and the deeper goal of the martial arts in China and Japan—in which the student of higher grades must be choked to death, then revived by his master-teacher—were to experience death and return to the body with a consciousness transformed by such an experience. In my opinion at least, Hindu yoga developed out of the experiences of the "Forest philosophers" of the early Upanishads period. According to the life-system codified in the Laws of Manu, during the last of the four stages of his life-span, the man of higher caste retired in the woods surrounding his village and, by detaching his consciousness from all the biological personal and social activities and interests to which he had been attached in the performance of his dharma, prepared himself for the transition into a transcendent metabiological and supercultural state which we know as "death." Eventually after a long period of nonmanifestation and absorption into the universal ocean of being, the unfinished business (karma) of the preceding life would reactivate the Soul-entity and impel it into a new body.

It must have occurred to some of the Forest-philosophers that, if through death, they could experience the transcendent after-death state of consciousness, and *then* return at once to the *same* formed body and its mature mental faculties, a step of tremendous significance would have been made, throwing a new supersensual light upon human existence; and that light would revolutionize philosophy, psychology and, in fact, the whole of man's culture. To this end the idea of *pranayama*, which literally means "the death (or suspension) of the breath," was developed into a definite and graduated practice; it was based on the archaic belief that the breath is the essential spiritual factor—the animating principle—in all living entities. The ability to experience states beyond the death-transition led to the realization of a condition of nonduality (*a-dwaita*; not-dual) transcending the level of life and all modes of existence based on the interaction of two polar principles.

3. The Cycle of Man According to the Symbolism of Number

1.   I have discussed this point in my recent book *Occult Preparations for a*

New Age (Quest Books, 1975) and to some extent also in the chapter "Fire vs. Seed," in *We Can Begin Again - Together* (Omen Press, Tucson, 1974)—a chapter mainly reproducing material published in a long out of print volume *Modern Man's Conflicts*: The Creative Challenge of a Global Society (Philosophical Library, N.Y., 1946-48). All developed societies embody a dualism of agriculture and industry. Agriculture is based on the power of Biological self-multiplication within the vegetable and animal seed—one seed being able to produce a harvest of similar seeds. Industry is founded upon the use of fire and heat in the process of giving specific and utilizable form to raw materials, and of transforming or transmuting them. The two types of activity can be symbolized respectively by Adam and Prometheus, or Abel and Cain.

2. The negative aspect of the civilization process when it produces large cities and agglomerations of lonely and insecure atomistic individuals without communal roots manifests at the biological level in characteristic diseases. The pioneer in the development of so-called "electronic machines" for the diagnosis and cure of diseases, Dr. Abrams, based his system on the concept that all illnesses could be found rooted in three fundamental diseases representing radical alterations of the life-force in the total biopsychic human organism. These diseases—syphillis, tuberculosis, cancer—need not manifest at all in terms of visible physical symptoms, but they exist at the level of "etheric" vibrations in the electromagnetic field of which the body represents only the physically material part. They may never manifest as visible illnesses, but a variety of secondary diseases are, as it were, their stepped-down manifestations or by-products. Hahneman, the founder of homeopathy in the early nineteenth century, had a similar theory referring to what he named "miasmas."

Following Abram's lead I related these three root-diseases to archetypal perversions at the mental (syphilis), the emotional (tuberculosis), and the strictly material-cellular (cancer) levels of the total organism of personality. If cancer is given so much prominence today it is because the negative aspect of civilization in the Western world has poisoned so many of the material substances of the biosphere, and the human body breathes and feeds on such deteriorated chemicals. Tuberculosis spreads most easily in social or personal situations involving great emotional tension and the breakdown of a person's or group's allegiance to ancestral beliefs and the sense of ego-security these bring. Syphilis seems to be spreading mainly in city-aggregations when the abuse, misuse, and perversion of sexual energies results from the atomistic and alienating type of existence to which individuals are subjects. Various skin diseases and inflammatory processes are the secondary or tertiary manifestations taken by that root-disease.

Dr Abrams claimed that smallpox inoculation introduced in the etheric body the syphilis vibration; more recent inoculations may have similar or different results. Abrams was fond of a pun he often repeated: Modern man may think of himself as civilized. One thing is certain: he is thoroughly syphilized.

3. In the Bhagavad Gita, the Supreme Spirit of human incarnation, states in chapter 10: "I am the beginning, middle and end of all cycles." On the other hand in the New Testament, Christ refers to himself only as the alpha and the omega,

the beginning and the end. The difference seems to be most significant, because Christianity devalued the existential middle of a cycle—its physical manifestation in Earth nature. The beginning and end of a cycle respectively constitute its spiritual and sacred origin in the creative Act (or Word), and its final consummation in terms of the Company of the Perfect, the White Lodge of Theosophical doctrines or the "Church triumphant" of Catholicism. Yet the deepest meaning of Christianity resides in the belief that God can incarnate, and has incarnated, even in the midst of an inherently sinful human nature. The tragedy of Christianity results from the idea that this divine Incarnation happens only once in human history. Popular Hinduism believes it occurs at the very close of all great cycles, providing a spiritual foundation for a new cycle; and the more esoteriiae etaphysical Hindu doctrines claim that the possibility of incarnation—or "descent"—of the Supreme Spirit can be realized in any individual person having reached an adequate state of development.

4. The terms *wilderness, garden, and castle* have a deep symbolic meaning as they refer to fundamental levels of human consciousness and man's attitude toward nature and society. Because all that refers to city life dominates the consciousness of human beings, and many people react to the artificiality and standardization of such an existence, "wilderness" has been given a glamorous meaning and the "life of nature" has been extolled at the expense of what the garden symbolizes. Thus a confused picture of the evolution of consciousness floats in the minds of emotionally disturbed and biologically frustrated people dreaming of adventurous safaris and of the exaltation which the "great wilderness" is supposed to inspire.

Actually a dialectical sequence in the successive basic approaches of man to nature, and in general the biosphere exists; its three terms should be well understood. These are: wilderness, productive fields, and gardens. In its truly wild state the biosphere is anything but friendly to human beings. If, during the summer, one goes to the Canadian forests below the Baffin Bay (north of Montreal) one finds oneself in an immense vastness in which small trees without enough space to grow big stand in crowded confusion in a very damp soil on which the snow has barely melted. Mosquitoes and black flies pullulate. Every few miles a river or narrow lake is found. There are no habitations except along the northern railroad line, and no road beside the tracks. When I was there, some forty years ago, I felt that the presence of man was totally unwelcome, and I was swept with a sense of the meaninglessness of man lost in such a wet inhospitable wilderness. An even stronger feeling would undoubtedly be experienced in Amazonian or African jungles, or in the wintry Antarctic or the Sahara.

Life in the biosphere is rough, cruel, totally uninterested in any *individual* organism, be it vegetable, animal, or human. What we call "life" operates on the basis of the law "eat or be eaten." The ideal of "reverence for life" is senseless in the wild state of nature. Life is violent and brutal, even if at times it can be exquisitely delicate, tender, and pervaded with glamor and possibilities. It is interested only in maintaining *as a whole* an intricately complex biospheric balance and symbiotic harmony; it cares not at all for what happens to particular single specimens, only to the species. When biospheric conditions change many species disappear. Other species may profit from their disappearance, but nature itself certainly is totally indifferent to their fate.

Only man may care; but even he not at first! He confronts the life of the biosphere with his mind, and in the seemingly totally unequal encounter the incredible, puny David stuns and makes a slave of Goliath, the life-force. He cuts trees, dries up swamps, irrigates deserts, and develops *productive fields*. He cultivates the soil; and soon develops a particular culture (and cults) which, like the particular type of cultivation he develops, takes form out of the pressures and opportunities of a particular soil, geography, and climate—and other magnetic and psychic types of conditioning.

While in the wilderness life's drives for survival, expansion, reproduction, and constant adjustment dominate, and the few relatively isolated groups of men can only adapt themselves to overwhelming pressures, in cultivated fields and energies of nature are the servants of men working in cooperative groups and societies. These energies are given *a human meaning* inasmuch as they are made to serve a human purpose and to satisfy human needs or wants. Unfortunately, this stage of antithesis (man's dominance) following the stage of thesis (nature's dominance), sooner or later takes on a character which gives it a negative meaning. The human master works his slaves so cruelly that they become ill; contagious diseases spread among them which in turn make the master ill and may destroy him and his grandiose unrealistic dreams. Generally speaking, in a dialectic process the stage of antithesis can be ultimately successful only if it reintegrates the once abandoned values of the thesis within an all-encompassing synthesis, a fact which as yet mankind has neither truly understood nor incorporated in systems of logical or social organization. When cultivating man understands nature and its wild spontaneous rhythms, he is able to build gardens.

A garden, in the ideal sense of the term, is the result of the cooperation of man and nature. In a garden there should be an area of controlled wilderness as well as cultivated fields and orchards. Ideally there should be bird sanctuaries. Everywhere man's genius should help nature to produce in the most constructive manner *and in terms of life's own values* what is latent and potential in its seeds. Thus the whole Earth could become a garden, which in a sense would reproduce the ideal preexistential state symbolized in the Bible by the Garden of Eden.

At the center of a garden man builds his home which, in the aristocratic tradition of a hierarchized society, is often symbolized by a castle. It should not be a fortified castle, but a structure made of translucent materials through which *light* penetrates into the man's inner being. It is this same light which, in *biospheric* terms, initiates the process of life. In terms of mind, it illumines the consciousness of the man who, because he neither fears nature nor is willing to be dominated by its unconscious and compulsive drives, has established a harmonious coexistence with it. Such a man lives a "natural" life; but in that life nature has become *humanized*. Having transcended the pitiless and compulsive state of the wilderness, it operates as a concert of peacefully interpenetrating energies whose cyclic development at all times is attuned to the rhythms of the harmony of the divine state. Earth nature, fecundated and raised to a spiritual level by the illumined mind and the sacralized will of Man, becomes divine Nature.

4. Toward a Companionate Order of Relationship

1. The Preamble of the Constitution of the United States states: "We, the people of the United States, in order to form a more perfect Union, establish justice, insure domestic tranquility, provide for the common defense, promote the general welfare, and secure the blessings of liberty to ourselves and our posterity, do ordain and establish this Constitution for the United States of America." It enumerates six basic purposes, the six most significant manifestations of the common will of "the people." This will and the collective character of the people constitute the seventh principle giving to each purpose its essential orientation and inner drive. These purposes are therefore: union, justice, internal peace, common defense, general welfare, liberty. The order in which they are stated has a great deal of meaning. Interestingly enough "liberty" is last.

The first three purposes are the most basic, corresponding to the "higher trinity" of principles in Man, according to the occult-theosophical concept. There can be no individualized existence for a nation unless all its constituent parts are united; but union is spiritually meaningless unless justice prevails, for only then can there be "tranquility"; only a tranquil lake can reflect the harmony of the heavens, i.e., divine Nature.

The last three purposes polarize the first three; they are the results of what the latter make possible. Without union the people would not have the possibility of defending themselves against an enemy, real or imaginary. Without justice there could not be general welfare. And liberty can flourish only in a state of internal peace; for wherever conflicts rage, either one of the fighting sides will inevitably not only oppress the people of the other side, but will also deprive its own people of complete liberty.

2. There are two kinds of time and the basic opposition between the "sacred" and the "profane" approach to existence and social activity are discussed in a remarkable book by Mircea Eliade, *The Sacred and the Profane* (Harper Torch Books, N.Y.; first printed in 1957). In this book some of the concepts developed by Rudolf Otto in his epochal volume *Das Heilige* (The Sacred) published in 1917 are carried much further. The fact that in the mind of archaic man the sacred refers to the creative beginnings of a cycle of existence, and of the world in general, is given its full meaning. Sacred time is a kind of ever-repeatable and changeless time which man can recreate (or existentially regenerate) through rituals in which he assumes the role and often wears the mask of a creative god. In order to reexperience the sacred origin of anything man must return to the source of the process, the creative and magical Act or Utterance—thus the importance of what we now call the Myths of Creation found in every culture.

This is also the reason why so many occultists or religious people are essentially conservatives, in politics as well as in other fields. Instinctively—which means compulsively and often irrationally—their consciousness is drawn back and worships the "Great Ancestor," or "the Tradition," and, in America the Constitution established by "the Fathers" of our nation. The revivification by rituals or sociocultural ceremonies of the original Impulse given by human beings, who sooner or later after their death, are endowed with a *transpersonal* character, constitutes a *hierophany*—a revelation of the Sacred *hieros*). Whoever reveals the sacred Word from which every existential manifestation is derived is a hierophant.

The great symbols of any culture are hierophanic agencies; they "re-veal" (veil again in metaphors) the sacred character of life. As Eliade states (p. 211): "It is through symbols that man finds his way out of his particular situation and 'opens himself' to the general and the universal. Symbols awaken individual experience and transmute it into a spiritual act, into metaphysical comprehension of the world." Metaphysics so understood is an intellectual path following which the mind can break out of its familiar "house of consciousness" and enter the subliminal realm where the Images of the creative gods are still impressed as timelessly active memories of the sacred origin of all creative processes. As we shall see later, a truly great creative artist—and particularly the supreme Artist of the Art of living, the Avatar—should be regarded as a hierophant.

3. The word "companion" literally refers to men who "eat of the same bread" (*cum-panis*). Bread here symbolizes spiritual sustenance—the consecrated bread which is transubstantiated into the body of Christ by a sacramental act. In French Free Masonry the second grade is that of the "companions." They are no longer "apprentices"; they are now totally committed and self-dedicated to the Great Work. This is the crucial phase of the process, during which the most severe tests have to be met before they can be "masters."

4. *The New State* was published in 1918 by Longmans and Green in New York but has unfortunately been so long out of print that it is practically forgotten. M. P. Follet was a social worker in New England who tirelessly sought to bring together management and labor. She was influenced by her studies in England with the philosophers of the Oxford School who spread the concept of wholes and holism—particularly Bosanquet and Jan Smuts. *The New State* is a remarkable book which should be read by everyone starting a commune.

5. Form and Creativity

1. cf. H. P. Blavatsky's *Secret Doctrine* I. 274-275: "The whole kosmos is guided, controlled and animated by almost endless series of Hierarchies, each having a mission to perform and who are . . . agents of Karmic and Cosmic Laws. They vary infinitely in their respective degrees of consciousness and intelligence . . . Each of these Beings either *was*, or prepares to become, a man, if not in the present then in a past or coming cycle (*manvantara*). They are *perfected* when not *incipient* man . . . None of these Beings high or low, have either individuality or personality as separate Entities, i.e., they have no individuality in the sense in which a man says, *I am myself* and no one else . . . Individuality is the characteristic of their respective hierarchies, not the units."

2. cf. *Bhagavad Gita*, end of the Tenth Discourse (p. 76, William Q. Judge's translation): "I established this whole universe with a single portion of myself, and remain separate." And the Seventh Discourse (p. 55): "I am the cause, I am the production and the dissolution of the whole universe," etc.

3. A few years ago in a mountain village of French Switzerland I met men who, when asked why they were performing at different times certain operations on their grapevines, answered at once—as if surprised by the question, "Because the plants like it that way." The father of a French Canadian composer, Alfred Laliberté, who cultivated a small farm, including woods filled with various plants and bushes growing wildly, had an extraordinary gift for selecting leaves or seeds with medical properties. He scorned ordinary doctors and no one in his family ever remained ill. Once with his abdomen smashed by the hoof of a rearing horse he directed his wife to get a number of plants and to make with them a poultice he appled to the wounds. After a week of rest he left his bed, showing no ill-effects. He "knew" that some plants able to stimulate metabolic functions when collected in the spring could be poisonous when used at the beginning of autumn. Yet he could hardly read or write and hardly ever went to a large town.

4. Sins of omission, more than those of commission, are very often breeders of tragic karma. It is the action that is not performed, when the particular phase of the life-cycle required its being done through the form then available, which may cause the deepest disturbance in the evolutionary process, whether for mankind as a whole or for an individual person. According to the occult tradition which inspired the writings of H. P. Blavatsky, it was the refusal of spiritual entities to ensoul the crude bodies of human beings living on now long-disappeared continents when it was their function (*dharma*) to do so, which led to the appearance and growth of evil on a planetary scale. These spiritual entities, emerging from a cosmic night of consciousness, became aware of the animal-like forms into which they were called upon to incarnate and were appalled by the prospect. As a result of such a refusal these animal-like bodies gradually developed into distorted and often monstrous forms through mating with even less evolved animals. When, later on, the spiritual entities found themselves compelled to incarnate in the perverted bodies lest worse might happen, some of them became caught in psychic whirlpools of biological energies and, losing the consciousness of their spiritual essence, allowed these energies to deviate their will and infuse it with lust, ambition, greed, the roots of "black magic."

This may be a myth; but myths are the fundamental realities of human consciousness, as they reveal the meaning of archetypal and cosmic processes. Who among us, modern men and women, has not at some time failed to perform an action which seemed difficult, boring or unattractive, yet—even if we did know it—was so crucially needed that dire results followed? If a vacuum is left in a process of relationship, some other factor usually fills it, and the character and quality of relationship may change so drastically that tragedy may ensue. In the life of any truly aware and consciously responsible individual a moment usually comes when he or she suddenly realizes that a few words have been said or an act performed whose traces can never be erased. It is irreparable; the whole life, the whole universe perhaps, will never be what it could have been if this vacuum had not been created by the failure to do or say what one's destiny demanded at that precise time. Such a realization of irreparability can be traumatic. It may be at the root of spiritual regression or psychosis, even if the realization is at once blocked and made to sink into the inner abyss of the unconscious mind. And the human race also has a collective unconscious mind!

This is the real meaning of what has been mythified in the "original sin." This sin of Adam-Eve—mankind at the level of dualistic consciousness—was not the eating of the fruit of the Tree which, together with the knowledge of the polarities implied in *any* existential process, brought to mankind the polarization of birth and death; the sin was the manner in which the man and woman *reacted* to the feeling of the irreparability of the act which closed to mankind the world of divine unity, even if what they experienced in the Garden of Eden was only a *reflection* (indeed, a mirage) of the divine world. Adam and Eve were *afraid*! Fear is the ultimate cause of evil.

5.   In my book *The Pulse of Life*, first published in 1942, now in paperback (Shambhala Publications, Berkeley, CA) the character and meaning of the zodiac and of each zodiacal sign is psychologically interpreted in terms of the ever-changing balance of what I called the Day-force (Yang) and the Night-force (Yin). These two polarities manifesting in *any* existential cycle can be most significantly defined as the *personalizing* (or individualizing) and *in-gathering* (or collectivizing) aspects of the dynamic process (cf. p. 27). It is the ratio between their capacity for effective action—thus the state of their power -relationship—which, as it constantly changes, defines on any day (and particularly at every New Moon) the essential nature of the energy produced by the relationship of the Sun to the Earth.

6. The Magic Will and the Esthetic Experience

1.   One of the problems faced by the student of esoteric philosophy seeking to obtain a clear picture of the processes of existence and of what may transcend the concrete reality he experiences refers to the necessity of not confusing potentiality with actuality. The confusion is easily made because it derives from the most mysterious of all concepts, that of Time.

As already stated, whenever we think of a *process* time is necessarily implied, because a process refers to a series of successive phases, each of which demands a particular kind or mode of activity. Every phase of an organized process contains in potentiality the succeeding phases. The Mind that conceived and planned the entire process may nevertheless have, to some extent at least, "visualized" (an inadequate term) the whole process in one act of conscious "seeing." Thus, at the level of consciousness at which this visualization occurred the whole process, from alpha to omega, *is there*. But what does "is there" actually mean? It only refers to potentiality, not actuality. To say that it *is* confuses the issue.

Potentiality is neither "being" nor "not-being"; it is the relationship between them; or, in another sense, *That* which encompasses both, just as in Chinese philosophy Tao encompasses both Yin and Yang. For most living embodied human persons to say "I am a Soul" is a misstatement. He or she represents a corporified set of potentialities which, together with many other sets constitute the Soul. Only an Avatar can say "I am God" because it is God that, having become focused *through* his total organism, utters the words.

This is what I mean by the symbolic phrase "infinite Ocean of potentiality." If we try to imagine *That* out of which everything and every possible universe emerges we should only speak of an infinitude of possibilities, but if we believe that *all* such possibilities of existential forms *will be* actualized in an infinite multitude of universes, then mere "possibility" becomes "potentiality." What is only possible might not take place; but the word, potentiality, should refer to possibilities which sooner or later, in one section of infinite Space or another, *must* become actualized.

If we wish to personalize this infinitude of potentiality we can speak of Brahman or, to use Meister Eckart's term, the Godhead—the word *God* referring to the One Being out of whom an entire universe develops; yet during the life-span of that universe only one particular (even if immense) set of potentialities is to be actualized by the end of the cycle (the omega state). But such a personification places "above" the infinite Ocean of potentiality an *actual* Being whose nature is totally unconceivable once we try to forget the easy, too easy, analogy of an artist in whose mind the possibility of a cast number of works of art is contained which he may or may not actualize. The nature of such an absolutely supercosmic Being is unconceivable because he would exist with reference to nothing at all, and the idea of "being" with reference to nothing at all makes no human sense. Some may call it ineffable; others, absurd. Whoever tries to hold such an idea as a psychological compensation for too large a dose of rationality may nevertheless state, with St. Augustine, *"Credo quia adsurdum"* (I believe because it is absurd).

The concept of an infinitude of potentialities—which, in order to be actualized require an infinite amount of potential energy—is evidently not much more easily understood; but we can get a more visualizable picture of it if we think of a *diffuse state of energy* periodically reaching a condition of *focused activity.* Whatever it is that constitutes the ultimate Principle-Substance-Energy can be easily conceived in two alternating, yet also in a sense simultaneous, conditions: diffuseness and focused condensation. What is in a diffuse state of nonactivity "longs for" the focused condition of activity through a focusing Form. Mind then is the formative agency—whether it be the cosmogenetic divine Mind or the creative human mind.

This is what I call the cyclocosmic world-view. It is developed in some detail in *The Planetarization of Consciousness* and in a smaller volume *The Rhythm of Human Fulfillment*.

2. What is meant here by "life-consciousness" is the central point at which the essential power exteriorized in all the members of a biological species *meets and interacts* with the collective response of all the cells and nerve-centers of the organism to any particular existential situation involving numerous stimuli and biological needs. The type of "knowing" involved in the magical operation has also been characterized as *knowledge by identification*. One can speak of identification if one deals with the level of consciousness; but at that of activity it is more accurate to think of attunement. One may imagine oneself as identical to any living organism; but the imagination needs the cooperation of the feelings in order to be effectual. In order really *to feel one with* another person, an animal or a tree, one's life-center has to put itself in a state of resonance to the life-center of the other organism. This is very difficult if that organism is enveloped in a protective covering of armor. Knowing magically the Name of the other being is like seeing naked a human being with whom one wants to establish a vital communication.

The relationship of naked being to naked being has recently been used in nudism and group psychotherapy. Each participant ritualistically and symbolically drops his or her psychological coverings, and is compelled to relate to the others in a totally deglamorized and deculturalized manner. Because sex-relations can dispense with and shed the intellectual coverings of the speech which the culture and the words of its language have built, such relations may serve highly significant psychological purposes. Yet they do so only if the partners are identified with *each other as individual persons* instead of becoming totally submerged by the stormy waves of biological compulsions. They should accept fearlessly the release of the life-energy, yet ride consciously over its waves as these beat upon the shores of their material bodies, using the power of life for metabiological ends.

A true clairvoyant, able to clearly perceive the play of changing colors and forms in the aura of a person, experiences a kind of knowing which has a magical character. The person facing him or her reveals his emotional and partially mental nature as if devoid of all psychological and intellectual coverings. In another sense, which theoretically should reach much deeper, an astrological birth-chart should reveal to the astrologer the fundamental dharma (and karmic background) of the person. The exactly calculated birth-chart represents the *celestial Name* of an individual. It reveals to some extent the individual's character and destiny—and deeper still, what he or she is *meant* to accomplish as a focusing agent for the fulfillment of a particular need of the whole universe in terms of the particular moment and place of the first breath—the original act of relationship linking the newborn and the cosmos.

3. In his book *Eskimo* (University of Toronto Press 1959) Edmund Carpenter, a Canadian anthropologist, deals most significantly with the approach of Eskimos, who do beautiful ivory carvings, toward the fashioning of their sculp-

tures and in general toward all relationships. The following paragraph is particularly revealing:

> They enter into an experience, not as an observer but as a participant. The artist participates in seal-ness, becomes one with the seal, and thus finds it easy to portray, for he is now, himself, Seal. As the carver holds the unworked ivory lightly in his hand, turning it this way and that, he whispers, "Who are you? Who hides there?" and then: "Oh, Seal!" He rarely sets out, at least consciously, to carve, say, a seal, but picks up the ivory, examines it to find its hidden form and, if that's not immediately apparent, carves aimlessly until he sees it. Then he brings it out: Seal, hidden, emerges. It was always there: he didn't create it; he released it; he helped it step forth. He has no real equivalents to our word create or make, which presuppose imposition of the self on matter. The closest term means to work on, which also involves an act of will, but one which is restrained. The carver never attempts to force the ivory into uncharacteristic forms, but responds to the material as it tries to be itself, and thus the carving is continuously modified as the ivory has its say. It is their attitude not only toward ivory, but toward all things, especially people: parent toward child, husband toward wife. Where we think of art as possession, and possession to us means control, to do with as we like, art to them is a transitory act, a relationship.

7. Musical Form and the Inner Space of Tones

1. Such a sequence of chords is found in the music he composed for some symbolic drama written by Peladan, who professed to be a "magus" along Rosicrucian lines. Satie's *Prelude pour le Fils des Ecoiles* (Prelude for the Son of the Stars) which I had orchestrated was performed by the Pierre Mondeux orchestra in a festival of "Metachorie"—an abstract symbolical form of dance performed in a thick atmosphere of colored light and burning incense and following the recital of a poem, given in New York at the Metropolitan Opera in April, 1917. This was Satie's pseudo-mystical period, years before he began to write pieces with spoofy titles. I had met him early in 1914.

2. In our Christian-European culture-whole the great bells of cathedrals, and even those of village churches, performed a function in many ways similar to that of Asiatic gongs. In China these gongs often had the shape of a heavy and deep bronze bowl, the tone being produced mainly by striking the rim of the bowl with a thick wooden stick covered with leather. Such a hollow shape resembles somewhat that of our church-bells, but it is inverted, as the bell hangs from its bottom, and the sound is produced by a metal clapper hanging *inside* the bell and striking its interior surface when the bell as a whole is rather violently moved. It is usually moved by a man pulling, *from below*, heavy ropes attached to the top of the bell. Thus the gong is static in physical space, while the bell releases its tones when in a dynamic state. This is a significant and symbolic contrast, because our Western culture represents a dynamic of transition between two fundamental levels of consciousness: the biological (local and tribal),

and the metabiological (global and universalistic). It is this dynamic character which Spengler symbolized as the Faustian type of human being.

3. While the problems related to the ambiguous relationship between the classical concept of tonality (especially after the adoption of the equal temperament system of tuning musical instruments) and the Harmonic Series of fundamental and overtones are too technical to be discussed at length in this book, a few basic points can be stated. These may clarify some points mentioned in this chapter. The whole issue is ambiguous because it can be looked at from various points of view, if one attempts to correlate the acoustical facts with principles referring to the development of cultu.·e and civilization, to sociopolitical patterns of organization, and even to what we may surmise of the order prevailing in biological and cosmic processes of unfoldment of creative impulses.

The first point to consider is the difference between arithmetic and geometric progressions, because it has played a most basic role in the formation of musical series, at least since the sixth century B.C. and the days of Pythagoras. The prototype of all arithmetic series is the sequence of whole numbers starting with number 1. An arithmetic series is produced when number 1 adds itself repeatedly to itself. Thus the series 1, 2, 3, 4, etc. can be written 1, 1+1, 2+1, 3+1, 4+1, etc. On the other hand a geometric series is a progression of equal ratios or proportions and, in music, of intervals. The interval of fifth represents the ratio 3/2; thus a series of fifth (3/2 + 3/2 + 3/2, etc.) is a geometric progression.

These two types of series are extremely significant when philosophically and metaphysically interpreted, and in the past I have given much time to such an interpretation, my last attempt being an as yet unpublished volume *The Magic of Tone and Relationship* (1972). What is called in music the principle of Natural Intonation is derived from the Harmonic Series of fundamental and overtones; it was particularly stressed by a great, but unfortunately almost forgotten, English musicologist, Kathleen Schlesinger, who made deep studies of Egyptian and archaic flutes and other instruments. She believed that all archaic music was based on that principle. Theoretically, Western Tonality in the beginning was also based upon "natural" intervals, but when the system of *equal temperament* came into widespread use in the early eighteenth century, partly because of Bach's sponsorship, tonality lost its "natural" character.

Equal temperament is essentially a compromise between the natural intonation principle exemplified by the arithmetic series of fundamental and overtones, and the principle of geometric progression manifesting in music as series of equal intervals, particularly of fifths (for instance the interval C to G in our Western scale). In the Harmonic Series there is a community of origin, the fundamental; but no two intervals created by its successive overtones are ever equal. It is a totally hierarchical system. It seemingly refers to the manner in which an original creative impulse spreads into space, then to the differentiation of the one primordial energy into an increasing number of secondary, tertiary, quaternary, etc., modes of cosmic and organismic manifestation. The original differentiation refers to the mysterious process whereby 1 becomes 2 *before* the appearance of a universe. Existence implies a dualism of principles (Yin and Yang in Chinese philosophy, Shiva and Shakti in India) and thus polarity; thus the manifested existential universe begins only when the 2 appears. In the Harmonic Series the relationship 2 to 1 is the first octave interval.

The octave is, yet is not quite, an interval. The two notes marking its boundaries are given the same name, for instance C; they may be called C1 and C2, but in some nonrational or superrational way, they are considered to be *the same* note, though obviously they do not refer to only one sound, but actually to two, each with a particular pitch. The octave relationship is then not a true relationship or we might say that it is a relationship of *identity*; but strictly speaking we should not refer to relationship between two entities which are identical.

The first octave of the Harmonic Series symbolizes the precosmic relationship of the creative *Principle* (God, the Creator) to the creative *energy* it released. That energy then operates as the cosmogenetic power actualizing itself in level after level of substantial manifestation. The first level of cosmic actualization is reached in the second octave of the Harmonic Series—let us say by the interval between C2 and C3, if C1 is the fundamental. Within that interval the second overtone, G, occurs. It corresponds to number 3 in the arithmetic series of whole numbers; and the relationship 3 to 2—thus of C2 to the G above—is the interval of fifth. The following interval, G to C3, is the fourth. A fifth plus a fourth $(3/2 + 4/3)$ equals an octave $(2/1)$.

This second octave of the Harmonic Series contains therefore two unequal intervals, the fifth and the fourth; it can be said to symbolize the noumenal world, or the realm from which the most essential cosmic Archetypes emerge. Duality then becomes a cosmic *fact*. When conceived as the relationship between 1 and 2—between the Creator and His creative energy—it is only a superexistential metacosmic *principle*.

If we understand this we can get a basic idea of the relationship between the musical space of seven octaves and that encompassed by a series of twelve fifths. The seven octaves are levels of *activity*; the series of twelve fifths symbolizes the archetypal process of functional organization which gives *form* to a cosmic whole.

The series of fifths produces the twelve *notes* of our chromatic scale (C, G, D, A, E, B, F sharp, C sharp, G sharp, D sharp, A sharp, E sharp—which on the piano keyboard is F). The thirteenth note produced by such a series would be a B sharp; it concludes this series of twelve equal *intervals* of fifths, because its frequency (vibrations per second) is nearly the same as that of a C seven octaves above the C that started the series of the twelve fifths. Twelve fifths are greater by a small interval, called the Pythagorean *comma* (about one-eighth of a whole tone) than the span of seven octaves, and the seven octaves define a complete cycle of existential manifestation operating at seven levels of activity.

These series of octaves and of fifths constitute a cyclic or "cyclocosmic" whole. The types of activity symbolized by the two series exist in the cosmos and indeed in all living organisms, but they cannot be exactly equated. The cycle of twelve fifths, when seen in relation to that of seven octaves, is not a closed cycle. At all levels of existence, trying to integrate the two series is a difficult problem or organization; we might call it the problem of reconciling the need for a hierarchy of command and the equally meaningful demand of every participating unit within the organized whole for a fundamental equality—thus aristocracy and democracy.

This problem takes a complex technical aspect in music, and our equal temperament system of tuning is the solution adopted by European musicians. Chinese musicians and (possibly before them) Pythagoras approached the problem in somewhat different ways. Our classical solution consists in clipping from each fifth-interval one-twelfth of a *comma*, so that after the operation twelve thus "castrated" fifths exactly equal seven octaves. Equality thus lost to hierarchy; and at the same time the whole principle of natural intonation became adulterated. Only the octave notes retained their truly natural quality.

This compromise was necessary because of the gradual complexification of music during the seventeenth century and the Baroque period (a strange name, this "baroque," for originally the meaning of this French word was "queerly formed and extravagant"). The increasing use of "modulation" from one tonality to another, and an ever greater dependence upon rigid keyboard instruments were mainly responsible for the need to develop the equal temperament system of tuning; but these factors too have a profound significance and reflect the system of values which developed after and even during, the Renaissance. These values and the cultural transformation they introduced had in turn been conditioned by the dogmatism of the Catholic medieval mind and the Aristotelian rationalism of the Scholastic philosophers.

Twentieth century composers are most eager to break away from what the concept of musical classicism produced; but in so doing they but too often react as emotionally to the past as Renaissance individuals, who had fallen in love with most incompletely understood and sadly intellectualized Greek theories, reacted against medievalism. The two types of series (arithmetic and geometric) and their musical embodiments, the seven octaves of a Harmonic Series of fundamental and overtones and the cycles of twelve fifths, should have their places in music, just as the "organic order" and the "companionate order" are today indispensable factors in a wholesome social organization. Here again we are dealing with the relationship between culture and civilization—between "life" and "mind."

8. The Interaction of Civilization and Culture

1. In several of my books I have referred to a person's birthchart as his or her "celestial Name." While the names given to a child by his parents are conditioned by culture, religion and family preferences or external occurrences, the birth-chart establishes the relationship of the newborn to the universe surrounding the birth-locality. It is the time-space formula defining the particular biopsychic rhythm and organic characteristics of the new member of the human species as a whole. With its first breath the newborn begins a mutual relationship with his environment, a relationship whose vehicle is the air he breathes, air being the unifying factor for all biospheric organisms. The birth-chart can thus be considered the "signature" of the newborn individual's existence; but at first it refers only to *potentiality*. The birth-potential is to be actualized throughout

the person's life-span. Psychological or Humanistic Astrology seeks to interpret the cosmic birth-pattern and its year-by-year evolution in order to assist the would-be individual to concretely become what he or she potentially is; and this means to fulfill his dharma.

2.   The first volume of Oswald Spengler's epoch-making work, *Der Untergang des Abendhandes*, was published in Munchen, Germany in July, 1918. The author states that it was mostly written before 1914 and fully worked out by 1917. The second volume came out in 1922. An English translation of the first volume appeared in 1926 under the title, *The Decline of the West* (Form and Actuality); the translation of the second volume (*Perspectives of World-History*) was published in 1928. Both volumes were published by Alfred A.Knopf (Borzoi Books) and translated by Charles Francis Atkinson. A one-volume condensed edition was also published in 1932. Spengler was born May 29, 1880, and died May 8, 1936.

Arnold J.Toynbee's monumental *A Study of History* in six volumes was published, the first three volumes, in 1933, the others in 1939. The whole work contains over 3,000 pages. A very fine one-volume Abridgement by D. C. Somervell was published in 1947 by the Oxford University Press.

3.   There seems also to be a vast area of *intergalactic* space surrounding our Milky Way galaxy and within which many "globular clusters" are located. That area could therefore be called the Milky Way's aura.

4.   The Abridgement of Toynbee's *A Study of History*, p. 25.

5.   The interested student of esoteric traditions would find much interest in studying a now rare book, "A Collection of Esoteric Writings" by T. Subba Row (Bombay, 1910). An *Appendix* written by H. P. Blavatsky (p. 34 to 37) is particularly significant in relation to the original source of the "Wisdom Religion" undertoning most of the great occult traditions and the mysterious place she calls "Sham-bhala." The importance of the Hindu Kush has also been mentioned in a book by Rafael Lefort, *The Teachers of Gurdjeff*, Victor Gollancz, London, 1968, cf.p. 128 etc.).

6.   Mani was a Persian prophet who sought to reconcile Christianity with the old Zoroastrian religion. He was a remarkable person with deep spiritual insight, perhaps the first religious leader to speak of a succession of great spiritual Teachers, periodically appearing in answer to new human needs and revealing new basic concepts concerning the relationship between God and man and the way of spiritual attainment. Another contender for religious leadership in the East Mediterranean regions had been Mithraism, strongly entrenched in the Roman army. But Mithraism was presumably more a revival of old vitalistic attitudes, while Manichaeism seems to have been more future-oriented and more esoteric.

9. Rhythms of Culture: From the Sacred to the Vulgar

1.   The cultural achievements of the Celts have been strangely played down

by historians, perhaps because of a Germanic or Anglo-Saxon bias. In a small book of Irwin St. John Tucker, *The Martyr People* (Chicago, 1919) a very interesting picture of what the Irish Celts did for Europe during the centuries following the total collapse of the Roman culture can be found, though the book is certainly out of print. The following quotations throw a significant light on what occurred:

When the Celts got to Western Europe, ethnologists say, they found there a dark people with a powerful priesthood, a ritual, and imposing religious monuments; a people steeped in magic and mysticism and in the cult of the Other-World. The Egyptian doctrine of the immortals was far more cheerful than that of the Greeks or Romans; and from them the Celts took their idea of a glorious immortality, which enchanted the Romans. From the Megalithic people the Celts took the religion of the Druids and the mystic doctrines of that strange faith, which had its origin in prehistoric Egypt. All over Europe the Druids held their colleges, and tens of thousands of the dominant race of Celts attended their schools. The British Isles, and especially Ireland, were to the Druid religion what Rome is to the Catholic Church. But this religion was Celtic; it was never shared by the Germans.

In Ireland the Druid colleges had their greatest development. When the Gothic wave beat down the defenses of Rome, Ireland remained outside the circle of destruction. And as soon as the Gothic invasion began to settle down into some sort of rude order—changed epochally from that which had preceded it—the land of Ireland became the beacon-light of the new world. (p. 13)

It was the Druid priesthood which held the Celtic empire together. Among the Greeks and Romans it was loyalty to the City or the Republic which formed the bond of union. Among the Germans it was fealty, loyalty to a personal chief, which held the tribes together. But among the Celts it was this priestly order which formed their bond of cohesion. (p. 14)

Very soon after the preaching of Christianity in Ireland we find the country covered with monasteries, whose complete organization and vast enrollments seem to indicate that they were Druid colleges transformed. Already the arts and sciences and philosophy of the Druids, together with Greek characters and literature, and the elements of a Greco-Roman commercial education, were given in these vast schools. Their Christian teachers added another element to the superstructure already existing.

As early as the year 450, Prince Enda founded a college at Aranmore, which attracted scholars from the whole of Ireland. Findian of Clonard, living from 470 to 548, spent some time in Wales; then returning to Ireland he founded the famous monastary at Clonard, about the year 520, in which three thousand students are said to have received instruction at one time. His college consisted of countless huts of wattles and clay, or of beehive cells of stone, built by the pupils and enclosed by a ditch like a permanent military camp. The pupils sowed their own corn, fished in the streams and milked their own cows, like a highly modernized Agricultural college of the Middle West today.

Meanwhile, the whole of Europe was being laid waste. In the year 406 hordes of Vandals from the upper Rhine invaded Gaul, ancient Germany, and Burgundy, and settled on the left bank of the Rhine, while the Huns under Attila made inroads upon these, and the Franks from the Lower Rhine burst into Gaul, making an end of Roman rule in that country. Angles and Saxons had devastated Britain, and what remained of Roman civilization in Upper Italy under the Heruli and Ostrogoths was destroyed by the Langobards and their allies. So vanished in the sixth century, at the hands of the German barbarians, the last remains of Roman culture which had lingered on during the first invasions. (p 14, 15)

When the darkness of Europe was at its worst, a stream of missionaries from Ireland began to flow across to the continent. In 543 Columbanus of Leinster went forth with twelve companions, and established first a monastery, then a university at Bobbio and at Luxeuil, in Southen Gaul. Settlements were also left by him at Anagratum, in the Bosges mountains. The university at Luxeuil was established within a deserted Roman bath. Bobbio, which is in what is now called Italy, at the foot of the Apennines between Milan and Genoa, continued throughout the Middle Ages as a seat of culture and high learning. The Irish monk Gallus founded the university of St. Gall, the chief seat of learning in ancient Germany. Cataldus established a monastery and College at Tarentum; Virgilius at Salzburg, Donatus at Fiesole, Kilian at Wuerzburg. At the beginning of the eighth century (about 725) a long chain of Irish missionary monasteries and universities stretched from the mount of the Meuse and the Rhine to the Rhone and the Alps. These monasteries were not only universities, but agricultural and industrial settlements, teaching the arts of civilization along with the Gospel of Christ.

Around these universities and settlements grew up cities, and around the cities states were developed. (p. 15, 16)

About the time that Charlemagne began to centralize power in Europe again and to restore some semblance of authority and peace, the Danes began their invasion of Ireland. Before the wave of their persecution the scholars fled to the courts of the European kings. John Scotus Erigena—a name which means "John the Scot Born-in-Ireland" and Alcuin of York, both Druid-Christian priests, were the shining lights of the age of Charlemagne.

Heinrich Zimmer, in a book called "Irish Elements in Medieval Culture," has given a careful history of the work of the Irish saints in reconstructing Europe.But the great tragedy of a study of this kind is that we are seeking a lost trail. The Druids left no trace of their teaching because it was strictly forbidden to commit their doctrines to books. Yet, on becoming Christians, they taught the world the art of illumination. Books made in Ireland were the most highly prized possession of a European establishment. From the libraries and archives of the ancient monasteries of Switzerland, Italy and Germany, precious documents are being dug out which show to what a height the Irish learning attained. (p. 17)

Ralph Adams Cram, in his book "The Substance of Gothic," finds himself unable to explain how the wonderful structure of Gothic art arose out of the barbarism of the Gothic tribes. For three or four centuries after the destruction of Rome, the barbarian tribes seem to have no impulse toward creating anything new. "Then suddenly, the Gothic civilization arose; perfect, exquisite, unlike anything which had preceded it."

The answer seems to be found in the Celtic grace which welded together rugged German and legal Roman into a structure whose variety of beauty exceeds the beauty of Greece, and which is the greatest sacrifice claimed by the holocaust of today. For it is on the foundations laid by the Celtic monks that the cathedrals of Europe arose. And it is the Celtic love of the little beasts of nature, the Druid adoration of the forests, which distinguishes Gothic styles. Classic styles were entirely artificial. Greek ornament must be so conventionalized that it lost its meaning. The Romans were too stupid to make anything but poor imitations. The Germans were barbarians pure and simple. But the submerged Celtic genius came to its own in the Cathedral-building (p. 19)

2.   In Vienna, Victor Frankl, the founder of "logotherapy" and the leader of the Third School of Austrian psychology, stresses the crucial importance of man's search for meaning, and the dire effects of the "existential vacuum" so prevalent now in our Western Society. His books and his lectures have received a warm response in many countries.

3.   The main figure in this little known movement which began in Paris around 1912, was the Italian-born Riciotto Canudo, who edited a magazine "Montjoie!" devoted to new esthetic ideas repudiating everything having to do with emotions and traditional ethico-religious ideals. This was to some extent related to the Futurist Movement which was then developing in Italy. Though he denied any connection with Futurism itself, the composer, Edgard Varese (born in France, but with an Italian ancestry) thought of music in a rather similar way.

10. Old Myths, New Myths, and the Creation of a New Culture

1.   For a more detailed formulation of the concept of cyclocosm and of the process of existence, the reader is referred to my book *The Planetarization of Consciousness*, Part 2 (Harper and Row, N.Y., 1970; paperback edition, ASI Publishers, N.Y., 1977).

2.   The never-ending number Pi, 3.14159 . . . rightly expresses the relationship of circumference to diameter, rather than to radius, because any radiation from a center inevitably, it seems, operates in two opposite directions. Any action moving to the right is, at least potentially, balanced by another moving to the left. Any release of potentiality into actuality can, and we must assume *has to*, evoke a release of power of opposite character. This is simply a corollary of the dualistic interplay of Yang and Yin. In this sense, cosmic existence is a Play, a *lila* of Brahma, a game of chess. But it is not a repetitive circular play. One side wins. The circle turns into a spiral. Yet, perhaps in one universe the spiral goes

"up," in another "down"—a matter and antimatter, the physicist would say.

3.   Some of the ideas stated here were developed at greater length and within a somewhat different frame of reference in my book *We Can Begin Again - Together*, Part One (Seed Center Publications, Palo Alto, California) written in 1970. In Parts Two and Three I outlined structural principles on which the eventual development of a new global society could take place. An earlier attempt, *Modern Man's Conflicts: The Creative Challenge of a Global Society* (originally entitled "New Goals") was written in 1945-46 and published two years later by the Philosophical Library, New York. This book has long been out of print.

11. Creativity and the Individual's Role in a Crisis Situation

1.   The word, "opportunity" literally means "reaching the harbor." When the sailor after a long voyage reaches a harbor he is challenged, both to adjust to a new situation in a totally different life-situation and to use the experience born of new relationships for his growth—personal growth, or growth of his wealth if he is able to sell products obtained from distant lands. The sailor may have to decide whether to return to his ship and his travels within a limited but totally familiar area of relationships, or to make a new home in a new country. This is a situation of crisis.

2.   Physicists have remarked, many years ago, that, in size, a human being stands midway between the immensely vast cosmos and the infinitesimally small atom or atomic particles. Is this a privileged position from the point of view of the cosmos and its Creator, or is it perhaps that, as the limits of man's capacity for perception aided by ever more complex and refined machines extend, they are extended at the same time and for the same reasons in *both* directions? If the second alternative is accepted, this means that the limits of the universe man can directly and indirectly perceive are determined by the human mind standing at the center of a circle whose radii simply reflect the acuity of that mind. The modern universe of science is therefore basically as anthropocentric as the world of archaic religions and philosophies. The world is our world, our mandala. It reflects what man is in any historical period. Our collective consciousness expanded when a vaster picture of the universe was presented to us by galactic astronomy and atomic physics; but this vaster picture resulted from the expansion of our intellectual powers. Thus the basic fact is not that man's mind has grown in scope thanks to science, but that science has expanded because the human mind has actualized, further than before, *some* of its inherent potentialities. The old statement, "Man is the measure of all things," remains as valid as ever. The today often repeated statement that man is an insignificant entity so small when he is compared to a galaxy reveals an irrational bias. Why not say: How vast is man's body compared to an electron? Both the galaxy and the electron simply reveal the phase in the unfoldment of consciousness mankind has reached today. Consciousness can not be quantitatively measured in

any absolute sense, any more than one can state *how much* of the "infinite Ocean of Potentiality" is actualized today. The recent mathematical concept of degrees or levels of infinity is essentially meaningless because, even if it can be intellectually justified, it simply pushes further the idea of infinity, as there could be infinite levels of "infinities."

INDEX

THE THEOSOPHICAL PUBLISHING HOUSE

Wheaton, Ill., U.S.A.

Madras, India   London, England

Publishers of a wide range of titles on many
subjects including:

Mysticism
Yoga
Meditation
Extrasensory Perception
Religions of the World
Asian Classics
Reincarnation
The Human Situation
Theosophy

Distributors for the Adyar Library Series of
Sanskrit
Texts, Translations and Studies

The Theosophical Publishing House, Wheaton,
Illinois, is also the publisher of

QUEST BOOKS

Many titles from our regular cloth bound list in
attractive paperbound editions

For a complete list of all Quest Books write to:

QUEST BOOKS
P.O. Box 270, Wheaton, Ill. 60187